IRREGULARITIES
Tidal Flows and Politics Along the Rockaway Shore

IRREGULARITIES

Tidal Flows and Politics
Along the Rockaway Shore

Selections from
"The Rockaway Irregular"
~ Straddling Two Centuries ~

Stuart W. Mirsky

To order additional copies of this book, contact:
Xlibris Corporation
1-888-795-4274
www.Xlibris.com
Orders@Xlibris.com
27058

CONTENTS

SCHOOL DAYS

THE GREAT DIVIDE

Making The City Better

Whither Rockaway?

Odd And Ends

For Brenda, my wife,
who had enough faith in me to let me try something new.

INTRODUCTION

I never voted for Ronald Reagan. This may come as a shock to some who are familiar with my politically conservative proclivities, but like many of my generation and milieu, I was raised in a household of Democrats. My earliest political recollection (I must have been four or five at the time) is of looking out a car window as my father drove us over the George Washington Bridge on the way to New Jersey, as my folks discussed the presidency of Harry Truman. Much later they actually voted for Dwight Eisenhower, a Republican, but that seemed more anomaly than the norm for them. Throughout the presidential race that year they were deeply drawn to his opponent, Adlai Stevenson. But I think they voted in the end for a war hero of their own era. Both my parents had served in the military during World War II and they lived always under its shadow.

But I grew up in the shadow of the Democratic Party and cut my teeth, as I came to political awareness, on the candidacy and presidency of John Fitzgerald Kennedy, the first national politician I was really aware of. Throughout the sixties my political sensibility was shaped by the Kennedy presidency and the sense of what it could have been, what I was convinced it would have been, had not an assassin's bullet ended it so abruptly and with such drastic effect upon the nation. I supported Lyndon Johnson as Kennedy's rightful heir thereafter but, with many of my generation, soon turned against him as the Vietnam War began to spin out of his control. I was draft age at the time and so had a vested interest in opposing the war though you tend not to think in such venal terms when the vocabulary of the moment is all about the morality of conflict and the "just" use and projection of power. Like many others, I was also steeped in the Civil Rights movement of that era and the subsequent assassination of Martin Luther King Jr. burned itself deeply into my consciousness.

Needless to say I did not support Richard Nixon during his years of campaigning and office holding, though his subsequent downfall, due to deep character flaws, struck me as approaching the tragic. Here was a man who had reached so high and driven himself, against all odds, to the pinnacle of his world, only to be tripped up by the very attributes that had gotten him to where he wanted to be. He seemed a ruthless and cynical sort, mistrustful of his fellow men (though not for want of good reason), a man utterly lacking a principled center. Yet Nixon was not unlike the rest of us in many ways, wanting so much and willing to do even more to get it.

But unlike many of my generation, I didn't really think ill of Nixon. I remembered that he had likely been cheated of the presidency once before by my own favorite, John F. Kennedy, and that what he did, however calculating and inept, was probably motivated, at least in part, by a desire to make sure that that never happened to him again. Perhaps he took the wrong lesson from his defeat by JFK and decided to be more ruthless and proactive than those Democrats who had somehow managed to stuff ballot boxes in Chicago and do even worse, as some have suggested, in the rural precincts of Texas when Kennedy beat him back in 1960.

When Jimmy Carter subsequently ran against Gerald Ford, who had succeeded the disgraced Nixon, I naturally voted for Carter . . . and continued to vote the Democratic ticket throughout the Reagan years. Reagan just seemed to lack the intellectual heft I wanted in my presidents so I was first a Carter and then a Mondale man, as Reagan ran for and won his two terms. But some time near the end of the second Reagan term I started to think I had been wrong.

Despite the steady media drumbeat against Reagan and his policies, and the Democrats' apparent efforts to do to the Reagan presidency, via the Iran-Contra scandal, what they had done so successfully to Nixon over Watergate, I noticed that Reagan had actually done what he had said he'd do back when he'd first won election to the presidency. The economy was growing again, after the Reagan tax and regulatory cuts, despite the Democrats' rhetoric to the contrary. And the Soviet Union, instead of becoming more bellicose and threatening in response to Reagan's military build-up and his assertive international posture, had begun, at last, to come around. Mikhail Gorbachev, the new Soviet leader, was making friendly noises as the Cold War began to taxi in for an unexpectedly soft, and long overdue, landing. I had not imagined that that would have been possible in my own lifetime. But Reagan had.

I voted for my first Republican president when George H. W. Bush succeeded Ronald Reagan, belatedly switching my party affiliation when I saw the harsh, partisan tactics employed by the Democratic leadership, and the mainstream media that seemed in perfect sync with them, against the senior Bush. So I'm probably the only Republican in the nation today who can say, in all honesty, that he became a Republican due to the first President Bush. It wasn't the senior Bush's eloquence or charisma that swayed me, of course (no one's ever accused him of those things . . . not to my knowledge, anyway). It was the sense I had that he was really a very competent chief executive who was following sound policies and doing a good job of it.

Against this stood the Democrats in Congress and elsewhere, who seemed bent on only one thing: regaining political power in Washington, at whatever cost to civility and the national interest.

But what did it mean to have become a Republican at that point, besides my merely expressing a degree of sympathy for an embattled incumbent? Certainly none of us should ever be so blinded by party or ideology as to disregard the qualities of the candidates we vote for or the positions they espouse and I would never lock myself into that kind of thinking. Indeed, I could have defined myself as an independent, voted for Bush, and blithely gone on with the business of living, party politics be damned.

Looking back on it I think the driving impetus for me was the realization that I was more conservative at heart than "progressive."

Not that I opposed change or improving things. I certainly believed there were many things that had to be changed . . . . and many good changes that we, as a nation and people, had effected in our history. But I began to recognize that what we had and might be losing, in the rush toward what many were calling progress, might just be too dear to part with. I believed that individual liberty, and the responsibility that went along with that, was paramount to the kind of nation we were and that this was jeopardized by the continuing unchecked growth of government-as-nanny-state that the Democratic Party seemed to be pushing. The big government solutions of the sixties seemed to me to have given us more, not fewer, problems in many ways. At the same time a culture of intolerant political correctness had taken hold in the wake of the great liberal victories of the past. Something was lost to us as a result of that era, I thought, as new orthodoxies took hold, orthodoxies that seemed to value change for its own sake, while devaluing the heritage and accomplishments of our past.

Conservatives, of course, have a vested interest in preserving what we already have, whether past or present, rather than rushing willy-nilly into the future. And that was what I saw in myself. Conservatives are not necessarily against change. Indeed, that would be absurd. We are, each of us, changing every moment we draw breath. Nothing can remain static, least of all ourselves. But the question before us is how shall we approach this change? Shall we deny what we have and blindly toss it all aside for a dreamed of better world? Or shall we proceed cautiously, holding the road as we drive into an unknown future whose prospects we can only guess at?

In today's political environment it's the Republican Party that is home to this sense of caution, this reverence for the here and now, and so I decided to put my money where my mouth was and forego the joys of nonpartisan independence for the rigors of party affiliation. This doesn't prevent me from focusing on character or the positions of candidates, of course. But it does align me with those who tend to think as I do, who revere what we have and counsel only the most deliberate advancement into the realm of what might be. But that's what party politics in this country is about after all, lining up with those who share our views on the big issues and making common cause with them in order to secure control of the government and guide its operations as we move resolutely forward into the unknown.

In the early nineteen-nineties, in the wake of my political shift and as the first Bush presidency came under increasing fire by its political opponents and the media, I found myself becoming more and more interested in local political concerns. As a result, I took to writing a sometime political column in a now defunct local weekly, the Peninsula News. It was, naturally, a somewhat conservative column, along the lines described above, but it had a very short shelf life. The Peninsula News shut its doors in the mid-nineties and the column died with it. I was already busy with my real career, in municipal government at that point, so I didn't have much time to worry about the column's demise. Besides, I had written and published an historical novel by then, a novel that was selling respectably (even if it showed no signs of making me the next J.K. Rowling). And I had plans to do one or two more in the same vein. So while the writing bug had indeed bitten me hard, it was finding its expression in other, less controversial venues.

Still, in 2002, when an opportunity to take early retirement from my position in the city bureaucracy suddenly came my way, I began to think about all this again. Since I was then less than happy with the New York City agency in which I was working, I thought I'd at last try my hand at writing full time, an unrealized dream of my more or less unrealized youth. So I took the final step and gave up my city position. Shortly after officially "retiring," I contacted the main newspaper in Rockaway, New York, and offered to revive my old Peninsula News column for them if they were interested. After some discussion, the editor of Rockaway's Wave agreed. And so began the second incarnation of "The Rockaway Irregular."

The pieces presented here span two centuries: the early nineties and the early 2000's, roughly a decade, with a hiatus of several years in between. Needless to say, I haven't reprinted all the old pieces (or even all the newer ones). They weren't all good enough for that and there is, of course, the little matter of redundancy. I didn't want to bore people to death and hopefully the selections I've made here won't.

The articles chosen, which are generally between two and five pages in length (reflecting the limitations of a newspaper venue), run the gamut of issues that concerned me, both then and now, including local conditions in New York's Rockaway community where I reside, municipal governance (particularly as it affects New York City), various social concerns and, of course, the overall political landscape which has always been front and center for me. Because these pieces are reprinted here, I also took the opportunity to correct certain errors that had managed to creep into many of them at their initial publication, as well as to restore some of them to their original form since editing constraints occasionally resulted in drastically shortened or altered versions. Because I also write for other papers at times, some of these articles may have also appeared elsewhere in slightly variant forms. Except for the introduction you are now reading and the final piece in this collection, all the articles here have appeared in one form or another in my "Rockaway Irregular" column.

Of course, the opportunity to re-do some of these pieces was too good to disregard and so I did some editing to clarify the writing in places where I'd originally been less clear, or less eloquent, than I'd have liked . . . and I've changed a few titles, here and there, when that seemed warranted. In some cases, I've also removed certain individuals' names, if they were private citizens without anything genuinely newsworthy about their activities beyond my reference to them. I've done this carefully, however, so it should not adversely affect readability or accuracy. In a few cases I actually altered a name by using a pseudonym (when I couldn't simply substitute a description or pronoun). None of this applies to public figures or to people reported about in the media as part of various new stories. Such people would normally be subjects of public discourse, based on their newsworthiness, anyway. Of course, political personalities get named here throughout . . . as they should be.

Beyond all this, I've also taken the liberty of adding some clarifying information here and there, either as endnotes or as interpolations in and around the text, to put the articles (particularly the older ones) in perspective. Interpolated text is shown in italics. Endnotes speak for themselves.

The material has been organized thematically, though sometimes themes may overlap. In such cases, I've chosen what I took to be the most important or dominant theme within which to place the article. Still, you shouldn't be surprised if you find yourself disagreeing with one or more of my decisions. It happens.

Within each thematic area, the material is arranged chronologically, or as close to that as I could get it. Sometimes articles that were written at one point in time did not appear until months later, making this all a little iffy. There were also a few articles which, when I checked back, were difficult to place as to actual publication date so all I can say is that I've taken my best shot with these.

As a writer I naturally hope others will find some of what I've offered here interesting and, perhaps, even a little useful. That's why writers write after all . . . to be read. I don't flatter myself that my concerns will resonate with everyone, nor is this a book for everyone. Insofar as it's overtly political, it reflects my own pilgrim's progress over a decade or so as I became more and more concerned with the need for a political alternative in my own local community. It also offers a history of some little known occurrences in the political life of Rockaway, information which would probably be lost to all of us over time otherwise. Finally, it contains a few of my own observations about how the business of government should and should not be done, particularly here in New York City, gleaned over a lifetime of working in city agencies, from my earliest days as a lowly welfare frauds investigator and as an assistant health inspector "in the field," to my final years as an Assistant Commissioner, lodged deep within one city agency's bureaucratic maw.

Finally, for those who may have wondered how "The Rockaway Irregular" column came by its name, I'll just add this. When I started writing it for the Peninsula News, I was reluctant to commit to a steady schedule of articles and so, of course, only promised it irregularly. This seemed an appropriate title at the time, too, since in writing it I was also expressing the guerilla-like views of a political upstart, someone who wasn't part of any "regular army" but who was fighting irregularly, without benefit of uniform or formal chain of command. So I saw myself as a "Rockaway irregular" in this sense, too.

But I tended to write the pieces more regularly than I'd planned and pretty soon was producing a fairly steady stream of them, despite the name I'd chosen for the column. Still, for the record and for those who have suggested otherwise, I want to stress here once and for all that whatever else the name was intended to suggest, it never referred to anything connected with a certain unmentionable biological function.

All Politics Is Local . . . Unless It Isn't

In January 1994, Rudolph Giuliani was sworn in as the 107th mayor of New York City. The campaign that preceded his inauguration had been a hard fought one and Giuliani only won his initial term by a very narrow margin, defeating Mayor David Dinkins, the Democratic incumbent and the city's first black mayor. Dinkins, who had defeated Giuliani the first time out, had gone on to become a divisive figure during his single term in office, appearing to allow some minority communities to ride roughshod over the city as local economic conditions continued to deteriorate and street crime seemed to be out of control. Giuliani, who was to serve two successive terms, was vehemently opposed in his initial run, and throughout his two terms, by self-styled "progressives" who objected to the assertive policies he would use to restore peace to New York's streets and in making government manageable again. Nothing Giuliani was to do in the course of his subsequent administration would assuage the grievances of those who opposed him on principle at the outset. But he won his second run for mayor decisively and left office as one of the most revered American political figures of his time, due in no small part, of course, to his role as mayor of the city during the terrorist attacks of September 11th, 2001.

USHERING IN AN ERA

(January 1994)

I got there late. The traffic wasn't bad but the parking was horrible. They had closed the municipal lot underneath One Police Plaza and "blue lined" the streets all around City Hall so you couldn't leave your car anywhere nearby. Still, I made it before the speeches, though not in time to get a seat or even to see more than the tiny speck of the new Mayor's head, bobbing up and down behind the podium especially constructed for the occasion. But at least I could hear most of what Giuliani was saying, despite the best efforts of the demonstrators on the other side of Broadway who strove, with uncivil disregard for their fellow New Yorkers, to disrupt and drown out the inaugural proceedings.

With whistles, left over New Year's Eve noisemakers, and loudspeakers, this crew of discontented refugees from the sixties and seventies refused to give up their right to be outraged and disaffected, rejecting the changing of the guard at City Hall. They flaunted banners and placards proclaiming "I Didn't Vote for Him" and "He's Not My Mayor" and "Jobs Not Jails" and "No Layoffs" and "Jonestown Was a Pentagon Plot" and any number of other complaints and charges which they hoped to level against the new administration. They waved rubber-edged squeegees in mock menace. And they chanted their oddly catchy refrain: "Racist, Sexist, Anti-Gay, Giuliani Go Away." But while they exercised their vocal chords and other instruments of disruption, the new Mayor clearly did not go away—as they must surely have known he wouldn't.

It rapidly became clear, as their efforts at disruption grew louder and more and more raucous during the national anthem and the invocation (by a rabbi whose name was lost in the cacophony of their discontent), that their strategy was not just to protest but to provoke the police who ringed the perimeter of City Hall. But while many irritated glances were exchanged among the patrolmen stationed all around us, none of them took the bait. And these hapless, perennial malcontents, who in other times and nobler causes might have inspired the sympathy of the general populace, were effectively marginalized.

While few of us would dream of denying any group its right to demonstrate or voice its political opinions (well, hopefully, few of us), it was strangely saddening to view the incivility with which this group of people chose to exercise their own civil liberties. Obviously, Giuliani didn't sweep into office with an overwhelming majority; and the job ahead of him is a daunting one. But don't we owe him the opportunity to prove himself? Didn't his predecessor have that? Yet while the new Mayor was up there promising new directions and new ideas and a unified city, this group could think of nothing better than to pelt him with insults and promise to drive him from office in, as one of their placards suggested "Ninety Days."

But the applause of the crowd in City Hall told a different story—that the new Mayor was not alone and that his vision is shared by many others in this City; others who believe, with him, that there's a need to try something fresh in a town that cries out for more than 'business as usual.' Civility, both in the streets and in the political arena, the crowd seemed to be saying, must be restored. The police did not react to these 'squeegee-men' of the political world nor did Giuliani succumb to the temptation to recognize them, either in speech or gesture, though their wailing rose to a desperate crescendo as he began to speak. In the end they filed off angrily, but without the confrontation they seemed to have come for. A few of them took on the police on Chambers Street and Broadway . . . and it appeared that one or two actually managed to get themselves arrested (to the tired refrain of "No Justice, No Peace") but, for the most part, they seemed disappointed as, indeed, they were destined to be on this day.

Who were these angry, unforgiving, lost political souls, these 'squeegee politicians' seeking to shatter the security of the streets near City Hall? Many of them looked familiar, if not in their specific features then in their clothes, their manners and in their strained and angry voices. They are the ones who used to bear so proudly those signs which proclaimed allegiance to the world socialist movement and which skewered America for any action it took. But none of those signs were in evidence today, perhaps because of the disrepute into which the ideology they espoused has tumbled.

In a democracy we must expect and, yes, endure these sorts of demonstrations while suspecting that the folks who engage in them would not scruple to prevent any of us from exercising the same option, were the power to do that ever to be theirs. But at least we now have the satisfaction of knowing this crew is, for the moment at least, without their historic moorings, adrift in a world of shifting ideas and beliefs. For however briefly we may see them for what they are, without the camouflage of ideology and 'noble' principle—perennial nay-sayers for whom no action, no government in this society can possibly be acceptable.

Does Giuliani want to introduce accountability and reason in the bureaucracy? Then "No Layoffs"!

Does he want to demolish governmental impediments and disincentives to doing business in the city, while restoring a sense of safety and order to the streets? Then "Jobs, Not Jails"!

With slogans they rage against whatever they oppose. But at least on this day their true nature was apparent—as was their isolation. With plastic pails on their heads and squeegees in their hands, they cavorted through the streets, climbing onto mailboxes and street lights, photographing and 'interviewing' one another, railing, all the while, at the police. But the crowd, who came to hear the new Mayor and join him in his effort to revitalize New York City, just pretended they weren't there. Except for those of us who came late, of course, and couldn't find a decent place to park.

HOW IT SHOULD BE DONE

(February 22, 1994)

One recent February morning, newly elected freshman City Councilman Al Stabile made history of sorts by meeting with orthodox Jewish leaders on the West End. According to several of the meeting attendees, this was the first time a representative to the City Council from this area had thought enough of them to sit down for a tete a tete.

In the past, Stabile's predecessor may have met with other groups and, certainly, he was famous for his "photo ops," but for some strange reason he seems to have overlooked Belle Harbor's orthodox Jewish community. Not the largest group on the peninsula, nor the oldest, nor the most politically connected, these people had come to feel somewhat disenfranchised—out in the cold, even before this season's arctic blasts reminded all of us what New York's winters used to be like. And *that* may help explain why we have a new City Councilman this year. Although Stabile didn't win the overwhelming support of this group in his recent run for the Council seat, there was more than enough disaffection on their part and on the part of other Rockaway communities to put him over the top.

As if in recognition of this nascent voter revolt, Stabile and a number of others braved the knee deep snow and ice on that recent February day to meet with the rabbis and some of their congregants and to listen to their concerns. Besides the Councilman, local Republican leaders Tom Swift and Tom Carney (who jointly footed the bill for refreshments) and Rockaway Action Committee counsel Jim Woods turned up. Also poking her head in was State Assemblywoman Audrey Pheffer who, though she hadn't been part of the original agenda, popped in late and left early. The new City Councilman, a Republican, gallantly invited the Democratic Assemblywoman to join him at the front of the room and there she sat, looking a trifle uncomfortable, but apparently as eager as Al to hear her constituents' issues.

The meeting, as it turned out, went on longer than anyone expected, as long unaired concerns spilled out onto the table, along with the donuts and the danish and the coffee (which everyone seemed to have forgotten about in the heat of the moment). They wanted to know why they had been left out of the peninsula's calculations for so long and expressed concerns about anti-Semitic incidents that many had encountered on the Sabbath, during the summer months when beachgoers from outside the area abound. But more than any of this, and strikingly, they wanted to know "what's going to be done to build up our area?"

Indeed, when all the personal matters of importance to this particular group were out of the way, their concerns were not so different from the matters which weigh on the minds of the rest of the peninsula's diverse communities and residents. "What about Beach 116th Street?" they asked as one participant bemoaned the fact that he couldn't send his children down there, on a warm summer's night, for ice cream or just to walk and enjoy an ocean breeze. "What about the businesses and the shabby appearance of everything? What about the panhandlers in the street and the litter and the lack of summer evening activities? Why can't we have the art deco look, like other communities have adopted, to make our businesses and stores a little more attractive?"

These were all familiar refrains and you might have heard their like at any community gathering in any neighborhood on the peninsula.

The Councilman promised a meeting with the local precinct commander to ensure greater police responsiveness, with, he stressed, a stenographer present to record any commitments obtained, and he spoke about a restaurant he was trying to coax into existence on 116th Street.

"Bringing in a business here and there is all well and good," said one fellow, "but how do you ensure that all the problems get addressed? How do you make sure the new restaurant, if it comes, doesn't go the way of everything else?" Give us a plan, he urged, not just a promise here and there.

Stabile seemed to be taken aback, but he recovered quickly. Though he had gotten off to a slow start with this group, and each side initially circled the other warily, the Councilman at last seemed to find his footing, even as the room heated up. And they began to warm to his simple, straightforward businessman's approach and the seeming sincerity of his manner.

"I'll do whatever it takes to address your concerns," he assured them and he began to write down issues on a napkin in front of him. An aide he had brought along was also taking notes and Tom Carney, president of the Gateway Republicans, was scribbling feverishly.

After the meeting, Stabile set a follow-up session with his legislative staff to integrate this group's concerns with everyone else's, in order to develop his long awaited plan for the Rockaways. He says he's looking to bring recreational attractions to the area's abandoned and underdeveloped sections, to restore Beach 116th Street to its former glory by getting the local merchants to pull together, and to enhance the peninsula's overall economic prospects by working with the Giuliani administration to target the Rockaways for environmentally friendly development. All tall orders, to be sure, and nothing that one City Councilman can accomplish alone.

But he's not alone, as the meeting showed. Nor are any of us or any of our communities. We're all on the peninsula together and we all have a stake in the quality of life we find here. If every group has its own unique concerns, each also shares the common goal of making a better home for ourselves and our families. That, more than anything else, emerged most clearly on that cold February morning, when everyone got so worked up they forgot about the coffee and donuts.

Historical Postscript (8/4/04): After serving two terms as City Councilman, Al Stabile left public life in 2001 and was succeeded by a well-known local Democrat when the Republicans failed to mount a strong race to retain the seat Stabile had won. During his tenure, Stabile did not deliver on all of the promises he had made on that February morning. Although new restaurants were ultimately established on Beach 116th Street (some successful to this day) and a business improvement district was organized to marshal the energies and resources of local businessmen, resulting in a cleaner and safer area, such gains did not endure. As of this writing (roughly a decade later), Beach 116th Street is again a community sore point for its lack of cleanliness and its general, overall shabbiness. Stabile was also unable to deliver on his promises of economic development or the introduction of a revitalized recreational franchise in this beachfront community. After splitting with local community politicos and activists in Rockaway over various issues, the Councilman closed down his satellite office in the area and devoted himself mainly to his constituents on the mainland. He also took the leadership of the area's regular Republican organization out of the Rockaways where it had historically resided. In his re-election bid for a second term, the Councilman's support from Rockaway was far less visible than it had been in the first run. Near the end of his second term, he was overtaken by allegations of scandal including claims of misused funds. Because of term limits, he was not eligible to run for a third term. After he left public life, the Republican organization he had built in the south Queens area seemed to go into hibernation and virtually disappeared. Still, what he did on that early February morning, after winning his upset victory against a twenty-five year Democratic incumbent, remains a textbook example of how and where political leaders ought to start: by listening and paying attention to their constituents' concerns.

THE GREAT GAME?

(June 7, 1994)

What's going on with Rockaway's Republicans? After a history making campaign last fall, when the party forged an effective alliance with fellow Republicans on the mainland to turn twenty five year incumbent City Councilman Walter Ward out of office—a scion and leading light of the entrenched Democratic political machine in this area—the Gateway Republicans seem to have lost some of their momentum. Only two months away from the start of a new fall campaign season, it's still not clear who's running for what. Or what kind of ticket the party is going to field in south Queens.

After a rambunctious and sometimes acrimonious meeting last month, the nominating process for the State Assembly seat seemed to stall as insurgent Republican John Baxter challenged the State Committeeman, Thomas Swift, for the party's nod and effectively blocked Swift's fait accompli endorsement by the County Committee. At the same time, Republican activist Mike Duvalle, who had been driving for the nomination for more than a year, found himself knocked out of the running on a technicality which left him feeling somewhat aggrieved toward the party's leadership. So far no one knows for sure where Howard Beach's Al Stabile, who recently took the City Council seat away from Walter Ward, will come down with his support, though the betting is he'll side with Swift.

Will there be a primary for the Assembly nomination and, if there is, will it hurt or help the Republicans in this area? People are of two opinions. Some hold that a struggle like this would split the party and open the way for another easy Democratic walk to victory by incumbent Audrey Pheffer in November, thus squandering all the gains from the successful Stabile and Giuliani campaigns last fall. Others, John Baxter among them, have argued that this kind of democratic exercise can only help the party since it will let some fresh air into a rather staid and musty political organization, an organization that, until last year's wins, hadn't experienced the exhilaration of victory for as long as anyone could remember.

The truth is that, while the Republicans are not used to open fights and want to shy away from them as overly risky, Baxter's probably right. Although out of practice and tending to take things a little too personally, the local Republican players, and the party as a whole, could benefit from the venting a primary would bring. New ideas and, maybe, new people would come to the fore and this can only liven things up. If it breathes some life into the party, this could be a boon to Rockaway . . . and all of south Queens . . . by helping restore the two-party system so that democracy, on the local level, can start to work again.

The big risk, of course, is that people get nasty with each other and vent their spleens, thereby severely damaging any eventual winner and/or making the Republicans the laughing stock of the area. The potential benefit, on the other hand, is that people sit up and suddenly notice there's another party around, realizing at last that they don't have to be prisoners any longer of a single party monopoly.

Which would be the likely outcome? Of course it depends on how the players conduct themselves. But one thing's for sure: it's a sign of how much the party's grown in Rockaway that there's talk of a primary at all this year. Used to be that you couldn't pay someone to run against the Democrats. Or that you had to.

GAME SET AND MATCH?

(September 6, 1994)

Do Rockaway Republicans have a death wish? After a bang-up 1993, with a mayoral and city council win under their belts and new members pouring out of the proverbial woodwork, you'd think the Republicans would be going into the '94 election loaded for bear. Well, not quite.

The local party organization had a number of eager candidates early on for the Assembly seat held by Democrat Audrey Pheffer but, for various and sometimes rather technical reasons, these candidates faltered. In the process, Gateway Republican club leadership (Rockaway's regular Republicans) fought a rearguard action to avoid a primary fight for the nomination which, they claimed, would be unproductive. They got their wish and avoided the primary, ultimately ensuring the nomination of one of their own—Thomas F. Swift, the local Republican State Committeeman. He got the nod, apparently, because the leadership was most comfortable with him, figuring his background, record and public positions were least likely to make their core constituency uneasy.

This will be Tom's second run against Ms. Pheffer. Last time he got 38% of the vote in a campaign which he started late and ran with no organization, no money and under a virtual media black-out. Tom's a decent and intelligent man who can claim a reservoir of goodwill up on the mainland (Howard Beach and Ozone Park), where people tend to think of him as a man of integrity. He's been a local Republican leader in the Rockaways and a leading light of the Gateway Republican Club since its rebirth a number of years ago. And if he's fought a number of tough, internecine turf battles and angered a few people along the way, well that comes with the territory.

But right after securing the nomination, Tom seems to have dropped off the scope. While incumbent Audrey Pheffer appears almost constantly in the peninsula's two main newspapers, and her picture and well known hairdo are, by now, fixtures in the local firmament (she pops up and gets photographed wherever more than three people have gathered), Tom has virtually disappeared from view. Presumably he's waiting for the autumn season to begin his campaigning. But in the meantime his opponent, with all the benefits of incumbency, is certainly not biding her time.

Apparently the local Republican organization, its leaders and friends don't think they need to do much more than nominate Tom. There's been no mad rush to fill his campaign coffers or to put together a grassroots organization to get his message out. Just as in the last campaign, they've left him pretty much on his own. At the same time a number of other Republican players, who might have been more vigorous in their efforts, seem to be sulking at the fringes, offended by the high-handed way the club leadership excluded them from the decision-making process or even from the opportunity to run for office themselves.

Tom, of course, knows this is his last shot at the Assembly. If he doesn't win it this time, it's highly unlikely he'll get the nomination again. He was banking on a stronger, revitalized Republican organization and on powerful support from the mainland where our new Republican City Councilman, Al Stabile, has his base. Al, whether people know it or not, owes a great deal to Tom since Tom led the Gateway Club into Al's corner when Al was just declaring. That decision brought Al a large number of Rockawayites and smoothed the way for Al with the Queens County leadership. While no one thing can be identified as the single factor which accounted for the Stabile victory (not even Walter Ward's incredible political vulnerability and overconfidence), Tom's actions certainly were critical and their absence could have derailed or seriously slowed the Stabile steamroller. (Many people, in fact, even on the mainland, think it was the Rockaway vote which put Stabile over the top.)

So Tom figures he can count on Al's support. But for Tom to pull off his own electoral upset, he's going to need more than a few kind words from the boys on the mainland. If they leave him on his on and he ends up running another shoestring campaign, he'll be starting off with an incredible disadvantage. The incumbent already has recognition (how many people know how Tom wears *his* hair?) and plenty of funds since the Democratic coffers are well-stuffed out here (though they don't like to admit it). And Ms. Pheffer has those infamous 'franking' privileges which allow an office holder to communicate with his or her constituents at taxpayer expense. Tom will be lucky if he can afford one mass mailing before the election. And, of course, Audrey Pheffer has a paid staff (once again the taxpayer is paying) and a real organization full of volunteers. Except for petition carriers and a few die-hards, Tom has none of that.

So what's Tom doing in the face of this growing debacle? We don't know. Presumably he's hunkered down somewhere, prepared to come out swinging in September. Maybe he's in talks with the mainland folks to generate some much needed support from that quarter. He's not saying.

As to Rockaway's own homegrown Republicans, after a session or two where lots of enthusiasm and pledges of goodwill were exchanged, nobody seems to be doing much of anything. Maybe they thought it was enough to nominate Tom, rather than take a risk on someone new who might make them uncomfortable? Maybe they're just worried about putting money up for a campaign that doesn't have much momentum to it—thereby all but ensuring that it never will generate much momentum. Maybe they just don't care much about winning. It's pretty easy being the party on the outside, after all—you can do all the complaining about the other guy without ever having to accomplish anything yourself. But if so, that's a shame. Because Rockaway is ready for a change. South Queens is ready. Last November's election proved it and this November's could confirm it. The same people have been in power way too long. They've gotten too comfortable—with us and with each other. They've come to expect to be re-elected as though it were their right, and they keep winning for lack of any real alternatives.

As a result, we are no longer represented by our fellow private citizens, as the founding fathers envisioned, but by a class of professional politicos. And now it looks like the Republicans out there want to be professionals too—professional also-rans.

FIGHTING CITY HALL

(October 11, 1994)

What's wrong with this picture? In the heat of a hard fought election campaign, City Council candidate Al Stabile jumped into a local issue here in the Rockaways—the fight against housing the homeless in Single Room Occupancy facilities (S.R.O.s)—and successfully forced the city bureaucracy to back down. A local hotel on Beach 116th Street, long a harbor for panhandling transients who intimidated local residents trying to make use of the area's shops, was finally shut down. The Mayoral candidate, running on the same Republican slate as Stabile, vowed that he would not send the homeless back there, once in office, and, along with Stabile, won his race. Thus the Beach 116th Street business district was set to live happily ever after, at least as far as this former S.R.O. facility was concerned, right?

Wrong.

The following fall, the new Mayor's own bureaucrats did exactly the same as the old Mayor's bureaucrats had done, sending homeless families back to this site as though nothing had changed. This, of course, partly reflects the fact that once you get below the very highest level in any city agency, the new Mayor's bureaucrats and the old Mayor's bureaucrats are likely to be the same bureaucrats— professionals who serve the agencies they run, rather than the Mayor or the people who elect him. They have their mandate and, in many cases, their own agenda, which does not necessarily coincide with the interests of the people in the communities their decisions affect.

So what did we, as a community, do? We got our new City Councilman, Al Stabile, to wade back into the fray. We got a meeting with the Deputy Mayor for Operations, number two in the City Hall hierarchy, and put together some demonstrations. Al filed a lawsuit on our behalf and City Hall was miffed with him, but he gamely promised to fight on anyway. The bureaucrats did agree to pull the families they had placed in the hotel eventually, but they refused to promise to refrain from placing people there again, should the need arise. So Beach 116th Street, finally on the road to recovery as a business center for the local community, seems to have weathered another temporary setback. But will the convalescence go forward or will this prove to be only the first in a series of further shocks which will permanently debilitate and bury this once proud seaside town? And do we have a chance of ever having any influence over the city which rules us, collects our taxes, makes the decisions we have to live with, etc., even after we had elected a Mayor who apparently understood the types of problems which beset communities like ours? Remember the question. There's still something wrong with this picture.

The other piece of this puzzle suddenly popped up in a New York Times article on September 28th, headlined "JUDGE CITES NEW YORK CITY ON HOMELESS." According to this little item, Judge Helen Freedman of the State Supreme Court held the city in contempt once again (she had done it during the preceding Dinkins administration, too—and the same thing was going on during the Koch years) "for leaving more than 100 families a night sleeping on chairs, tables and the floor of a city office while they waited for shelter . . ."

The article went on to note that the judge, as part of her decision, ordered the city to pay $2.5 million in fines "to thousands of families who had overnight stays between September 1991 and December 1993, and more fines are expected for that period as more families come forward to claim them."

Each family, the article tells us, is "entitled to $50 for the first overnight in the office and $100 for each night thereafter." The judge told the city it must not only pay those it failed, in the past, to house immediately, but must also pay this fine to all future families it does not immediately place. The Department of

Homeless Services complained that they were experiencing a seasonal glut in demand, but homeless advocates decried this, saying it's the city's fault because of the budget cuts, and declared that the incidence of non-immediate placements "in the last two months has been off the map." A frustrated Commissioner of Homeless Services notes that the fines are just an added incentive to people, who consider themselves ill-housed, to enter the city's shelter system, further straining city resources.

Still trying to figure this out?

The problem isn't of City Hall's making. Our Mayor and the bureaucrats who work for him have their own troubles which, as these affect their ability to manage city resources, impact us as taxpayers and citizens as well. Who says you have to have immediate placements, that a little inconvenience for people seeking a city service, especially one as costly as housing, is unacceptable? Who made the rule that enables a sitting judge to disregard the city's fiscal crisis and, in fact, make matters worse by imposing penalties on an agency which hasn't been able to address this problem as far back as the Koch years?

We keep fighting City Hall and railing against the bureaucrats who, heaven knows, certainly deserve our ire at times. But they can't fix this one by themselves, at least not in the short term. According to the Times article, a state ruling imposes this particular burden on the city. Where do such rules come from? Two places: the state legislature passes the laws which establish the framework for our locally administered social services programs and the State Department of Social Services make the rules, based on these laws, which New York City is obliged to follow. The governor appoints the head of the state agency and all of its employees report to him.

So why do we keep beating our heads against the wrong wall, year after year? Because you always hurt the one you love or, in this case, the bureaucrat closest to you. But there's a statewide election coming up this November for Governor and for the legislature, and we have a classic confrontation in both areas. In the local Assembly race, especially, incumbent Audrey Pheffer (a liberal Democrat) is running against conservative Republican Thomas

Swift. Audrey and the Democrats have been in control for years and we got S.R.O.s in our main business district, facilities we still can't seem to permanently get rid of. Want to change things? Then let's apply the lever of outrage where it will do the most good—the statewide elections. Maybe a new legislator representing our community will help change the rules of the game and allow the city to finally get out from under its current burdens. At the least, it doesn't make sense to keep sending the same people who gave us the problem back to the scene of the crime year after year, while we go on demonstrating and shouting ourselves hoarse down here.

HOW WE KNOW THEM

(October 18, 1994)

She was sitting on the table next to mine, moving her legs up and down, the weights strapped to her ankles. Or at least I imagined it that way, since I was too busy pumping my own weights and working up a sweat to notice. The physical therapy technicians moved about between us, giving instruction, applying heat and cold, electrical stimulation to our weakened muscles and something they euphemistically called "ultra sound"—though heaven knows you couldn't hear anything coming out of those little gizmos they kept rubbing against our injured areas. I don't know when we got into it, maybe the therapist himself sparked the conversation, but I asked her, at one point, who she planned to vote for in the upcoming election for State Assembly. That's the seat that Audrey Pheffer currently holds in our district. Since this was in Ozone Park, I figured it was hers, too.

"Who's running?" she asked, rather too naively.

"Audrey Pheffer," I said. "And Thomas Swift."

"Well I know Audrey so I'll probably vote for her."

"Why's that?" I asked. "You know Audrey personally?"

"Oh, no," she replied, "but I see her in the papers all the time. She's always doing something. I never even heard of this Swift guy."

"But wait a second," I said. "You don't have to do something to get yourself in the local papers. All you need is to show up at the events with your photographer in tow, get a few good snapshots, and send them off to the local newspapers."

"Well," she said, "you can't get in the papers if you're not doing something."

"Not true," I insisted, "especially where the small local papers are concerned. It helps, of course, if you know the editors or if they're sympathetic to your party or positions, but basically they print whatever gets sent to them."

"Well, what does the other guy stand for?" she asked at long last.

"He's a Republican and a conservative," I said, "while Audrey is a liberal Democrat."

"Well, I'm a Democrat, too," she said, "so I guess I'll still vote for her."

"Who'd you vote for in the City Council race? Ward or Stabile?" I asked.

"Stabile."

"He's a conservative Republican," I said.

"Yeah, but I knew who he was . . . and what he stood for."

"Because you saw his name and picture in the papers?"

"Partly," she admitted.

"Then you could vote for Tom," I said triumphantly. "They're both from the same end of the political spectrum. In fact they're political allies!"

"Well, if I knew what he stood for, maybe. I vote issues, not party."

"So what would it take for Tom to win your vote?" I pressed.

"Tell me what his positions are . . . I'm a pretty independent voter," she shot back.

"Well, he's for the death penalty," I said, knowing that this particular position of Tom's made me somewhat uncomfortable. "And he's against abortion on demand, although he's more restrained on the subject than many conservative Republicans. He wants to rein in government spending, too," I added.

"He doesn't sound like my kind of candidate," she said. "I don't like anyone who wants to interfere with women's reproductive rights."

"You ought to at least give him a chance," I said. "A state legislator doesn't have any say on abortion anyway. What if you saw him in the papers more?"

"Maybe. But it probably wouldn't matter. He sounds too

conservative for me. Besides, I hate all politicians anyway . . . I don't trust them, so it doesn't really matter what they say."

"But wait a second," I cried, fairly leaping off the table. "Isn't that crazy? You say you hate all politicians . . . but who are the ones you hate? The ones you know about, right? Because if you didn't know anything about them, you wouldn't know enough about them to hate them. But those are the very ones you say you're willing to vote for . . . because you know who they are from the newspapers. Someone you've never heard of before, like Tom, can't give you any reason to mistrust him, can he? You don't know him from Adam. It's the ones you know about who give you reason to dislike politicians. So why keep voting the same ones back into office?"

"I'd rather not talk about it," she said abruptly.

She got up then and began to put on her shoes, preparing to leave.

"We should talk again," she turned to me at last, on her way out the door. "I'm pretty open-minded. Tell this Tom fellow to come to Ozone Park and let's hear what he has to say. I'm willing to listen."

"I suppose it would help if you saw him in the papers more, too," I called after her, still lying on my table, an ice pack wrapped tightly around my injured knee.

"Yeah," she said. "That wouldn't hurt either."

CREDIT WHERE IT'S DUE

(November 1, 1994)

I recently received a phone call from Congressman Schumer's office concerning a piece I did, not long ago, about a local hotel. It seems I noted that City Councilman Al Stabile "successfully forced the city bureaucracy to back down" on the use of the aforementioned facility as a way-station for homeless families in 1993, but failed to mention the involvement of others. Schumer's spokesperson reminded me that Councilman Stabile was a private citizen at that time (he was running against then-incumbent Walter Ward) and so, in her opinion, could not be credited with actually having effected the closing.

According to the Congressman's office, he and Democratic Assemblywoman Audrey Pheffer had actually done the deed. I mentioned to the spokesperson that I specifically recalled Stabile making this a campaign issue and actually conducting a rally outside the hotel in question during his race for the councilmanic seat. (I also recall being advised at the time that the aspiring Councilman was "working behind the scenes with his government contacts" to assist the local groups who were fighting this use of the facility.)

Nevertheless, she told me, it had been Schumer who accomplished the closing, since Stabile as "a private citizen" was not in a position to do anything more than speak out back then. This got me to thinking about how we credit people for doing what they do. Certainly the fight over the S.R.O. hotel had been going on for quite some time and many people, public figures and otherwise, had taken positions on the subject over the years. Stabile was only one of these. However, he was unquestionably one of the major players, once he got involved. Many local people still think they owe him a special debt, since they believe his involvement is what tipped the balance during that crucial period.

It often takes lots of people and lots of noise to get something done. But, ultimately, it takes the decision by someone in charge (often a government official) to do it. So who gets the credit? The official who says okay, let's do it, or the person or people who demanded that it get done? If the wheel doesn't squeak, the guy with the oil can doesn't know he has to oil it, right?

Of course, even this is a simplistic model of how such things happen. The truth is, somebody screams about an issue and others hear it and join in until they raise a loud enough cry to attract more major players. Stabile was pulled into the battle in this way and so was Congressman Schumer and, according to Schumer's office, Assemblywoman Pheffer. Stabile was still in that nether world of semi-public people (he had not yet achieved public office though he was vying for it), while the latter two were already public officials. But they all joined in the fracas and came to the aid of people whose support (read votes) they coveted in the future.

Once the major players got involved, the crescendo of discontent grew loud enough for the officials in charge to hear and react, although it's unclear which particular "major player's" entry represented the tipping point. No doubt, though, that the hotel's closing, however temporary, was facilitated by the fact that a very tight election, both locally and citywide, was then under way.

Schumer's person says *he* got it done. Stabile's people, and others, swear *he* was crucial in the chain of events which brought the matter to a head. (Pheffer's people haven't made any special claims in the matter, to my knowledge, and most of my information concerning her involvement comes from the off-handed inclusion of the Assemblywoman by Schumer's spokesperson while claiming credit for the Congressman.)

From what I can see, a lot of people can get on this credit bandwagon—not just these three elected officials. In fact, I remember a press release at the time from Boro President Claire Shulman's office at the time, claiming the hotel was closed due to her intervention . . . and, just as Schumer's spokesperson had done, it tacked on the name of Assemblywoman Pheffer, too. The interesting thing is that, once something popular gets done, the public players all clamor for a piece of it with a plethora of press releases and, sometimes, phone calls, as in this case.

So again, who gets the credit? The ones who got their press releases out first? The ones who manage to get their press releases picked up while the releases of others languish unnoticed? Or the ones with the perseverance to follow up with the press, years later, to make sure their guy doesn't get forgotten? Or the ones who get included, perhaps as a professional courtesy, in other people's releases? In fact, Assemblywoman Pheffer's current opponent for the State Assembly, Tom Swift, was also a player in the matter since he was the one who organized the Stabile rally in front of the S.R.O. facility in 1993 that raised this issue up a notch in the public debate. But nobody ever did a release on his role in all this.

I told Schumer's person, as she earnestly spelled out the Congressman's contribution, that I had respect for her guy since I thought him one of the smartest, most effective politicians in the local firmament. Indeed, you have to acknowledge a competent pro when you see one. A guy like Schumer is very likely to be going places. Since his advent on the Rockaway scene, in fact, all the local Democratic office holders seem to have become marginally more effective. He knows how to organize them and get things done so he's obviously the bullfrog in our little pond. More, you can see his hand in the recent "toll wars," in the decision to create a local resident discount thereby deflating what had been, until then, a growing source of discontent on the peninsula. (People might have really thrown the incumbents out across the board if something hadn't been done on this one, given the rising level of anger over the tolls!)

Accordingly, I don't have any problem acknowledging that a pro like Schumer probably did have a hand in shutting down the S.R.O. hotel in question. But I balk at any suggestion that he did it alone. He was certainly one of the links in the chain, but would the chain ever have been strung, or would it even have reached him, if others hadn't gotten involved earlier to raise the ruckus that eventually caught his eye and alerted him to an issue which cried out for his attention. Yes, he probably deserves some credit for this effort and, because of his political skills, likely a fair amount. But don't tell me he did it alone. Or just with some other local politicians his spokesperson thought to include in our phone conversation as an afterthought.

PROGNOSTICATIONS

(November 15, 1994)

Time to eat some crow? After the recent elections there must be plenty of folk out there ready to acknowledge how wrong they were. No doubt plenty of Democrats feel that way—and plenty of pundits. One of my fellow columnists in this paper made a big to-do about his predictions for the congressional races, going out on a limb in the October 18th issue of this paper with his prediction that "there will be no major shift in House seats, Clinton's lack of popularity not withstanding."

Based on historical comparisons, he posited that, since Clinton had failed to win by a landslide in his run two years ago, there was no major swing to the Democrats to "correct" this time so no seismic shift to the Republicans was to be expected. As this gentleman himself has since acknowledged, he was using a form of reasoning known in stock market circles as "technical analysis." This differs from so-called "fundamental analysis" which purports to look at the underlying factors which drive markets. The only problem is that, while fundamental analysis is tough to do (hard to identify and correctly weight all relevant factors), technical analysis can be even more unreliable, since it assumes that patterns which occurred before are likely to occur again—and yield roughly comparable results. Unfortunately, past performance is no guarantee of future returns—as they tell you in the fine print in those mutual fund advertisements.

On the other hand, my fellow columnist did better in his prediction of the Governor's race. There he called Pataki by a nose, which turned out to be right on. I, however, blew that one, since I predicted Cuomo would edge out Pataki from the beginning, even though Cuomo was already trailing in the polls. Whoops. Although I never went public with that call, I feel obliged to 'fess up anyway, out of a sense of honor, since I'm reminding my colleague here of his miscall. His other calls, by the way, were split. He got the Comptroller's race right, but blew it on the Attorney General. Given the relatively few races to bet on, vs. the vast number of stocks in the investment universe, I'd have to say his track record doesn't appear much better than that of the run-of-the-mill investment adviser's or money manager's.

Apparently, though, these investment gurus have even less to fear from me. Besides blowing it on Cuomo vs. Pataki, I also got it woefully wrong on the local Assembly race. Although not expecting a Tom Swift victory (given all I'd seen in the run-up to the election), I was fairly confident he'd at least match, and maybe do a little better than he did the last time he ran against incumbent Audrey Pheffer when he garnered 38% of the vote on a shoestring campaign. Apparently, Ms. Pheffer thought so too, since she spent a bundle on mass mailings before the vote. As it turned out, it's hard to see why she went to all that trouble. Swift did even worse against her this time: 29% to Audrey's 71%.

Ms. Pheffer thinks this shows she has gotten her message out and that the voters are happy with what they heard. Swift, on the other hand, has taken the position that Pheffer just out-spent him. At the risk of offending both parties, and hoping my lousy prognosticator's record won't prejudice anyone's opinion, I'd suggest that neither of them have it right.

Pheffer is entitled to claim a mandate, since the lopsided vote for her occurred in an election year when Democratic incumbents were literally being swept out the door in other venues. She is also entitled to our support and respect as our duly elected representative to the state Assembly. Still, this was not the blanket endorsement of her record she thinks and I hope she will not take it as a signal to continue confining her efforts to handholding at community meetings and demonstrations, however important that practice is, or to just channeling dollars into those local organizations which have come to depend on her as a funding source.

We send a legislator to Albany to legislate for us and it is there, I fear, that Ms. Pheffer has yet to distinguish herself. I was serious when I wrote recently that the way to address the ongoing S.R.O. issues in our community is to attack the underlying legislation which makes it possible for judges to force city officials to turn local hotels into warehouses for the homeless. But Ms. Pheffer so far has shown little interest in pursuing that question. And that's where I was hoping Tom Swift would make his mark.

But Tom started his campaign late (he diddled around from June to late September); and seemed reluctant to develop a substantive agenda, beyond some general philosophical statements about the death penalty, the "three R's" and lower taxes and spending. He largely failed to give the voters any substantive hooks to hang their collective hat on, or any sense of what he was besides a "conservative Republican" . . . whatever that is. Worse, he made very little effort to reach out to the wide range of ethnic groups on the peninsula or the mainland. This led to misunderstandings about him. (I've recently heard that rumors were flying, in the eastern part of the peninsula, that he was an "anti-Semite"—be assured, he's not, and I would know.) Tom, unfortunately, is rather introverted for a politician and has trouble reaching out to his own ethnic group, let alone to others.

So from what I can see, the fact that Tom did so much worse this year than two years ago, despite the tidal wave in favor of Republican challengers around the country, has little to do with how much money he spent. In fact, despite the slow start and lack of funds, his presence was greater this year than it was before. He even managed to draw Audrey into a debate. What went wrong, sad to say, was Tom, himself. A decent, honorable man, Tom missed his cues, even telling voters, in his closing remarks at the debate, that the reason to vote for him was because he probably wouldn't be around that long anyway!

With all due respect to Ms. Pheffer, she won her landslide because the more the electorate saw of Tom, the better she looked to them. She was more energetic and more specific at the debate (after a slow start) while Tom faded half-way through into terse ambiguities.

Given that, Tom should now recall another of his campaign promises, that he'd just quit if he thought he wasn't doing a good job, not wait around to be voted out. Given this, it's time for Mr. Swift to accept the role of elder statesman among Rockaway's Republicans, for whom he's already done so much, and step down as State Committeeman in favor of younger blood. If Rockaway's Republicans want to get on the train now leaving the station for the next century, they'll just have to learn to do better than they've done so far.

CHANGE IS NOW

(January 18, 1995)

Events seem to outrun our ability to write about them in these unusual times. Not long ago I called on our State Assemblywoman, Audrey Pheffer, to take a stand on the question of those state mandates which forced City Hall to provide immediate placements for the homeless, on pain of contempt-of-court citations and burdensome fines. My argument was that it was this kind of onerous and unrealistic mandate that was causing City Hall to "dump" homeless families in one of our local hotels on Beach 116th Street and that, until this was addressed, all the screaming and demonstrations and lawsuits we could muster would only be like sticking our fingers in a dike. I also pointed out that, as citizens of New York City, we had another, larger interest and that was fighting to keep our town governable and economically sound—things which become harder and harder to do as mandates are piled on top of mandates.

Assemblywoman Pheffer responded to me in a letter to the editor, disclaiming any direct involvement in the matter since, as she put it, this was an issue between City Hall and the courts. She completely ignored the thrust of my argument which was that courts enforce laws, and the regulations which arise from them, and that, as our state legislator, a law-maker, she was uniquely situated to raise this issue at the state level. As I pointed out at the time, the courts, in this case, were enforcing certain state regulations that had been promulgated by then Governor Mario Cuomo and his State Social Services commissioners. The regulations ostensibly elaborated on a state constitutional requirement to care for the needy. The Cuomo interpretation of that, in the matter of housing the homeless, was to oblige local social service jurisdictions to do this "immediately" whether the resources for this existed or not.

I argued that the most effective way for local people to fight use of the S.R.O. hotels as warehouses for the homeless, and to protect their interests as citizens of New York City, was to vote the Democrats who have given us this problem out of Albany. I also suggested that, if we couldn't get the Governor to rescind this burdensome mandate, our representatives in the state legislature could still deal with this matter for us, "if not by a bill than at least by a legislative review," with an eye toward effecting legislative changes to provide the sought-for relief. Ms. Pheffer finessed this question by largely ignoring it and called, instead, for more demonstrations and solidarity in the battle with City Hall.

Her opponent in the recent elections wasn't much better in this regard. When called on, in his debate with Pheffer, to indicate what could be done to protect local communities from laws like this, which imposed unfair and unjustifiable burdens, erstwhile Republican candidate for the State Assembly, Thomas F. Swift, declared "there isn't much anybody *can* do" (emphasis his). The panelist who posed the question seemed stunned by the non-response.

But now it looks like we'll be getting relief in this matter after all. In an eleventh hour bow to the conservative tide which swept him from office, outgoing New York State Governor Mario Cuomo rescinded the "immediate" placements rule in favor of a forty-eight hour timeframe which does not legally require placement, even after the initial timeframe has elapsed.

Odd that Cuomo chose to do it now, since George Pataki, his successor, was probably set to do it anyway. More to the point, if Cuomo thought it was the right thing to do, why did he wait until the last minute to do it? On the other hand, if he still thought it was wrong to remove the problematic rule, why do it at all? Leave it for the new guy to grapple with. What, we may wonder, occasioned the outgoing Governor's change of heart? These are just more questions to bedevil Cuomo watchers, if there are any left, for years to come. But as for us, we have got our relief, without having had to force our hapless Assemblywoman to take a stand against a Governor of her own party—or replacing her with a Republican legislator who seemed uncertain in his own mind as to what a legislator is really supposed to do.

My original point, on the other hand, still looks good, i.e., that the way to solve these sorts of problems is to change the people we send to Albany . . . and to Washington. Does anyone seriously think that Cuomo would have reversed his own longstanding policy if he were beginning still another term in the Statehouse, after December 30th, rather than heading out the door? Or that the new faces in Albany and Washington do not herald a lot more sensible changes of this type? The American electorate, in general, voted for change in '94 and change is what we now have a right to expect.

LATE TO THE PARTY?

(February 7, 1995)

While Republicans, nationally and statewide, are basking in the warm afterglow of their recent electoral sweep, Rockaway's own homegrown GOP is still reeling from what looks like a stunning reversal of fortunes on the local scene. After tossing out a 25 year Democratic incumbent City Councilman and delivering a solid vote for a new Republican Mayor, the Gateway Republicans went down to defeat in '94 as the party's local standard bearer, Thomas F. Swift, was convincingly trounced in his second bid to replace Democratic Assemblywoman Audrey I. Pheffer.

The Gateway Republicans, which had seen a groundswell of new membership after the '93 victories and which had the local Democratic machine suddenly looking nervously over its shoulder, abruptly went from rising political star to plummeting meteorite in a single electoral cycle. So in this year of Republican revolution across the country, with Newt Gingrich making Bill Clinton seem increasingly irrelevant on the federal level, what went wrong in Rockaway?

Part of the answer, of course, lies in the little black box that is Republican politics in our part of south Queens. The leadership of the Gateway Republicans squandered their momentum coming out of '93 because they didn't understand that a successful political group has to reach out to the general electorate—not just preach to the converted. The party's local standard bearer and titular head, Tom Swift, a decent enough fellow, didn't grasp the need to develop an agenda of issues defining himself to voters. He thought it was sufficient to say "I am a conservative and my opponent is not" to get the votes he needed to make it to Albany as our Assemblyman.

Tom thought all he had to do was speak in generalities and count on folks nodding their heads and saying: "Yes indeed, he's one of us, so I'll vote for him." But it didn't work out that way.

Tom and the Republicans out here got their heads handed to them in the recent election because they made no effort to reach out to the broader electorate and to address the many and varying concerns these groups have. The Gateway Republicans, in the end, is a small, insular group which so far has shown no ability to attract a broader spectrum of people to its banner. Its meetings tend to be uninspired affairs and its leadership a small group of individuals who seem to have a proprietary interest in "their" club. At the same time, its philosophy and ideals remain rather vague and ill-defined. Of course, it's understandable that the few people who were instrumental in reviving the Gateway club, after it fell on hard times a few years back as a result of a local school board scandal, would want to retain their pivotal roles in that organization. But there's no excuse for these people trying to hold onto the club's leadership indefinitely. If they really want to "grow" their club and have an impact on local affairs—and maybe even elect some candidates to office—they're going to have to open themselves up to other people and other perspectives.

Although conservatism is what generally distinguishes Republicans from Democrats today, and what the Gateway Republicans espouse, there are actually many different kinds of conservatives in this country—though you wouldn't know that from the club's leadership. There are, of course, the social conservatives who dominate the Gateway Club. These are folks who favor restoration and strengthening of traditional social values as manifested in a respect for the institutions of our society, such as marriage and family, and for standards of individual responsibility, respect for life, etc. Opposition to abortion on demand and belief in the death penalty for heinous offenders stand high on the list of issues dear to social conservatives. Similarly, these folks have a profound respect for traditional religious teachings and beliefs.

But there are other, related conservative groups. One is represented by the so-called fiscal conservatives whose main issues revolve around balancing budgets so that spending does not exceed the revenues taken in. People with this view also tend to be strong supporters of the business sector in society, seeing it as the engine of true economic growth and prosperity, which must be sustained and enhanced in order for us to continue to live well as a nation.

Then there are the small government conservatives who tend to be libertarian-oriented and favor limiting governmental growth by lowering taxes and tightening the constraints on permissible governmental operations. These libertarian types, not to be confused with liberals who favor larger government (and are most prevalent in the ranks of the Democrats), believe in minimalist government, where feasible, on the grounds that this is our best defense against tyranny and is what the founding fathers actually had in mind when they set up our Constitution.

These various forms of conservatism can be quite different and can lead adherents to advocate very different positions. Libertarians, for instance, usually oppose government intervention on the abortion question, either pro or con, whatever their personal feelings may be on the issue. They also tend to oppose government attempts to foster values such as pushing prayer in public schools. On the other hand, they are very sympathetic to the old-fashioned values many social conservatives long to see reinstated in our communities and institutions, i.e., that people should be encouraged to stand on their own feet and not depend on the stultifying largess of government. Fiscal or economic conservatives tend to be somewhat socially conservative too, even if this is not the focus of their political philosophy. And, of course, libertarians in their support for smaller government, are in concert with those who want to unbind the private sector and who want to rein in government so that it cannot spend more than it takes in or grow to the moon on an unlimited power to tax.

The point here is that conservatism is a fairly broad web of ideas and principles, many of which overlap and some of which actually appear contradictory. But it's rather an extensive net, capable of gathering in a lot of fish, and this should not be overlooked by those attempting to build a new political base in Rockaway.

Many people today see the benefits of smaller government and of economic growth; and they are not to be found in one community only. But this fact seems to be lost on the Gateway Club leadership which, in the person of Thomas F. Swift, thought it could win an election without any sort of broad appeal across communities.

"Conservatism" may be a single word but it is also an often complex philosophy that cries out for definition, for engagement, for an agenda. Only in that way can it be successful as an alternative to the tired liberalism of Rockaway politics which seems to win elections, year in and year out, for want of any serious alternatives. Do Rockaway's Republicans really want to start winning elections again or are they content to remain political also-rans, talking only to themselves and to those who think and look like them at their regular monthly meetings? If they're serious about participating in the nationwide resurgence of Republicanism, they'll just have to do better than they've done so far and build a bigger house for themselves. And maybe even invite the rest of us inside.

Historical Note: In the mid-nineties the Peninsula News, which had carried the Rockaway Irregular column since 1993 shut its doors and the Irregular at last fell silent. But this would only be a hiatus. In 2002, The Wave, Rockaway's oldest newspaper and premier news weekly, picked up the column and a new era of commentary was initiated. Many of the same themes continued to be plumbed.

The November 2002 elections, like those in 1994, proved to be another apparent milestone in the shift that had been underway since the mid-twentieth century . . . reflecting the increasing influence and success, nationwide, of the Republican Party. A minority party nationally since Franklin Delano Roosevelt forged a national consensus in favor of the Democrats during the Great Depression of the nineteen-thirties, the Republicans had been fighting their way back ever since, in an effort to establish a new national consensus in their favor. The leftish leanings of the Democratic Party had gradually become more pronounced, as big spending, greater governmental activism in domestic and social matters, and an aversion to a strongly proactive internationalist stance— left over from the country's divisive Vietnam experience—pushed the Democrats further and further away from the moderate political center.

In the 2002 elections, the Republicans convincingly, if narrowly, took control of both houses of Congress for the first time in recent memory, thereby reinforcing an earlier marginal win by their presidential standard bearer, George W. Bush, who had squeaked into the White House amid much controversy two years before. As subsequent events would show, the Democrats were not only taken aback by their surprising losses in 2002, they were galvanized to do whatever it took to reverse them. But even while the Republicans had racked up electoral wins nationally and at local levels at an unprecedented rate, Rockaway remained a community apart, where Democrats continued to have little if anything to worry about.

CLOSING THE GATE

(December 28, 2002)

A recent note in this paper told us that the Gateway Republican Club was shutting its doors for the second time in a generation. This group, revived in the early nineties by two gentlemen sharing the same given name, Tom Carney and Tom Swift (old-line Republican politicos both), had tried valiantly for over a decade to restore the two-party system to Rockaway politics. Alas, it was not to be. The two Toms worked diligently throughout the nineties to bring in new members and drum up attention for the Rockaway-based Republican club in what is, in essence, a thoroughly Democratic town. Why did they bother? The usual reasons: interest in politics, a commitment to Republican ideas, frustration at being frozen out of the process here on the peninsula, a desire to accomplish something and, perhaps, to win an elective office.

While Tom and Tom were running things, local Republicans in Rockaway were galvanized. I was there with them, myself, when they reached out to Al Stabile and offered him the club's endorsement. And I worked closely with Tom Swift in his several abortive runs for the State Assembly. It was invigorating. There was a sense that we could make a difference and that we might even make the Democrats out here stop taking us for granted.

I had my own reasons for getting involved. Having been a lifelong Democrat I watched with fascination as Ronald Reagan accomplished things with his Republican philosophy that Democrats had only talked about. Although I had never voted for Reagan, by the time George H. W. Bush ran, I had decided to cast my vote for a Republican on the national level. Later, when I saw how shabbily the media and mainstream Democrats treated Bush senior, who I thought had performed quite well in his single presidential term, I decided to formalize my switch and made the jump to the Republicans (making me probably the only Republican in the country who can trace his party conversion to the senior President Bush).

I chose to become actively involved with the two Toms when former Councilman Walter Ward's staff blew me off over a local property fee the city wanted to levy. That clinched it for me and I decided that all organizations, even the Democratic Party, needed a little competition if they were going to perform at their best! So I sought out, and found, Tom and Tom . . . . and went on to join the Gateway Republican Club, a group they had only recently revived after some earlier scandals and political floundering had prompted a previous shut down of the club. And together we all made a bit of noise.

But, unfortunately, we never got any real traction out here in Rockaway. The Democratic Party was too strong, perhaps because local folks are just more comfortable with the statist philosophy of the Democrats, or because most people don't like to buck the trend. In the end, Tom Swift's several abortive runs for Assembly made no ripples on the pond and club membership did not swell. Our biggest success was supporting Al Stabile in his effort to unseat Walter Ward. But Al seemed to have other fish to fry than what was to be had in Rockaway and his two terms were marked by disagreements and rancor with Rockaway's Republicans. John Baxter, then a mainstay of the Gateway Club, went over to the Independence Party out of frustration and his brother, Owen Baxter, did a brief stint as club president after Tom Carney stepped down. Tom passed on not long afterwards, unfortunately, leaving a big gap for the club. Tom Swift, sadly, also left us around the same time, due to a heart ailment.

We went into a long period of decline as Al Stabile shifted the focus of his own peculiar brand of Republican politics over to the mainland, leaving us a club more or less out of water. I allowed my own membership to lapse since the club's monthly meetings had begun to seem pointless. Nothing of any note was happening and there was no fire left in the collective belly. Attending the meetings began to feel like the proverbial exercise in futility. Local Republican activist Kenny Huhn tried to keep the club alive but even he, in the end, saw the hopelessness of it and recently announced the club's untimely second demise.

But where, then, does that leave Rockaway? Well, John Baxter has been trying valiantly to build a grassroots organization for the Independence party here but this has never really caught fire. So what have we got left? Just the Democrats . . . multiple iterations of this party in fact, including a western branch and an eastern (to make room, I suppose, for all those trying to play in the lone Democratic tent). Yet, Rockaway is not the better for this.

Monopolies lead to stagnation and institutional unresponsiveness (as I found out when I needed Walter Ward's help so many years ago). They are also characteristic of the one party politics of the old Soviet Union, a system that seems the very antithesis of what we pride ourselves on. It's better to have a choice and know that our political representatives really do have to stay on top of issues if they want to keep their jobs, isn't it? A political civil service system, with more or less guaranteed tenure, is just as bad as the civil service system that weighs down our city agencies. Yet, without a viable political alternative, that is all we can hope for.

Is there any reason to be a Republican instead of a Democrat in today's New York, besides the desire to have some choice in our elections? I would suggest that there is. Democrats stand for more robust government which includes a greater emphasis on services to the public and the taxes needed to support and pay for those services. What does the Republican Party stand for? Aside from our current mayor who often seems unsure whether he is really a Republican at all, Republicans in general stand for more restricted government. This is not the same thing as no government, or even minimal government (you need the Libertarians or anarchists for that). Rather, restricted government means tighter reins on the governing agencies in terms of ensuring a finite, not infinite and inexhaustible, flow of available resources and stronger requirements for operational accountability. In short, an emphasis on tighter management over more expansive government.

On the Democratic view, what is really needed is more funding for all those added programs and services, thus higher relative taxes. On the Republican view, the funding spigots should be opened only reluctantly and with care to reduce government's tendency toward profligacy and waste. Thus, in principle, Republicans are for lower taxes.

Obviously this doesn't always work out quite so simply in the real world but, I submit, there is a genuine philosophical difference between the two parties. And a reason for some folks here in Rockaway to choose the loyal opposition.

With the demise of the Gateway Republicans for the second time in 20 years, we are all a little worse off than we were before. But this needn't be the end of it. Surely there are still a few registered Republicans left here in Rockaway, Republicans who haven't yet gone the way of the Dodo Bird but can, like the piping plover, be called back from the brink of extinction. The Gateway Republican Club may be gone again from our midst but there is still room enough, and time, for the party of Lincoln and Teddy Roosevelt and even George Bush to come up for air for a third time in the rarified waters of Rockaway. And like they say, maybe the third time is the charm.

REPUBLICANS VANQUISH DEMS! WHITHER ROCKAWAY?

(March 22, 2003)

Now that all the shouting and campaigning is over, and the politicians are sorting through the fallout, one thing is painfully obvious: the Democrats got served with a wake-up call this past November 5th. Throughout the nation, hotly contested races fell to the Republicans in the wake of George W. Bush and his party's efforts to convince voters that his administration had a vision which addressed America's needs . . . and that Democratic control of a portion of Congress obstructed that vision.

Gains in the House and a retaking of the Senate virtually assure Bush that he will have a chance to implement some or all of that vision. Moreover, they give him a patina of legitimacy that many Democrats had striven to deprive him of, since his own narrow election in 2000. And so the worm turns.

Does this mean we are in for a Republican majority for the foreseeable future? Hardly. The Republicans now have the enviable, if risky, chance of actually putting our money where their mouths are . . . . and trying to make things better. There is homeland defense to attend to and a sharpening up of the still-listing economy. There is a need for tax reform and to get judges in place, too. Bush has been admirably low-key in the shadow of this past Election Day's decisive turn of events but he has given every indication that he understands that the onus, as well as the opportunity, is now on him.

What about Rockaway? We're still decidedly in the Democratic camp, given the recent electoral results and that means we're still a one-party town. But, if it's a good thing to have more than one party operating on the national scene, isn't it also a good thing to have that on the local level? For years, one of the main reasons people flocked to the Democratic Party in the Rockaways has been the perception that the Democrats were the only serious political alternative. Republicans rarely, if ever, won elections out here and they had no organization to speak of on the local level. If you wanted to get things done, it's always been the Democrats who were positioned to accomplish things.

Of course, there are many who genuinely believe in the Democratic Party's core positions: more government involvement, increased taxation in order to fund that involvement, re-direction of resources from the wealthy to those who are not, unqualified support for work rules that may insulate a workforce from accountability, etc. But many others have gravitated to the Democrats merely because they were perceived to be the party with the power. But that leads to arrogance and hubris for the Democratic leadership. In a democratic society it may also lead to a shifting of the political plates, as we have just seen on the national level!

With Republicans beginning to demonstrate that they represent a serious and respectable alternative, we have watched as they incrementally re-took the reins of power at the city, state and, once again, the federal levels of government. The Republican view, shorn of some of the hardcore nonsense of yesteryear which reflected an almost atavistic, and to New Yorkers, unattractive social conservatism, has reshaped itself into a philosophy of limiting government by imposing greater accountability (as opposed to their older cry of shrinking it at any cost!) and of placing primary emphasis on ensuring effective management. Bush has exemplified this by the seriousness with which he staffed his cabinet and in the professional response he and his team provided to the attacks of September 11th and afterwards.

What's needed in Rockaway now is the development of this same, serious alternative. It does no one any good to be represented by a monopoly party . . . except, of course, those who control that monopoly. One of the things that brought down the old Soviet

Union was the popular realization that Russia was being ruled by a monolithic political dinosaur, more interested in its own longevity and survival, its own retention of the levers of power, than in new ideas or in being responsive to the needs of its people. The beauty of democracy is that there is room for more than one party and that having more than one is best for the body politic. This has been proved out, in the long run, both for nations and individuals time and again over the century just passed. In fact, you can't have a real democracy without competition.

In light of this latest demonstration, on the national level, that there is life outside the Democratic Party, isn't it time Rockaway, too, heeded that song? Isn't it time for a return to real two-party democracy at this most local of levels, time for a revitalized Republican camp here on our own small peninsula? And isn't such competition a good thing for all of us . . . even for the Democrats?

Historical Note: In March 2004 a new Rockaway Republican club opened its doors with a kick-off meeting in the Belle Harbor community. Begun by a few concerned supporters of President Bush's "War on Terror," and initially meeting in one member's garage during the preceding winter months, the newly named "Rockaway Republicans" quickly attracted a surprisingly large and energetic following. Unfortunately, it did not garner speedy support from local and county Republican leadership and so had to find its own way. Perhaps that was a good thing, since it meant members of the new group had to proceed on their own devices and their club would not develop as a dependent of some larger organization. Left on their own, without feedback or support from the regular party organization, the new Rockaway Republicans began reaching out to other like-minded groups around the city.

STAR-CROSSED IN BROOKLYN

(May 28, 2004)

Back on April 1st, a contingent from the newly minted Rockaway Republicans joined their Brooklyn counterparts at a borough-wide reception in Mill Basin hosted by Brooklyn State Senator Marty Golden from Bayridge. Like an old time revivalist, Golden whooped up the crowd, pushing three items: renewing Republican strength in New York City, re-election of George W. Bush, and praise and support for New York's own Mayor Mike Bloomberg. (Bloomberg came charging into the hall about an hour late, due to traffic delays, he said.)

Golden surprised his Rockaway guests by publicly singling them out and introducing them to the Brooklyn crowd. Among the Rockaway Republican club members present were Tom Lynch, the club's foremost spokesperson, as well as Pete Stubben, Robert Smith, Mike Bracci, Tom Hannan and Gerry Cronin. I went along for the ride, too. The surprised Brooklynites gave their visiting Rockaway neighbors a fierce round of applause as the State Senator urged Brooklyn and Rockaway to join forces in pursuing a revival of the Republican Party in New York City.

Golden used his time to praise President Bush who, he said, "had made the tough decisions when others could afford to sit on the sidelines and criticize." He lauded the Bush tax-cuts as measures to "bring long-term growth" and called on his audience to close ranks in support of the president and to assist his re-election effort through vigorous volunteerism. Then, introducing Mayor Bloomberg (when the mayor finally arrived), Golden talked up the

Mayor's own courage and achievements, including his tough stand against social promotions in schools and his efforts at bringing new development to the city.

Following the Senator on stage, Bloomberg told the audience he had no interest in raising taxes beyond where they now were and that he was, in fact, looking for ways to lower them. (One has to wonder how that will be possible, given recent forecasts of city budget deficits ahead . . . though such forecasts may just be another move in the intricate minuet that city labor negotiations represent.) Bloomberg reiterated his call for passage of a one-time real estate tax rebate to homeowners but added, in response to a question from the audience, that "someone still has to pay taxes" if the city was going to deliver all the services its citizens expected.

Unfortunately, no one asked him about progress (or the lack thereof) re: improving government efficiency by tightening up on wasteful practices and inefficiencies. As I've written in this column many times before, there are many opportunities for this, including improving the city's management of its own real estate portfolio, tightening city personnel practices, and modernizing and streamlining the city's management of capital projects. But it's difficult to get governments to focus in these areas . . . even Republican-led governments.

Responding to another question, Bloomberg also reminded his audience that a number of the tax increases he pushed through earlier in his term "go away by law between this year and next" and promised to fight to ensure the laws aren't changed to prevent this. He concluded by noting that "I wasn't hired by you people to cave in to every pressure group. I did what I had to do to balance the budget. I tell my staff, don't worry about what you look like in the tabloids each morning, worry about what you look like in the mirror."

The Mayor ended by praising Bush and promised a strong welcome for Republicans at this summer's planned national party convention, even though he admitted he expected large protests.

After the meeting, Belle Harborite Tom Lynch led his group around the hall to get better acquainted with the Brooklyn

Republicans. Lynch noted admiringly that "the Brooklyn groups seem to have found the secret that still eludes us in Queens."

Expanding on his theme, Lynch bemoaned the fact that "there doesn't seem to be the same kind of cohesion or excitement among Queens groups" as we were seeing in Mill Basin. Although he recently led his membership into alliance with the Forest Park Republicans (an insurgent Queens Republican group on the mainland), since he's been unable to achieve symbiosis with Republican leaders closer to home (Broad Channel and Howard Beach), he insists he's not ruling out closer ties with these nearby communities. "We still want an alliance with them," Lynch told me, "to build the kind of borough-wide organization the Brooklyn party has. But if we can't get that, maybe the next best thing is to try to hook up with Brooklyn. Many Rockawayites came from Brooklyn, after all, and our peninsula is certainly closer, physically, to that borough than to the rest of Queens."

After listening to him and seeing the Brooklynites in action, I couldn't agree more.

THE POLITICS OF COMPETITION

(July 2004)[1]

A recent piece in another New York paper decried the loss of democratic competitiveness in this city and suggested the way to restore real competition may actually lie in switching New York's electoral methodology to a proportional system. In such a system each party gets legislative seats according to the percentage of votes it receives in the overall election rather than through direct election of individuals as is currently the case. In fact, this has been tried before. The city briefly experimented with proportional voting shortly after World War II, only to decide it was a bust when tiny factional parties, including groups like the Communists, ended up with legislative seats. This actually made governance more difficult not less.

Reengineering our voting system, while superficially attractive, is not the answer. You can't legislate competitiveness. You have to have the right conditions for it and these are precisely what are currently missing in large parts of New York City, leading to the virtual one party system we now have. Indeed, the solution is not to replace current problems with older ones (a one-party monopoly with fragmented factionalism). Rather, we must find and restore competitiveness in the places where it naturally arises . . . at the grassroots, where true democratic politics is born.

A good part of the reason there is such ideological homogeneity in local government in this city today can be laid at the doorstep of the main opposition party itself. New York Republicans have relentlessly institutionalized their own minority status by embracing that role in a generational retreat to "safe" bastions for their leaders . . . at the expense of fielding vigorous opposition across the city's communities. In the borough of Queens, alone, the Republican "leadership" has shrunk in on itself over the years, in order to preserve a few precious positions. Public offices held by Republicans grow fewer and fewer as district after district falls to the Democratic machine.

In a kind of pyrrhic retreat, the Republican leaders in Queens County have preserved what little they have left by ignoring, or in some cases actually working against, any real grassroots activity for fear this may result in new people coming to the fore, thereby opening up the possibility that current leaders might actually have to campaign and run for their positions in open elections in order to retain the perquisites of power. But what are such "leaders" leaders of then, having given up the possibility of developing a vibrant membership within their own party?

In the few "safe" Republican pockets around the city, current leaders manage to hold onto their seats in government by avoiding challenging the stronger Democrats in adjacent and neighboring communities, while many cling to "appointive" leadership posts, secured through the good graces of the Albany machine rather than via the rough and tumble (and risks) of grassroots competition.

The result is an atrophying Republican Party in New York City that bears little resemblance to Republicans in other parts of the country . . . a party that is fatally weakened by its own oft-espoused, self-fulfilling prophecy: 'avoid challenging the Democrats in hopes they won't challenge you.' But it's exactly this decision to accept what is, in essence, a 'non-compete' clause with the Democrats, that makes the Republicans in this town as weak as they are.

If we want to change the look of local governance and see real political opposition again in places like the City Council, then the answer is not to be found in re-engineering elections to create a less responsive proportionalized system where we vote for parties, not people. Rather, the key is to revive politics at the grassroots. This is already happening in some places. In the past six months in the Queens community of Rockaway, a new Republican organization recently raised its head after being crushed over the years by a system that preferred quietude and job security to giving the voters a genuine political alternative. In neighboring Forest Park, another Queens community, the same dynamic has been occurring on a parallel basis for over five years now. There's ample reason to believe there are other areas in Queens, and elsewhere in the city, where this is also happening.

This year, with a Republican president in surprisingly dire straits, due at least in part to a relentlessly hostile mainstream media, some locally based Republicans have finally been galvanized to raise the flag of opposition. The newly formed Rockaway Republicans recently held two gatherings to support President George W. Bush and saw record turnouts in their area, the most Republicans in one place in some twenty years. They did this without the support, or even encouragement, of the county level organization and with minimum publicity and ballyhoo. Although "leaders" are supposed to get out front in these kinds of things, sometimes it just doesn't work out that way.

If genuinely competitive elections and real voter choice is to return to New York City, it will have to start at places like this, at the ground level, and not depend on reengineering from the top. That's the only way to turn the tide of oppositional quietism which has made politics in our city as stultified and undemocratic as the worst that the old, and thankfully now extinct, Soviet Union had to offer.

ALL THE NEWS THAT FITS . . .

TELLING IT LIKE IT WAS

(June 28ᵗʰ, 1994)

Remember the terrible eighties? You know, that horrible decade when the hard-hearted Republicans let loose the economic dogs of war upon an unsuspecting American public by cutting regulations and supporting the free enterprise system? When the rich got richer, while everyone else suffered the financial ignominy of an allegedly shrinking share of the pie? When minorities and the middle class were told they had been left behind by all those greed mongers on Wall Street and by the bogeymen of Big Business?

That's what they told us, anyway, in 1992 when the mainstream media and Democratic politicians combined to castigate the Reagan-Bush years, finally convincing the American people to cast out those awful, business friendly Republicans in favor of "New Democrats" sworn to advance the liberal social agenda, tax increases or no. That's why Bush lost to Bill Clinton; because Bill "cared" and was willing to show it by pumping up government programs and spending, and by enlarging the bureaucracy's role in our lives.

Well guess what? Maybe the eighties weren't so bad after all! At least that's what the New York Times suggested in a recent front page article which pointed out that "driven by striking gains in the 1980's among working wives and immigrants, the median income of black households in Queens has surpassed that of whites."

Hold it. Did we read this right? In the eighties? But we were told that that decade was a time of suffering and economic deterioration for minorities and the middle class. Isn't that what the mainstream media (including the Times) was saying just a short time ago? That's certainly what they were saying throughout 1992 when the presidency was up for grabs, making all of us feel a whole lot worse about a shallow recession which now appears to have ended in 1991.

But there's more. The Times article goes on to say: "A fresh analysis of 1990 census results found that . . . economic progress by blacks in Queens . . . was built largely on a traditional foundation of family solidarity . . . Married couples made the greatest strides . . . (and) . . . Among immigrant families, black couples earned a median household income of $48,800 . . . appreciably more than the $40,500 reported by whites born abroad." And again, according to the Times, "Blacks had higher household incomes in more than 130 cities and counties in the United States." Looks like this wasn't just a one-town phenomenon!

Of course, this information isn't really new. A number of pundits and analysts tried to buck the trend in 1992 and afterwards, pointing out that jobs creation had surged in the eighties, that the alleged gap in income gains was more apparent than real, since Americans typically progress through various economic strata as they age, and that the supposed "worst recession since the thirties" (according to candidate Clinton) was really quite mild by historical measures and nothing to compare with the deep downturns of the seventies.

But sailing into the headwinds of the mainstream media and their liberal political allies, who sought to recapture the levers of power in Washington, it was hard to be heard above the squall. Tired of a "blue blood" president, who valued competence and dickering with world leaders over a nutra-sweet embrace of the public's problems, a la Bill Donohue, folks wanted to hear that Washington would be there to take care of them again. In truth, people tend to believe what they want to believe, whatever the facts say, and to listen to the voices that tell them what they want to hear. And so it was in this case.

People were ready for the "caring politician," completely forgetting that politicians, like most other people, really don't care all that much about anyone but themselves. But, of course, that's not necessarily a bad thing either, since our whole democratic republic is premised on the belief that, when people are free to pursue their own interests, they really serve everyone else's interests too. That's why our system has all those safeguards—to prevent government from getting too big, too out-of-control and, thereby, jeopardizing our civil liberties; smothering initiative and the freedom to do business (among other freedoms). That freedom which made the eighties such a remarkable period of economic expansion, after the sour seventies, when liberal policies fed the monster of big government—a period which everyone now seems to have conveniently forgotten. A period of gas shortages and wild inflation; of job shrinkage and slow growth and dramatically lowered expectations; of turning the lights off and the thermostats down.

That's what everyone forgot in '92 in the rush to change administrations. They forgot how bad it *had* been. And they refused to see which policies had been associated with the change from the seventies to the eighties, when prosperity made America, once more, the premiere nation on earth and the envy of the world. But now that the presidential campaign is over and those reprehensible Republicans have been safely unseated, the New York Times can at last tell us about all those economic gains people made in the eighties when things were so "bad," right? No one can construe this as providing aid and comfort to an incumbent Republican administration that might somehow have been associated with those gains. The Times is free at last to tell it like it is and again uphold those high standards of journalism they profess to believe in. After all, the Democrats are safely back in power . . . aren't they?

FITTING THE PRINT

(May 23, 2003)

Surprise, surprise: The New York Times has an agenda! It's all over the news media these days. Turns out the venerable paper, whose slogan is "All the News That's Fit to Print," has been shaping what it reports in accordance with its own point of view . . . a very questionable journalistic practice, to say the least.

I first noted this in print back in the nineties when I was writing this column for another newspaper, remarking then how the Times slanted its economic and social coverage in order to advance a liberal agenda. This was not just a matter of tone or emphasis either. It often seemed to involve actual misrepresentation and/or suppression of information. And it was not just reflective of the Times' editorial page. It showed up in actual news stories where the Times slanted its presentation to suggest that economic conditions were much worse back then than the financial press (where business coverage really counts!) was then suggesting.

More recently, in the January 4th edition of this paper, I noted, among other things, how the Times had misrepresented a statistical survey it was reporting on in its headline and lead-in text, leaving the impression that the survey's findings were very different from what they actually were. Now it turns out, with the revelations of plagiarism and fictitious reporting, and new information about the opinions of its staff, that this is a deeply embedded part of the paper's culture. Times reporter Chris Hedges was recently booed off the stage at a Rockford Illinois commencement ceremony for inveighing against U.S. policy in Iraq even as Times executive editor Howell Raines admitted he let his belief in affirmative action affect his judgment in the plagiarism matter concerning disgraced Times reporter Jayson Blair.

But, as Andrew Sullivan, a blogger and occasional contributor to The New York Sun, recently wrote: " . . . while Mr. Raines was promising a new commitment to accuracy and openness, another one of his acolytes, Maureen Dowd, was up to her usual tricks of dissembling the truth."

Sullivan went on to note that Ms. Dowd, a regular Times columnist, known for her peculiarly petulant vitriol against Republicans and especially the Bush family, misquoted President George W. Bush in order to suggest that he had mistakenly claimed to have rendered al Qaeda "not a problem anymore."

Sullivan offers us the actual quote, filling in Ms. Dowd's strategic omissions (which clearly alter the sense of what President Bush said), and challenges Ms. Dowd to retract. Don't bet on that one!

Indeed, on the very same weekend that Sullivan's article appeared in The Sun, Ms. Dowd offered another one of her zingers in a column comparing two newly released films, "The Matrix Reloaded" and Renee Zellweger's "Down With Love". What had any of this to do with Bush?

Everything per Ms. Dowd, who reserved the final three paragraphs of her article for a gratuitous swipe at our 43rd president, suggesting that Bush and his policies are all about "testosterone as a campaign accessory."

Hey, I guess you hadda be there.

So maybe she's not stooping to misquotes this time, but her constant tendency to take cheap shots of this nature betrays something quite a bit more serious: an agenda which has little or nothing to do with facts, but a great deal to do with savaging those with whom she disagrees.

Sure, she's writing a column, an opinion piece, but even columns need some degree of dispassion and deference to the facts, don't they?

But in the New York Times these days, this commitment to dispassion seems to have been lost. As Holman W. Jenkins Jr. notes in a May 21st opinion piece in the Wall Street Journal, the Times has a history of getting it wrong in order to advance an agenda. From misreporting a quote from a Texaco executive in order to support allegations of racism, to trying to stir the pot in the Augusta National Golf Club brouhaha, Jenkins suggests: "The Times can't find enough racist behavior to suit it, so the paper has to resort to dubious statistical and other means to create the story it's looking for."

Now comes disgraced reporter Jayson Blair who, in the face of Howell Raines' claims to have given him "one chance too many" because of his race, avers that Times editorial management, in fact, just weren't too bright since he, Blair, was able to fool them so thoroughly concerning the phony articles he was writing for them.[2] Blair then goes on to accuse the Times staff of racism and of holding him down.

So the Times is hoisted on its own petard. Shaping its coverage to advance an agenda of liberal social activism and affirmative action, it's tarred, in the end, with the brush of racism and unintelligence by the very man its management claims to have bent over backwards to excuse for his excesses in the course of promoting diversity in the workplace.

Maybe there's a message here?

PUPPETS, SCHMUPPETS

(August 29, 2003)

New York Times syndicated columnist Maureen Dowd, the writer who takes the prize for showing the most contempt for a sitting American president since the media feeding frenzy of the Nixon years, has done it again. On the August 24th Times Op Ed page, in a column headed "Gotta Lotta Stigmata," she gives us one of her typical anti-male screeds, going after all those awful male politicians who affect a strong (read "manly") stance for the media. Of course, after taking a few obligatory swipes at John Kerry, Howard Dean and even "wonky Bob Graham" for aping George W. Bush, "immortalized with an action figure in a flight suit and the leg hugging harness that made Republican women's hearts go boom-boom," she tells us, and after having gone after Arnold Schwarzenegger for being, well, Arnold, she finally gets down to what really yanks her chain.

Ms. Dowd, who recently gained national notoriety for misquoting Bush by lopping off part of what he said in order to make him sound as though he'd said something entirely different, can't quite contain her feminist outrage where the Bushman is concerned. Noting that some conservative writers, and especially some women, see in Bush a president who "does what he says, whose every speech and act is not calculated"[3] Ms. Dowd let's go with both barrels blazing.

Reporting that one David Gutmann, a professor emeritus of psychology at Northwestern University, says of Bush that he "bears important masculine stigmata: he is a Texan, he is not afraid of war, and he sticks to his guns in the face of worldwide criticism,"

Ms. Dowd opines "Stigmata, schtigmata. Shouldn't real men be able to control their puppets?"

Who and what does she have in mind with this latest swipe at the President? Well, it's about Iraq, of course.

"The Bush team could not even get Ahmad Chalabi and the Iraq Governing Council to condemn the U.N. bombing or feign putting an Iraqi face on the occupation," she proclaims and then proceeds to add that "the puppets refused, because they didn't want to be seen as puppets."

Continuing, she informs us that "Rumsfeld & Co." erred, "thanks to the phony optimistic intelligence fed to them by the puppet Chalabi."

Come again?

Maybe I missed something but, despite current and not unexpected difficulties in stabilizing post-war Iraq (everyone knew it was going to be tough . . . that was one of the reasons many were uneasy about undertaking this effort in the first place), I seem to recall that the war, itself, achieved its goals with surprising speed and record low casualties thanks, in no small part, to the intelligence fed to our military about what was waiting for them. The "puppet Chalabi" was not without some small involvement in this matter.

But more to the point, in Ms. Dowd's mind, the Bush administration nefariously established a puppet regime through Mr. Chalabi (we *know* they're puppets, of course, because Ms. Dowd has told us), and yet the administration lacks the machismo to make them act like the puppets she tells us they are. Sounds a lot like Ms. Dowd's stacked this deck, condemning her favorite testosterone-producing whipping boys, Bush, Cheney, Rumsfeld, et al, for puppeteering . . . and then going after them for not keeping their erstwhile creations on a string.

But at least one slightly more rational scenario is also possible here: that the "puppets" aren't acting the part because they aren't puppets at all.

Holy smoking gun, Batman, maybe the Bush administration is serious about rebuilding a free, independent and modern Iraq, despite Ms. Dowd's protestations to the contrary? Maybe they really are working to set up an independent Iraqi government? But such logic seems to have no more impact on Ms. Dowd's thinking than actual facts . . . as in accurately quoting what presidents really say.

After poor-mouthing George Bush Sr., in the nineties, for being a privileged preppie without much backbone, she seems to think the son is, of all things, just too macho. One begins to get the sense that something else is going on here. Maybe the good Professor Gutmann needs to look a little more closely at Ms. Dowd's own "shtickmata" to see why she has this thing about Republicans, the Bush family and testosterone?

"BUSH ACTS AGAINST CRITICS . . ."

(February 14, 2004)

The New York Times has actually been showing some improvement over the past few months, since its recent false reporting flaps. As public scrutiny zeroed in on the Times' news and editorial staffs, and people began to talk about the paper's obvious liberal bias, management finally took action (after decades of self-satisfied inaction) and fired their top editors, replacing them with individuals thought to have a less obvious agenda.

The new executive managing editor, Bill Keller, actually supported the Iraqi war . . . while criticizing the Bush administration's reasons for undertaking it and how they handled it. (Well he did get tapped to run the Times, didn't he?)

Times management also added a new conservative columnist (David Brooks) to its stable, presumably to offset such strident anti-administration stalwarts as Paul Krugman, Maureen Dowd and Tom Friedman. And they put an editorial ombudsman on the payroll to write a twice-monthly column addressing reader concerns about bias and unfairness at the paper. Most recently the Times announced its intention to "cover conservatives." (One has to wonder what a newspaper that prides itself on reporting "all the news that's fit to print" thought they were doing all these years if they haven't been covering conservatives until now!)

So things are better, right? Well, as I said, there have been some noticeable improvements. Some of the really egregious, partisan anti-conservative, anti-Bush, anti-Republican stuff has been toned down. Maureen Dowd, for instance, Bush basher par excellence, has not been quite so outrageous as she's been in the past. (This doesn't mean she's suddenly become a Bush fan, of course . . . but she hasn't been quite as shrill lately, even occasionally turning her attention to some other targets besides favorites like "Junior," "Rummy," et al).

Still, it looks like it's hard for even the venerable New York Times to completely turn over a new leaf. The selection of readers' letters reprinted on the editorial page remains almost uniformly and aggressively anti-Bush. Well, you could argue that that's just the kind of readership the Times gets. Shucks, they can't control who sends them what, can they? Of course, we have no idea what the actual distribution of their letters looks like . . . we have to take their word for that.

But one thing is certainly evident: editorial interest in casting Bush in a bad light continues apace. Reading through the "paper of record," last Saturday morning, I noticed a front page piece headed "President Acts on Two Fronts Against Critics." It caught my eye but not enough to demand immediate attention. I passed over it as I read through the paper, intending to come back to it later. But, as I was leafing through various articles, I suddenly came to the continuation of that front page story. And here's the headline that arrested my attention:

> **"Bush Acts Against Critics on National Guard Service
> Records and September 11 Commission."**

Whoa, I had to catch myself when I saw that. Bush acts against critics? I had visions of storm-troopers streaming out of Washington, making house arrests and herding the president's critics into secret star chambers, never to be seen or heard from again. At once I turned back to the first page and began to read the article from the beginning.

Want to know what it actually said?

> *"President Bush moved on Friday night to try to stem potentially
> damaging election-year questions about his military record and
> whether the White House mishandled intelligence threats before
> the September 11th attacks."*

Desperately fearing the impending mass arrests, I read on:

> *"In dual announcements capping a week of intense political pressure on Mr. Bush, the White House said it had decided to release all documents from the president's National Guard files and, within hours, disclosed that Mr. Bush would appear before a commission investigating terrorist attacks."*

So this was what the headline was about? An article detailing Bush's response to his critics! Could the Times, perhaps, have found a less misleading, less inflammatory way of writing this headline? How about:

> *"Bush to Respond to Critics"*

or

> *"Bush Responds to Critics by Releasing Guard Records and Agreeing to Testify"*

These aren't particularly hard headlines to write . . . and they're certainly much closer to what the article is about. In fact, they *are* what the article is about. No star chambers. No purges. No arrests.

A sigh of relief!

So why would the Times headline writers present such a misleading caption in the first place? Think it could have had anything to do with opposition to Bush, his administration, Republicans or conservatives?

Even with all their recent changes, supposedly intended to remove any concern about bias at their paper, they still give us this?

Of course, people don't always read every word in every article. But headlines usually get read. And headlines shape perceptions.

> *"Bush Acts Against Critics . . ."*

Do you think it's possible someone at the Times wanted to send the paper's readers a subliminal message, a message that plays to the outrageous claims and fears about secret Republican cabals and alleged attacks on our civil liberties by the stifling of dissent? Is this any way to report the news . . . or to facilitate a free and democratic electoral process?

This is shaping up as one of the nastiest, dirtiest campaigns for the presidency in living memory. And our friends at the nation's premiere liberal newspaper, the New York Times, have done precisely as they always do . . . weighing in for "their side" with barely more than a nod to the usual niceties of journalistic evenhandedness.

STAYING ALERT,
NEW YORK TIMES STYLE

(June 25, 2004)

When U.S. Attorney General John Ashcroft and FBI Director Robert Mueller recently held a televised press conference to announce that terrorists were seeking to strike at us this summer, and publicized mug shots of some of the suspects in the process, I turned to my son and laughingly said: "Just watch what happens now! Either the criticism's going to be 'why is the Bush administration alarming the public unnecessarily?' Or 'why are they racially profiling these suspects?' Or 'why didn't they tell us sooner?' Or 'why do they have to tell us at all, since it only increases the danger by giving the terrorists advance notice that we're on to them!'"

One way or another, I assured my son, the media and their left-leaning political allies are going to find a way to attack this latest administration effort. Of course, the 9/11 commission investigation is about exactly this sort of thing: What did Bush and company know before 9/11, and what should they have known . . . and what should they have done differently from what they did? The whole point of that exercise seems, more and more, to be about raising doubts in the minds of the public about Bush's performance in the months preceding those devastating attacks. And it has had exactly the corrosive effects its proponents had hoped for.

Now, imagine if we do get attacks this summer of the sort alluded to by Ashcroft and Mueller and it turns out afterwards that the Bush administration had had in its possession photos of real suspects, just like those mug shots they showed us on TV, but for whatever reason had neglected to share them with the public. Wouldn't *that* be an invitation for renewed accusations and investigations? Wouldn't that lead to still another commission whose not-so-hidden agenda would be to stir the political pot, create further embarrassment for the President and erode the levels of confidence the electorate had placed in him? Just imagine the brouhaha if it came out, after such an event, that our government had had advance information about a potential attack but hadn't fully publicized it.

So can anyone blame the administration for wanting to go public now and get the information out? Well, it seems the New York Times can.

Still, they managed to come up with a negative spin on this that even I hadn't thought of. It seems that Homeland Security Chief Tom Ridge was not present at the Ashcroft-Mueller press conference and that he did not raise the administration's color-coded alert status in sympathy with their announcement. So the Times moved in swiftly to the attack:

> "Attorney General John Ashcroft and Robert Mueller III . . .
> created unease on Wednesday with their vague warning
> that Al Qaeda is planning an attack in the United States."
> (The Times editorial page, May 29th)

"It wasn't so much the grimly familiar warning. It was the absence of Tom Ridge," added the editorialist. Mr. Ridge, he noted, "had been on television that very morning assuring viewers that there was no new intelligence requiring an increase in the threat level. That left everyone wondering what to make of Mr. Ashcroft's different message."

So the Times was confused along with "everyone" else?

Funny, I didn't feel the least bit confused. The color-coded threat level system that the administration instituted after 9/11 has often been derided as imprecise and likely to lead to a growing complacency. When you raise the threat level every time a new hat drops, it not only increases costs for federal, state and local authorities, it causes people to become jaded and pay less attention to the warnings. And, of course, the Times has been among the color-coded system's most vocal critics for just these reasons.

So why should we expect the administration to link every announcement concerning the ongoing risks of terrorism to changes in the threat level as the Times now seems to demand?

The Times itself noted that "the official explanation is that Mr. Ashcroft just wanted to show the pictures of wanted terrorists . . ."

Hmmmm, well, that seems like a perfectly rational explanation to a simple guy like me. Should the administration, on the Times' view, raise the threat level *every time it needs to put out new information?* Imagine the crescendo of criticism that would create in the media and from anti-Bush partisans.

Of course, the Times sees through the smoky haze here. Ashcroft's comments, they tell us, "about terrorists perhaps wanting to disrupt the election, presumably to hurt the incumbent, were horribly inappropriate . . . the administration needs to be far more competent and consistent—and apolitical—when it talks about threats."

So, on their view, Ashcroft really had an ulterior motive: to win sympathy for the president!

Never mind the need to apprehend terrorists before they can act or to make critical information available to the public in advance, in hopes that public awareness might contribute to terrorism prevention. No, says the Times, Ashcroft's announcement is nothing more than a political ploy designed to help the President. Well, I have to wonder what sort of ulterior motive the Times itself has when it relentlessly attacks Bush for not acting preemptively before 9/11 but then for acting too preemptively afterwards . . . or for raising the terrorist threat level too frequently, but then for not raising it at the drop of every new FBI hat? Does the Times always have to operate on a double standard like this when it considers the actions of this administration? Or is it just something unique to this present, unfortunate hour on our political clock?

WHO'S GOT GALL?

(July 23, 2004)

A couple of months ago I was doing an errand up in College Point . . . picking up a new toilet, actually. Why all the way up there? A long story. But some time before 10 A.M. I was in my car on the road back, spanking new bowl safely in my trunk. I had the radio on, listening to the New York Times classical music station, WQXR. Yeah I know, the New York Times. But what can I say? I like the music and there's minimal commentary . . . and I always listen to their news reports with a skeptical ear anyway, so it seemed safe enough.

So there I was, heading toward the Van Wyck Expressway when the show's host, one Jeff Spurgeon (I think that's how you spell his name), came on and gravely informed his listeners that Attorney General John Ashcroft had been hospitalized that morning. I'd actually heard Ashcroft was in intensive care due to an inflamed gall bladder before I'd set out on my hunt for that special bowl so I didn't pay particularly close attention to the report.

Spurgeon continued: "I was surprised to hear about Ashcroft's hospitalization for gall bladder disease."

His voice slid off into steady and mellow tones as the music faded.

A pause, as for a moment of studied reflection.

"But then," added Mr. Spurgeon, "who's got more gall than John Ashcroft?"

I nearly drove off the road.

Here's the Attorney General of the United States, one of the highest officials in the federal government and a fellow human being, apparently facing a life threatening illness, and this fellow

Spurgeon could not resist a snide remark as he delivered the news to his listeners.

I was still thinking about this, having safely returned to my lane, when Mr. Spurgeon abruptly returned to the airwaves to tell us: "never mind."

His voice was apologetic. He seemed suitably chastened, unnerved by some reaction or other that his words had apparently triggered somewhere out of broadcast earshot in his station . . . and, perhaps, more widely.

"I shouldn't have said what I said," he opined in his mellifluous voice. "No need to call in, the phones are already lighting up I see . . . but I wasn't thinking when I spoke . . ."

He went on: "It's the earliness of the morning, I guess, people just going to work and all. They're telling me here I shouldn't have . . . well, never mind, I take it back."

I smiled to myself and thought that at least someone at that station had shown some sense.

And then a pause.

And then, as though mumbling to himself, as he allowed the music to gently take over again, Mr. Spurgeon softly added: "Still, I'm not THAT sorry."

I couldn't believe what I was hearing on this presumably respectable radio station, a station owned and operated by the nation's "newspaper of record," the self-declared paragon of the journalistic virtues. First Mr. Spurgeon insults a government official and fellow human being, without any apparent thought for the state of the man's health or his feelings . . . or for the feelings of his family.

And then he apologizes.

And then he takes back the apology in almost the same breath. Is that supposed to be it? Everything's okay now because hey, Mr. Spurgeon misspoke but he apologized for it . . . well, sort of, anyway, if you can ignore his parting retraction of his retraction.

The elite liberal establishment makes a big deal these days about so-called conservative and Republican negativity, and decries the allegedly negative talk on certain conservative media programs.

Fox News, for instance, is always catching it for presenting the news in a way that questions various liberal conceits. (Hey, you're not supposed to do that, right?) If the mainly liberal media is to be believed, this is enough to make Fox News a mere conservative house organ. Better to listen to CNN, they seem to be telling us, or to one of the major broadcast networks, or NPR, or, of course, the esteemed radio station of the New York Times itself. These outlets know how to tell us what's really going on which seems to be mostly a matter of continuously trolling for scandal on, and taking potshots at, the Bush administration.

Of course, I expect the usual slant from the usual suspects whenever I listen to the various news shows on the different stations. But while listening to a music program? And from a fellow whose main job is to select and play tasteful selections for his listeners as they wend their way through early morning traffic to their jobs?

The problem seems to come down to an ongoing sense of grievance that has infected the liberal establishment and its supporters, prompting a guy like Spurgeon to think there's nothing wrong with insulting and demeaning a public official while he's seriously ill. Hey, he's only a Bush cabinet member, right? I mean it's not like he's worthy of serious consideration or sympathy.

It's not enough, it seems, for a man like Mr. Spurgeon to oppose a set of policies, which he presumably does, or to argue for a change on his own time and, perhaps, to work, off-hours, for President Bush's opponent in the upcoming campaign. No, Mr. Spurgeon apparently feels perfectly justified in exuding his snide disdain for this president and his administration, even as he conveys what should have been a simple news item.

Mr. Ashcroft is in the hospital in critical condition? Well, people like Spurgeon seem to be saying, it couldn't happen to a nicer guy. A lot of gall, Mr. Spurgeon? Yes, but it's not John Ashcroft, then lying sick in intensive care with gall bladder disease, who has it.

SCHOOL DAYS

THE LEFT REVIVES

(November 8, 1994)

My eighteen year old daughter started college this year. I don't know why, but it seems like a milestone—for both of us. Of course I'm rather proud of her, especially of her ability to think and question what she hears. And, from the looks of things, she's going to need all the ability in that area she can muster.

The whole family was sitting around last weekend, listening to Heather read excerpts from one of her college texts: "Social Problems: A Critical Power Conflict Perspective." Well, I took a look at this text book and can agree that it's certainly "critical," although not in the normal, academic sense of that word. On the other hand, it doesn't offer very much in the way of "perspective." What it does do is advance a decidedly left-wing agenda which one would not have been surprised to encounter in the old Soviet Union. Of course, the Soviet Union doesn't exist any longer, having imploded because of the failure of its ideology and the system which that ideology gave rise to. (There must be some truth to the claim that one of the few places left in the world where you can still find committed and believing Marxists is on America's college campuses. And this one is right across the bridge since Heather is attending Brooklyn College.)

Well, what does the book have to say for itself? It offers a sweeping indictment of capitalism and capitalists, dividing society into classes (a la Marx) and concludes that America's system of democracy is "corrupt." It's chock full of statistics purporting to show this, as well as shockingly offensive political cartoons demonizing our politicians and businessmen (presumably intended to reinforce its main point about the nature of the American system). According to this book, women, workers and minorities always get the short end of the stick, largely by design of the "ruling class." And wages, the book asserts, are nothing less than theft from workers because what is paid to workers is always less than what the products are sold for, given that profit margins are built into the items when the businessmen who pay the wages turn around and sell them to customers. (Of course, this is a classical Marxist premise).

Now you can argue that this is a legitimate intellectual and political point of view, however wrongheaded it might be, and that it deserves to be taught along with other viewpoints. I certainly would be the last to object to that. I happen to believe we *should* expose ourselves to all kinds of thinking in the marketplace of ideas. But exposure is not what's going on here.

This assigned text my daughter is reading only presents one side, the left's side, and has nothing good or even neutral to say about any other theories or perspectives that may inform this debate and which have been developed and advanced by an array of scholars and economists over the years. Worse, it has nothing good to say about our legitimate American traditions, including individual liberty, despite the fact that it is presented as a survey of American society. Yet it's so full of "statistics" intended to bolster its positions that I didn't know quite where to begin responding when my daughter asked me to comment on it. Of course it's easy to compile statistics to support almost any case you want to make, but this doesn't mean the statistics are reliable or even the full picture. Statistics can appear extremely compelling when presented in certain ways in support of particular agendas and if you don't have access to alternative information, they can mislead. The problem is, what do our children know when they encounter this sort of thing? How prepared are freshmen college students like my daughter when handed a book that appears authoritative as it disparages our nation and system of governance? Don't all such tables and charts look like "facts" to those who are as yet unschooled in the broad array of ideas that are out there and who may lack the critical background one must bring to such material? Are the statistics offered in such books as authoritative as they may appear to the uninitiated?

Well, that seems to be what the author of this book wants his readers to think (and, presumably thinks himself). How can we know, how can my daughter know that there's something wrong with a book like this, so full of deceptively appealing numbers and presented as a scientific analysis of American society? (Marx called his theory a science, by the way, though it went on to fail miserably in the empirical world.)

As it happens, leafing quickly through the material, I found a little nugget on page 101 which is a dead giveaway for the book's agenda and reliability. Once noticed, the intelligent reader should readily be able to see that, with this book, we are in the hands of a propagandist, not a social scientist. "Conservative elected officials . . ." it says, "have often circulated misinformation about individualism and competition, welfare programs, and the poor . . . (while) progressive officials and professionals, particularly those in welfare agencies, have tried to counteract stereotypes by issuing research reports or publicizing facts . . ."

In other words, says this book, conservatives lie, but progressives give us the facts. Whatever anyone may think of the merits of the arguments about individualism, welfare programs, government intervention and the like, we must at least admit that there are well-intentioned people on both sides of these arguments. Yet this author cannot conceive that there can be any truth to those opinions which are contrary to his. Worse, he wants to convince his readers that the other side of the debate is insincere while he, and those who share his views, are the epitome of rectitude. Well, at least he's not pretending to put any stock in that old American value of fair play.

The point is that even his method of arguing conjures up the kind of diatribes the old line communist ideologues (when there were still people willing to call themselves communists) used, when they used to hurl their indictments against America and the capitalist system. But I noticed something else as I waded through this book in response to my daughter's comments and questions.

All of the positions espoused by this author are the so-called politically correct ones of the day, the kinds of positions modern day liberals are advancing as nostrums for what ails the social corpus.

In my day, when I was coming up in the sixties, liberals believed in the American system and traditions, just like conservatives. Both sides agreed that the free-enterprise system was superior to command economies, that individual liberty was essential to the kind of democracy which made this country a haven for the oppressed throughout its history, and that there were generally two, and often more, sides to most questions. Where liberals and conservatives differed was on how far government should go in getting involved in solving society's ills. Now, however, something new has occurred. In the face of the collapse of the world socialist experiment through the failure of the communist Soviet Union, the liberals seem to have slid, without fanfare, into the socialist camp. There no longer seems to be a great deal of difference between liberals and socialists, at least in their prescriptions for society. And that's scary because socialism is a discredited philosophy throughout much of the world. Yet its solutions seem to have found their way into mainstream American thinking.

Worse this plainly bankrupted approach to social analysis seems to have found its way into the canons of the academy, where the future thinkers and leaders of our nation are being formed. What happened to the real liberal arts education, the one which sought to open, not close, the minds of our young people? And what, I can't help wondering, will happen to my daughter, after four years of being force-fed this stuff?

THE COSTS OF
AN EDUCATION

(January 17, 1995)

Just a brief follow-up to my eldest daughter's first semester college experience in the City University system. As some of you may recall, Heather was enrolled in a required sociology course (they call them "core" courses now) at Brooklyn College, in which one of the main texts was an obviously left-wing, anti-American tract that demonized American political and democratic values, along with the nation's leaders and businessmen.

After roundly castigating what it characterized as phony American democracy, this book presented a panoply of socialist-type solutions for what it alleged was ailing us. Socialism is laudable, of course, in the ideal. But as a practical philosophy or as a blueprint for a society it is largely discredited today. Still, this was to be the main text of the course, a primary means of imparting to students that knowledge they would have to have if they were to pass this required course.

How did Heather deal with this? In the end, she swallowed hard and struggled to parrot the professor's party line so she could be assured of a "good grade." She did note, however, that many of the students in the class were skeptical of the one-sided message which passed for scholarship there, but that all ultimately gave up on the chance for meaningful engagement with the professor when they found him evasive and unresponsive to questions. "We'll get back to that," he told them. Or, "Hold that for later on in the course." But, Heather tells me, promises to revisit issues were never kept. And, as the sessions wore on, so did the students' boredom and disinterest.

On top of this according to Heather, the professor routinely cut classes by as much as a third of the allotted time. His explanation? He taught another class right after theirs and needed some time to himself, before then "to rest." Did the students see anything wrong with this?

No, said Heather, since they found him so boring anyway they were grateful for any opportunity to spend less time with him.

But what about the money we were paying in tuition? Did she think she was getting her money's worth since we paid by the credit (which reflects the number of hours each course covers)? Or that this professor was fulfilling his responsibility to his students and to the college administration which hired him?

Heather said this didn't matter because he was tenured and couldn't be fired in any event and that he had told them as much. Besides, she saw the course with him as a burden she was obliged to carry, not an opportunity for gaining new knowledge. The less onerous the burden, the better!

Of course, this professor's class time policy had other implications. Three quarters of the way through the semester he suddenly announced that he had to race ahead to cover all of the course requirements since they had "unaccountably" fallen behind in the work. Whoops!

As a result, after spending more than half the semester on the anti-American tract already mentioned, and, as Heather noted, on Marx, he now had to teach the Federalist Papers and de Tocqueville (the French commentator who first observed and marveled at the workings of our Republic in its earliest days) in whatever time remained—but without compromising his need for a rest period between classes, of course. As it happens, Heather tells me he spent one day on de Tocqueville and one day on the Federalist Papers. Not a whole lot of time, considering what he allocated for some of the other stuff.

Did she think there was equity in the presentation? No, said Heather, but added that she really hadn't expected there to be, given his obvious bias. Besides, she noted, she was already preparing her schedule for next year and quite beyond caring about this semester's work.

What about the professor? Did she think she had learned anything from him?

"Well," she allowed, "he did teach us about how we can all be victimized by the establishment and the people who control it."

"How so?" I asked.

"For one thing," she explained, "he told us how we're victims of the Republican victory last November, because they're going to dry up federal funding so that schools like Brooklyn college won't have enough money to hire more professors. Then the professors already on staff will have to teach more classes."

"How does that affect you?" I asked somewhat naively.

"Because then our professors won't have enough time to teach our classes the way they should. Or give us any special attention."

"I guess they'll need longer rest periods between teaching sessions, too," I suggested.

"Yeah, something like that," Heather said.

DIALING FOR DOLLARS, BOOKLYN COLLEGE STYLE

(March 21, 1995)

Here's another update in the ongoing saga of my daughter Heather's first-year venture into the groves of academe. As some readers may recall, last semester (her first at Brooklyn College) Heather took a course with a professor who insisted on teaching his left-of-center agenda in lieu of the course requirements, thus ultimately failing to cover the material Heather and her classmates were expected to know for their final exam. He did this, at least in part, by routinely cutting class time by a third (explaining that he was overworked since he had to teach two classes, back to back). At the same time, he generally bored the students to death by refusing to respond to their questions when they disagreed with things he was teaching, telling them there wasn't anything they could do about it if they were dissatisfied since he was tenured. He did warn them, however, that they could expect horrible things from the recent Republican electoral sweep (November 1994) since the newly elected officials were likely to cut public funding of education, among other cuts. Thus, he noted, professors like him would be kept busier than ever so students could expect to lose out on the individual attention they should otherwise expect to be getting from their teachers.

Well, he was right about the funding cuts, in any event. Turns out, Governor George Pataki's new budget will not hold the city or state university systems harmless. Like the rest of us, they stand to experience their share of fiscal pain. (I guess that means it'll hit Heather too, since Heather's tuition will be going up, as a result of these cuts—and my other daughter, Elissa, is now only a year and a half away from starting *her* college career.)

The four year colleges in the City University of New York (CUNY) system have a budget of $900 million ($300 million comes from tuitions and $600 million in state subsidies), according to a recent article in the New York Times. Current cuts recommended by Pataki's administration in Albany amount to about $116 million (to be made up through tuition increases) and an outright cut of $41.5 million. Thus the overall CUNY budget for senior colleges is expected to be reduced by roughly 4.6% ($41.5 million as a percent of $900 million). I guess I should be complaining as loudly as anybody since the bulk of the cutbacks will be made up on the backs of people like me, through our tuition payments. But it's a funny thing—I can't help thinking a college education at CUNY prices, even after an annual tuition raise of about $1,000 (the expected increase), still looks like a bargain when you compare it to the outrageous tuitions the private institutions are getting.

I'd be a lot happier, of course, if some of the professional staff at Brooklyn College were a little more diligent in doing their jobs. But, believe it or not, I have no quarrel with exposing my kids to left-wing views. In fact, I think it does the kids good, opening their minds and forcing them to think. Still, it would be nice for the faculty to allow equal time for other reasonable points of view.

So how are college staff and administration handling all this? According to the same New York Times article, tenured professors in CUNY have "begun frantically sending out resumes and scrambling to seek jobs." CUNY's Board of Trustees has declared a "financial emergency" for the system's two year colleges and voted to participate in the state's retirement incentive program, a prelude to staffing cuts at all the institutions in the system. This will enable the administration to offer buy-outs to tenured professors (who, according to their union contract, must be given twelve months' notice before being dismissed). At the same time, some faculty members in attendance at the recent Board of Trustees meeting, where these decisions were being made, were reported as being rude and disruptive—until threatened with eviction from the hall.

What about Brooklyn College? Well, Heather recently obtained some material which was being distributed to students by various members of the faculty. It included a memo from the college Dean which "urges" faculty members to distribute sample protest letters to students, along with a list of local state legislators, and to read them excerpts from the Dean's memo. In the memo the students are warned about the dire implications of the upcoming budget cuts and advised to send protest letters to Albany.

The text asserts that the impending cuts "will deprive of thousands of students from a CUNY education."

No kidding, the above quotation is *not* a typo; it's what appears in the Dean's actual memo! Although he doesn't tell us how you go about depriving people "from" something. Well, maybe he's not from the English Department?

The sample letter, which students are instructed to "personalize," goes on to offer two possible texts for student use: If you're full time, it says, you're supposed to say you work to support yourself and depend on financial aid to get by. (But what if you don't like my daughter, Heather, who neither works nor depends on financial aid? Well, I guess it does say "personalize.")

If you're part time, you're supposed to say you receive financial aid, too, and that attendance at college will "advance my career and increase my income thereby increasing taxpaying dollars to the state." (Personally, I wasn't aware that dollars paid taxes, I always thought people did.)

Finally, the instructions on the attached list of legislators conclude with a message that "we stand to loose more than 25% of our budget . . ." (I guess we could *lose* some of that money, too. Hey, maybe spelling's not the Dean's strong suit either.)

At any rate, setting aside the question of whether it makes sense to continue pouring money into an institution of higher learning that offers the foregoing standard of literacy (on the evidence presented here, maybe CUNY's not such a bargain after all!), there is a more serious issue: should the faculty be engaged in politicking their interests during class time when they are supposedly being paid to teach—not advocate. And should taxpayer dollars (yes, you *can* describe dollars in *that* way!), intended to pay for this teaching, be used to support special interests for more taxpayer dollars? That's not what the state is subsidizing them for, to the tune of 600 million of our hard earned dollars, is it?

Well, the Dean only "urged" faculty members to distribute this material, right? He didn't say they had to do it. But I wonder what happens to any instructor who hasn't yet achieved tenure, if he or she doesn't?

THE GREAT DIVIDE

BUSH VS. REAGAN?[4]

(August 16th, 1994)

In a July 5th piece in this paper, one of my fellow columnists took me to task for painting former President Bush as a conservative and for asserting that Bush lost to Clinton because Clinton and the media fooled people about Bush's record. Bush, says my colleague, deserved to lose because "he stood for nothing" and didn't have a "clue about how people were suffering and what to do about it." The writer goes on to remind us that Bush raised our taxes and was not as ideologically pure as his predecessor, Ronald Reagan.

These last, at least, are quite true, but my point was that the media and liberal politicians generally misrepresented the conditions of the country at the time in order to cast doubts on Bush's stewardship. It wasn't that Bush was more or less conservative than anyone else that did him in. Americans were receptive to the media's message because they were looking for something Bush was not capable of offering—a bear hug embrace to help them feel better about their perceived problems. Of course, if the problems were not so big, they would not have "needed" the bear hug. Therefore the media felt they had to magnify the problems. It was this deliberate distortion of reality that did Bush in at the end.

Although my colleague apparently agrees with me as to the tacit (and sometimes not so tacit) media conspiracy to portray Bush's tenure in a dismal light, he thinks they had plenty of raw material to work with in George H. W. Bush. I would suggest that this is not quite true. Bush, while no great intellect,[5] is an intelligent man who had a record of demonstrated managerial and diplomatic competence. If he appeared to lack strong convictions on the diplomatic front and tended toward the pragmatic, he certainly showed backbone in the matter of Saddam Hussein's seizure of Kuwait and in facing down the Israeli lobby (a good thing for this country, even for those of us who support Israel's right to exist).

He was also responsible for a number of successful initiatives to address problems of the sort that heads of government in this country often have to deal with but which are also easy to forget about once they've been solved and are safely behind us. On coming to office, Bush immediately tackled the Savings and Loan and Latin American debt crises, two situations which threatened the financial stability of this country. Ignored during the Reagan years in favor of other priorities, Bush chose to deal with them head-on.[6]

While the Resolution Trust Corporation (which Bush's administration set up to handle the Savings and Loan problem) was expensive, it did not turn out to be anywhere near as costly as pundits had predicted and, of course, we avoided the dreaded crisis in our financial institutions which many anticipated would be triggered by the S&L disaster. Similarly the Latin American nations ultimately were made whole and most are now rapidly becoming part of the economic revival in the Western Hemisphere. Bush was also responsible for guiding us into NAFTA although it fell to his successor, Bill Clinton, to take us over the final barriers and make NAFTA a reality. Since its inception, NAFTA has come to be generally recognized as having a net positive effect on our economy, H. Ross Perot's giant sucking sound not withstanding.

If George H. W. Bush was unsuccessful in terms of domestic legislative initiatives, perhaps, just perhaps, this was due to the obdurate opposition of Democratic politicians who dominate Congress—especially Senator George Mitchell of Maine, who time and again blocked the movement of White House bills. It may also have been partly due to a conservative philosophy which holds that government should be sparing in its actions. Thus, then-President Bush may simply have chosen not to meddle in the wide range of issues which draw the "new" Clintonian Democrats.

As to his retreat on taxes, while to my mind a mistake, it pays to recall the context in which it occurred. Bush was faced with the same stubborn Senator Mitchell and company he had been dealing with since he entered the White House, while trying to hammer out a federal budget. At the same time the crisis over Saddam Hussein's invasion and annexation of Kuwait, and the need to form a consensus to deal with it, was already looming.

Did Bush err in previously supporting Saddam against Iran's Ayatollahs? It looks that way from our current vantage point, but it was certainly not an unreasonable diplomatic sally at the time. And, of course, Bush shepherded us through the diplomatic thicket of crumbling political structures which rung down the curtain on East European communism. That was certainly not "nothing," however undramatic, compared to the confrontations of prior decades.

In sum I would suggest that my colleague overstates the Bush flaws (which were certainly there) while giving no credit to Bush's many accomplishments. Was he less ideologically pure than his predecessor? It certainly seems a reasonable surmise. Was he a failed president as my ideologically conservative colleague alleges? Certainly not.

But the media and even the American public wanted a change. They wanted someone more lovable, more cuddly, more sensitive. We got Bill Clinton. Hopefully he will grow more presidential with time.

DEFENDING BUSH AGAIN[7]

(October 4ᵗʰ, 1994)

I told myself I wasn't going to do this but the recent response by my fellow conservative columnist in this paper to my earlier response to his initial article pillorying me for a still earlier column (sounds like an infinite regress, doesn't it?), in which I suggested the American electorate was snookered in regard to the economic and governing record of the Reagan-Bush years, has been gnawing at me (as I suspect my colleague hoped it would). So I'll take one more swipe at setting both Bush's and my own record straight. But I promise I won't bring this subject up again . . . if he doesn't!

In his rather emotional attack on Bush, my fellow columnist evinces an apparent belief that Bush somehow betrayed the conservative agenda, presumably because he didn't appear to be as wedded to the full gamut of Reaganite positions as Reagan himself was. If this opposition to Bush, then, is a visceral reaction by my counterpart based on his sense of ideological betrayal, I suppose it is understandable. But it is also unrealistic. One of the things I have discovered in this world is that there are very few pure anythings (including politicians) and, when you find them, they usually turn out to be fanatics, not the kind of people you really want running your government. Even Ronald Reagan famously made compromises.

My colleague's citation of known conservative pundits, true believers and periodicals in support of his contention that Bush betrayed the conservative cause is, however, not enough to wean me from the view that Bush was a substantive and successful president. As I said before, and will reiterate here, Bush had a number of very marked accomplishments to his name and his main flaw, it seems to me, was his inability to touch a responsive chord in the common man the way Clinton obviously can. He was more pragmatic than the man he succeeded, but I don't count that a flaw at all though, arguably, it led him into some mistakes which, I imagine, he came to regret (e.g., the reversal of his "no new taxes" pledge).

According to my colleague, I would adjust my views if only I'd read what Peggy Noonan and the National Review and "EVERY (sic) Republican economist," had to say about George H. W. Bush. They really know the true story, he suggests, and are the proper interpreters of conservative orthodoxy to which I, like any good conservative, ought to adhere. Well, of course, that's not a fair test. While I do consider myself conservative, it is not to the bible of the prophets of conservativism (whatever or whoever these may be) that I look for my views. Believe it or not, I suspect that even the National Review can sometimes be wrong. And I'm not convinced that every Republican economist held the same view about Bush's alleged responsibility for the 1990-1991 recession, as my fellow columnist rather cavalierly suggests. Economists are notorious for disagreeing about nearly everything much of the time, though historically, when they all do line up on the same side, they are nearly always wrong—just look at the stock market.

In fact, the conservative spectrum is a much more varied one than most folks give it credit for. Even I manage to find an intellectual home of sorts among fellow conservatives, though I don't follow every "mainstream" conservative opinion. I oppose the death penalty, for instance, which the majority of conservatives today support, including Bush. I oppose governmental involvement on the abortion question except in very specific and limited circumstances. I oppose government trying to mandate or enforce social values, although I certainly am comfortable with governmental policies intended to support, and not undermine, values which I take to be essential to the functioning of our free and open society.

In sum, as a conservative, I sometimes find myself supporting candidates or other individuals with whom I am not in total agreement. Well, that's life. I don't imagine I have dibs on all the correct opinions in the world. And I don't expect everyone to agree with me all the time. What I look for in politicians and government officials are: 1) a philosophy with which I am generally comfortable, i.e., belief in smaller government and lower taxes (since low taxes help shrink government while fueling economic growth, thus serving society as a whole); and 2) real, demonstrated competence. I think Bush, while generally uninspiring, qualified on both counts. I certainly don't think he should have been penalized for his lack of charisma and "star quality."

Did he blow it on the tax question? It looks that way in retrospect, but as I said once before, you have to see matters in context. He was facing down Saddam Hussein at the time, as well as the United States Senator from Maine, George Mitchell, a particularly partisan Democrat. So Bush had to choose where to make his stand. Many of us might not have chosen so differently, had we been in his shoes.

As to the other main knock against Bush offered by my fellow columnist, that Bush abandoned Israel, I'm not sure that putting a little pressure on a foreign, even if friendly, government, in order to prompt it to be more cooperative in terms of American policy concerns is such a bad thing. Recall that Bush did roll back the Saddam Hussein gambit in Kuwait which threatened the balance of power in the Middle East and, ultimately, the world. In this he certainly acted in a way that was protective of Israel's interests, even if only indirectly. And this altered perceptions enough to revitalize a largely moribund peace process. Israel has certainly benefited from this. At the least, Israel is still there and Saddam is no longer a looming threat to them (though many of the people who opposed Bush's stand against Saddam, subsequently castigated him for not following up and leveling Baghdad, taking over the country and ousting Saddam—some people are never satisfied, especially when they don't have ultimate responsibility for other people's lives and the national interest.)

Finally, my colleague alleges that George Herbert Walker Bush just could not feel others' pain. While I think that's really a public relations issue (i.e., Bush was just not very good at appearing empathetic), I would just add this: Mr. Clinton is outstanding in this area and it has not yet made him a better president. I don't vote for a man on the strength of his ability to make me feel better about myself when he is talking to me via the TV screen and I hope that my colleague doesn't either. Unfortunately the electorate, as a whole, sometimes does.

A READER RESPONDS[8]

(December 6, 1994)

I like responses to my columns as much as the next guy but a recent muddled and rather mean-spirited letter to the editor, taking me and a fellow columnist to task for our alleged hypocrisy and "blatherings" because of our supposed "right wing" and "Reaganite" sympathies, kind of got my Irish up. (I use this latter term without any intended offense since, while not of the Irish persuasion, I've always had an intense feeling of kinship for that North Atlantic folk—especially for their "pipes" and folklore.)

The author or the letter, a certain Mrs. Kaufman, whom I do not know and have never met, proceeds to assert that we two "hypocrite columnists" are "typical fans of Bob Grant and Rush Limbaugh" but since we do not have our own businesses, we have no right to say the things we have been saying in our columns.

"Fellas, you should practice what you preach about self-reliance," says the irate Mrs. Kaufman, "and open your own businesses, make your own payrolls and take your own risks." Otherwise she seems to think we should just shut up. As though freedom of speech and the right to hold unpopular opinions in this country have suddenly become constrained by the position one occupies in society or how you make a buck! This is an odd reading of the First Amendment, especially coming from someone who is so manifestly of the "liberal persuasion."

Well I won't attempt to speak for my fellow columnist (I suspect he's more than capable of coming to his own defense), but I would like to respond briefly for myself. Mrs. Kaufman, you are certainly entitled to hold and express the opinions you do (although you seem to want to deny me the same right), but you should at least be aware that you have misread both me and my columns. Although conservative, I hardly think I qualify as a "right winger."

If you had been reading what I have been writing, you would know that I have expressed opposition to the death penalty and to government's over involvement in the abortion question (I think that is usually a matter best left to the individual). Nor have I ever expressed support for former President Reagan (although I am comfortable with many of his policies), since I never thought him intellectually qualified or personally suited to hold that high office. (*Note to readers: since I wrote this back in 1994 I have undergone a sea change in my opinion and have concluded that I, like many northeasterners at the time, underestimated Mr. Reagan . . . in sum I was wrong about this and now believe that he was not only much smarter than he was given credit for, I also think he was a very successful president. So Mrs. Kaufman had me pegged right back then on this issue, though she had no written statements of mine to hang her hat on!*)

Further, while expressing strong support for President Bush (a fairly unpopular position, even among conservatives), I have acknowledged that President Clinton may very well have had the higher IQ of the two men (though perhaps he was less well-seasoned) and that conservatives ought to get off Clinton's case on issues like Whitewater and Paula Jones and let him govern the country since that is what he was elected to do.

That said, I would reiterate my views that Clinton's policies are basically wrongheaded, since he seeks to increase government involvement in our lives. This can only swell the bureaucratic monster, thereby sucking up more and more of our tax dollars, wasting large quantities in the process, and imposing a horrible drag on the private economy—that sector of society which drives everything else and makes it possible for enough people to earn enough money to pay taxes and support the government.[9] This, Mrs. Kaufman, is not to say there is no place in the economic structure for government and its employees, but only that they are dependent, in the end, on other parts of society which misguided governmental policies have, over the years, adversely affected.

Which brings me, Mrs. Kaufman, to your odd assertion that as an employee of others, I am being hypocritical when I support a program of shrinking government, by opposing higher taxes, or when I come out for self-reliance rather than dependence on governmental largess. I don't know where you get your information from, madam, since I have never mentioned how I make my living in any of my columns, nor is it common knowledge as far as I can tell since I'm not exactly a well known personality on the peninsula. Nevertheless, I will not deny that I am a government worker since I see no reason to be ashamed of it. In retrospect, I probably should have chosen another line of work but it's too late for such regrets now. On the other hand, my occupation certainly cannot and should not interfere with my right to hold the opinions that I believe are correct—or do you have to be from one "side of the tracks" only, before you can express "Republican" opinions? If that were true, Republicans could never win any elections since most people, almost by definition, work for someone else.

Your view, Mrs. Kaufman, is one which sees society divided into classes, us against them, and, if you're one of us and you vote for (or support) one of them, you're either a hypocrite or a traitor. I should, I suppose, at least be grateful you have only accused me, so far, of hypocrisy.

But your view, ultimately, is silly and unrealistic. Not everyone is cut out to be a businessman or entrepreneur. Or to be rich. What you end up doing with your life is partly a function of brains, partly luck and partly attitude (ambitions, desires and how you express these). One of the beautiful things about our society is that it does not have rigid classes, since anyone with the right combination of factors can end up pretty much anywhere. That we don't all end up in the same place merely reflects this dynamic. As the fall of world socialism has recently shown, when you try to take this potential away, you create a static society where everyone has less. Such societies cannot compete with the more dynamic, capitalist variety.

But Mrs. Kaufman, you seem to think that, as a government worker, I am somehow on the dole and have thus forfeited my right to honestly rail against oversized government. Well, Mrs. Kaufman, let me assure you that some government workers do earn their pay and, working where they do, may actually be better placed than others to see what's wrong and needs fixing. You don't have to be rich to believe that everyone has the right to become rich . . . and you don't have to be in business to believe government should get out of the way and let entrepreneurs do what they do best.

Still, I can't shake the feeling that if I had, in fact, been a well-off business person instead of just someone's employee, you would be attacking me anyway—only this time for being a fat cat "right wing hypocrite" who has no right to be saying conservative things since I couldn't possibly hope to understand the needs and concerns of working people.

Damned if I do and even if I don't?

THOSE DARNED REPUBLICANS!

(February 28, 1995)

In a recent release reprinted in this paper and elsewhere (and picked up by the major dailies), Congressman Charles Schumer listed a litany of pain which he says we New Yorkers can expect in the wake of the recent Republican electoral sweep at the federal and state levels. According to the Congressman, we can anticipate service cutbacks across a wide range of areas including funding for education, social services and mass transit. All of this, he suggests, will negatively affect the quality of life here in New York, hurt those most in need, and disproportionately impact urban areas such as our own. Unfortunately, some of this may actually be true, especially in the short term. But it's not the whole story.

Of course it's not surprising the Congressman would take the stand he has—as a leading light among Democrats, both at the local and national levels, it is his job to stake out the Democratic turf. And it's in his interest to do so. Still the Congressman, in his partisan role, misses the point. If belt tightening is not attempted now, if we defer making the hard choices while we still have a sturdy economy and the global winds at our backs, how much more difficult is it likely to be, trying to put our fiscal house in order when the impact of spiraling budget deficits in the face of a shrinking workforce (as the baby boomers age) finally begins to be felt?

It's not balancing the budget per se that needs to be accomplished—the strong growth inherent in the American economic machine can handle that over time—it's the need to get this crazed governmental growth back under control, before it overwhelms and sinks us all. That's the essential Republican insight in this last decade of the 20th Century—an insight which the Democrats briefly flirted with in the 1992 presidential campaign when Bill Clinton flashed his "New Democrat" credentials for the electorate to see and approve.

Today just about everyone seems ready to sign onto the principle of making government manageable again and Congressman Schumer, of necessity, has to tread carefully through this thicket, raising the liberal banner for his historical constituency without losing sight of the real need which most Americans (even New Yorkers) now seem to agree is paramount. Balancing the budget is the symbol, of course, even the first salvo in this "cut-backs crusade," but it is fiscal accountability that is the ultimate issue. Schumer and his staff see pain ahead and call on the Republicans to rein in the horses, positioning the Congressman to pick up the standard if and when the pain becomes too great—as it may at some point, thus sparking the inevitable reaction. But the Republicans dare not hold back. Just as Schumer, one of the remaining champions of late 20th Century liberalism, cannot fail to defend the castle on which his political fort has been raised, so too the Republicans, having mounted their successful assault with a call to arms against the monster of big government, cannot now forsake their principles and lay down with the beast. Thus the battle lines are drawn.

But merely because each side is impelled by its own historic dynamic does not mean there is not a right side and a wrong side in this epic struggle. Indeed, readers of this column will know that I have long advocated a restoration of government manageability through increased fiscal accountability, even when it was still relatively unpopular. So it will come as no surprise to those readers to learn that I think Republicans have it right in this cycle and that Gingrich, Pataki and Giuliani represent the positive force in the political pendulum's latest stroke, while the Democrats are the drag on the clock, essential to keeping the pendulum from swinging out too far and snapping the mechanism's inner workings, to be sure, but largely a reactionary force which must now be resisted. Schumer, sharp as he is, is part of that reactionary force.

When Schumer says there will be pain and calls on us to vote out the pain-givers, he must be resisted. His is a siren's call, with all the sweetness marshaled by those mythic creatures as they sang to Odysseus and his crew on their long journey back from Troy. Yet the sirens summoned that hapless group of men to their own destruction on rocks which lay just beneath the turbulent coastal shallows they were trying to steer past. Sure it's tempting to think about answering their call. But it's also deadly.

If we do not fix things while we have the chance, the economic and social seas on which we sail are likely to become a great deal more treacherous in the coming decades. Costs of governing will mount, as will the cost of being governed (read taxes), and the economic machine will begin to grind itself into a condition of unhealthy stasis. Then jobs will shrink (as they already have in New York, after ages of liberal spending growth) and, with them, the tax base, which will mean, in its turn, that the cuts we are now likely to make will be even more draconian and recessionary to implement in the future.

Is Schumer's appeal, insofar as it highlights the risks to the poor and underprivileged, an appeal to out better natures? Only partly. Indeed, most of us feel concern for those who are less well-off than we are. (Yes, even conservatives have a heart!) But how much worse will it be for the poor, and how many more of them will there be (and how many more of them will be us!), if we don't make the hard choices now? Locally all of us New Yorkers, the poor and the non-poor, are likely to feel some short-term pain. Welfare benefits and services may see some cutting, public transportation costs may rise (although they seem to rise pretty regularly anyway, even in flush times), and funding for various local programs may shrink.

Here in Rockaway we are certain to see some of that. And then, given the essential selfishness of local politics, we can expect to hear the cry go up: "Cut his program, not mine, because mine is essential!" But we must resist the temptation to indulge in that sort of caterwauling, if we are to successfully address the future needs of our communities—and our nation. Won't it be better to have the shackles lifted and Rockaway growing again, a part of a vibrant New York City and State, with jobs and money flowing, than to have us continue subsisting on a bevy of government handouts and grants, begging City Hall, our Councilman, and our federal and state representatives for yet another financial "fix"— a fix which must ultimately be pulled out of our own pockets, thereby draining us of the capital which keeps us afloat and enables us to continue on our course into the future, sailing, like some latter day Odysseus, until, after a harsh and arduous journey we find our way once more to the front steps of our own half-forgotten homes, amidst the welcoming cries of dogs and kin, in far off Ithaca?

Historical Note (August 5, 2004): A lot of water has passed under the proverbial bridge since this piece was written. Congressman Schumer is now Senator Schumer and a major mainstay of the liberal establishment within the national Democratic Party. The cuts and belt tightening introduced by the shift to Republicans in the mid-nineties elections did help reduce the national budget deficit, as predicted, and the latter half of the nineties proved to be boom economic times. In New York City, Republican Mayor Rudolph Giuliani demonstrated that the city was, indeed, governable and altered the public's expectations concerning that. His embattled campaign for welfare reform bore fruit on the local level just as President Clinton's willingness to work with a Republican Congress nationally, to "change welfare as we know it," made inroads on this issue across the country. The reduction in dependency led to an infusion of new people into the workforce that further served to inspirit the economy in those years. But as is so often the case, good times prompt politicians to loosen up and open the spending spigots. By the end of the Clinton years, states and municipalities were overspending again and even Mayor Giuliani was showering largess on his city's employees. With the terror attacks of September 11th, 2001, spending at all levels blew back through the roof. In New York City alone, overtime costs were astronomical as the city mobilized to respond to the most massive attack on American soil in our history and to a series of anthrax mailings that took the lives of innocent civilians in New York and elsewhere around the nation. The shock of the attacks and the infrastructural and psychological damage done, cost the economy billions and stymied growth. Costs to respond to newly discovered security needs skyrocketed. Coming as they did, after the bursting of the dot.com bubble in the last year of the Clinton presidency, and exacerbated by a series of major corporate scandals that shook the confidence of the markets, the economy went into a steep decline. The tax cuts of the second Bush presidency, and continued shrewd monetary policy on the part of the Federal Reserve, kept things afloat until real economic momentum was finally restored. However, in retrospect, the boom times of the late nineties apparently came much too soon on the heels of the fiscal restraints introduced by the newly elected Republicans across the country. Republicans, like their Democratic colleagues, proved no stronger at resisting the siren call of overspending, leaving us in worse fiscal shape than they should have when the crises of 9/11 hit. Many opportunities to restructure and rationalize government were missed or forsworn when the need no longer seemed so pressing. As a result, there remains quite a bit left to do today, if we are really serious about getting government under control. Alas, we're now engaged in a war with terrorists who want to bring us down, even as we face new fiscal problems. When you're in a war, of course, the first and only real priority must be to win it. Cost consciousness has to take a back seat until it's over.

ON GOVERNING

(March 1, 2003)

"Democracy is the worst form of government there is," said Winston Churchill back in the mid-twentieth century, "except for all the others!" Some have ascribed this quote to the French statesman Clemenceau, instead of Churchill, but whoever said it certainly had a point.

I was reminded of it recently, as I listened to the pundits and commentators holding forth after the Bush State of the Union Address.[10] Here we had a president who took office under an electoral cloud, a man who seemed a rank amateur to all and sundry, unable to inspire confidence even in many of those who had voted for him, who then went on to surprise us all with his clarity and steadfastness in response to the terrorist attacks on September 11, 2001. A president who literally blossomed before our eyes from laughable verbal bumbler to plain-talking orator. A man genuinely able to move a nation with his own special brand of Texas straight-shooting. A man who reversed the terrible sense of vulnerability that beset us after al Qaeda did its worst. And yet, as a people, we can't seem to stop our carping or complaining.

After Bush's recent performance before Congress, what did the talking heads have to say? Well, they were all over the map, as usual, dissecting and deconstructing the president's words, evaluating his speech as though it were just another entertaining moment on television . . . which, to some, I suppose was all it was. The absolute dumbest complaint I heard after the speech was on the cable television program known as "Buchanan and Press" where Press, the non-Buchanan half of the show's eponymous analytic duo, announced that what really got him was that Bush "failed to introduce his guests." The "guests," of course, are those private citizens from various walks of life who are routinely invited to attend the annual joint session of Congress as proxies for all the rest of us.

They always introduce the guests, Press averred, it's a tradition. But Bush just ignored them. Ouch, that criticism must have really struck home at the White House!

There is something about the dynamic of democracy, I think, that makes it hard for citizens to pull together. The opportunity to speak freely and to vent seems to draw out the worst in us, encouraging everyone to advance an opinion, whether he or she knows anything about the subject or not. Any old opinion will often do, it seems, as long as it questions the judgment of those who are charged with the thankless job of governing the rest of us.

Do we face an unpleasant and high-risk decision re: dealing forcefully with a dictatorship that threatens world stability and our own long-term security because of its history of ill-intentioned aggression and lust for weapons of mass destruction? Well then, every individual in this country knows what's best to do, no matter what the Executive Branch says. Every commentator knows how to handle those bellicose Iraqis and North Koreans better than the men and women who are paid to do this for us. And every congressman or woman knows too. Of course, the opposition party knows (almost on auto-pilot, you might say) that whatever the President proposes is dead wrong from the get-go.

Was Bush too isolationist when he ran for the presidency in 2000? Well, yes, that's what his opponents and the media told us back then. But isn't he too interventionist now? Wouldn't it be better to mind our own business and allow the community of nations to maintain the status quo, relying on continuing sanctions and containment of Saddam Hussein's Iraq, than to risk proactive intervention? You betcha, says the loyal opposition today. Nation building is a good idea if it doesn't cost too much and if the other party isn't in favor of it. But it ain't so hot, when the other party suddenly sees the light.

And isn't Bush being too unilateral in insisting that America must go it alone if it has to, in order to deal with a rogue dictator like Saddam? Of course, says the opposing party.

But when the president recently tried to multilateralize the effort to deal with North Korea, given that the North Koreans are much more of a military threat than the Iraqis at this point, what happened? He was castigated by the same opposition for being too wishy-washy on the issue and for not taking the lead to deal with the matter head-on as he is doing (albeit wrongly, they tell us) with the Iraqis.

Of course, the word from institutional punditry at this point, no less than from the loyal opposition, is that Bush, himself, caused the problem with North Korea by his blunt talk, getting that nice, mild-mannered Kim Jung Il all riled up at us by naming his country as part of the now infamous "axis of evil". Never mind that what came to light, after Bush's words, was nothing more than an acknowledgement by the North Koreans themselves that they have been violating the nuclear non-proliferation accords consistently since these were negotiated with them by former President Carter on behalf of President Clinton back in 1994! Sure the North Koreans have been lying to us all this time . . . but they never would have had to tell us they were lying, if Bush hadn't gone and made them mad like he did.

I remember how the loyal opposition railed against Bush's father, the former president, when he determined to intervene to reverse Saddam Hussein's seizure of Kuwait back in 1990. It's all about oil they cried. He really just wants to go in there and push Hussein out to grab those oil fields Iraq possesses. The proposed liberation of Kuwait is just an excuse, they cried.

So what happened? Bush pere got castigated in the end for not going in and finishing Saddam, once he had accomplished what he had said all along was his sole goal, to liberate Kuwait from the aggressive Iraqi dictator. (And in retrospect it does look like it would have been a good idea if the first Bush had gone further, but, of course, if he had, the same people who opposed the Gulf War in the first place, and then condemned the former president for not following through and taking the war to Baghdad, would have been the first to cry foul, saying 'see, we told you Kuwait was really just a pretext and all Bush really wanted was to dash up to Baghdad and seize Iraq and its oil!')

So how do you govern in a democracy where everyone wants to second guess you and the institutional opposition sees dissent as a veritable obligation, no matter which policy choices you make? The younger Bush has metamorphosed into a strong, competent and inspiring leader. But to his political opponents this just means they must find a different brush with which to tar him. Well maybe he's not as dumb as people thought after all? So, maybe he's really too smart for his own good![11]

It's all in the spin and the democratic conceit that every decision is everyone's to make. It sometimes amazes me that anyone wants to risk being president at all. They insult you, belittle you, parse your every word. Every decision you make is subject to perpetual national backseat driving. The first slip-up and they cry for Congressional investigations and, if that isn't enough, an independent prosecutor. The national media are forever on the alert for something dirty in your past. Does a big fundraiser or political supporter stumble? Where's that smoking gun to connect the president with the debacle? The media and the loyal opposition are forever in feeding frenzy mode, barely able to wait for that next big gaffe.

And, while all this is going on, the man or woman (since a woman will certainly achieve the presidency one day) who is charged with leading the nation must maintain a level head, must not grow angry, must keep his or her judgment sharp and hand steady. The president's senior staff, too, must remain self-possessed and not bend with every ill wind that blows in from the likes of Chris Matthews, Bill O'Reilly, Pat Buchanan, et al. Nor must they let themselves be bedeviled by all those "experts" who are incessantly paraded onto the tube by the talking heads, both the "experts" who predicted a quagmire before the 1991 Gulf War (nearly all of them) and those who loudly proclaim the inadvisability of acting preemptively in defense of world stability today.

Listening to Bush deliver his State of the Union Address and its loquacious aftermath, observing the second-guessers' industry in its usual high dudgeon, made me wonder how we can ever expect to get good government from the men and women we select for this purpose. And why there are still any around willing to undertake that role!

But then again, what's the alternative? A government like the one Saddam Hussein provides for his people, where he sits and smokes his odorous cigars while his generals and other lackeys compete with one another to shower him with blessings and praise? Or a government like the now defunct Taliban regime where women were obliged to walk the streets in body bags . . . or be summarily beaten and, possibly, executed?

So maybe Churchill had a point after all. I just wish we could figure out a way to make this democratic free-for-all of ours a little less messy.

NATION BUILDING IN THE MIDDLE EAST?

(March 6, 2003)

There's a new complaint about George W. Bush's plan for military action in Iraq these days. He wants to go in there (shudder) and do some (gasp) nation building! Who are we to think we have a right to change Iraq's form of government, the critics complain. Where do we come off thinking our way is the *right* way? I mean, they have their own traditions over in the Middle East. Who says they have to have freedom of speech and press, the right to trial in credible courts, and to democratically elect their leaders? That's not what they want or what they're used to, goes the argument, so why do we think we ought to spend our treasure and blood to give it to them?

So what *do* they want? More Saddam Husseins? Some Saudi princes, perhaps?

Not long ago everyone was actually taking the Bush administration to task for not going public with plans for a post-Saddam Iraq. Then the knock on Bush, and one of the reasons to oppose military action in Iraq, was that his policy would allegedly destabilize the region and allow some other power-mad dictator to come to the fore who might be just as bad, or worse, than Saddam because the Bush folks had no plan to make Iraq better than they found it. The Bush administration wasn't thinking about what comes after, was the criticism of the day not so very long ago.

In fact, that's what they tell us happened in Afghanistan in the eighties and nineties, i.e., the U.S. supported the mujahedeen against the Soviets and then walked away, leaving that country to the warlords and a weak central government. American policy makers, internal and external critics opined, just washed their hands and walked away when the Soviets withdrew, leaving Afghanistan in a state of anarchy, after supporting a war that had wrecked the national infrastructure. And lo and behold they tell us, we got the Taliban, those oppressors of their own people and allies of our self-declared enemies, al Qaeda.

Instead of "nation building" in Afghanistan after the departure of the Soviets, the U.S. left that land to its own devices and that was wrong.

Bush, of course, campaigned in 2000 in favor, apparently, of just such hands-off policies. When Bush spoke disparagingly of "nation building" back then, the critics all said he was disengaged and isolationist and hit him hard for that.

So what happens now? Bush reverses himself in the aftermath of the attacks of 9/11 and calls for changing the political environment in the Middle East and the first thing people start carping about is that he's trying to impose our system on people who are not asking for it. He wants to "nation build."

I'm bemused by it all. With Bush it's always damned if you do/damned if you don't. If he tries to be multilateral with North Korea, they say the U.S. should deal one-on-one with Kim Jong Il (because that is Kim's demand, of course). If he tries to deal one-on-one with Saddam because others, particularly at the United Nations, refuse to support his actions, they say 'don't be unilateral, don't act without the agreement of the United Nations.'

And now comes this foolishness about it being wrong to plan to introduce democracy into the Middle East. First of all, democracy is a good thing for people in that it leads to open societies and human freedoms. Second it's a system of government that may finally wean the populations of that part of the world away from the medieval mentality that has created the bloody mindedness that brought us September 11th, 2001 (and many other atrocities). Third, democracies tend to be more peaceable than dictatorships or other forms of despotisms. Fourth, I don't think the Germans or the Japanese hold it against us that we brought them democracy after World War II (whatever other petty resentments now seem to be rearing their awful little heads in those and other countries). In fact, those countries are surely the better for our efforts in that arena. Just ask the Eastern European states who had Stalin as their post-World War II midwife instead of Truman and Eisenhower.

It may be the case that in a perfect world everyone ought to be free to choose to be just whatever he or she wants to be, even if that means choosing to live in an autocracy or worse. But recent events have shown us quite clearly that this world is far from perfect. We cannot afford to sit around while the Saddams and Osamas and Kim Jong Ils (and their ilk) strengthen their positions and prepare to launch attacks on our cities, buildings and people. It's very nice to advocate peace and non-intervention. But that doesn't prevent us from being attacked or from facing a more dangerous world in the future as these characters proliferate and gain access to more and more dangerous technologies.

Bush's announced decision not to walk away from Iraq, after Saddam is removed, but to remain in place in order to stabilize the region and introduce democracy, is laudable, not reprehensible. Or should we have walked away from conquered Germany and Japan after World War II and left them to stew in their own juices as happened to the defeated nations of World War I? As George Santayana said, "those who do not learn from history are condemned to repeat it."

It's to the Bush administration's credit that they are facing the future with their eyes open and have the courage to proceed (along with Tony Blair), despite the short-sighted opposition that is being marshaled against them at every level. An opposition, I might add, which only encourages Saddam Hussein to resist, thereby making war more likely, not less (as Elie Wiesel recently noted). In fact, if the world were to line up firmly behind President Bush's intention to enforce the past U.N. resolutions now, Saddam might actually see that his choice is between a war he cannot win and giving up his dreams of empire in the Middle East. But as long as the world doesn't, as long as other nations continue to maneuver to block U.S. action, they give Saddam hope and make it that much less likely he will begin to cooperate, which is the only truly viable way he can avoid a U.S. action to remove him and his heinous regime now.

This is not about American imperialism, despite what the critics want to claim, and frankly the best way to prevent it from ever becoming a question of imperialism is for the world to join us now and do what has to be done jointly, through the United Nations, rather than force America to act on its own. As Bush said recently on national television in his own awkward way, we ask no one in the world for permission to act in our own defense and so will do what we think needs to be done with or without U.N. support.

But obliging America to act alone now is only going to establish a very bad international precedent and begin to create an imperialist mindset in America that will start to be felt more strongly in future decades. Moreover, it will seriously weaken the United Nations when we need to strengthen that organization. But if the U.N. now goes the way of the League of Nations, its member nations will have only their leaders to blame and in particular France's Jacques Chirac and his minion, the French Foreign Minister, Monsieur Dominque De Villepin.

BLOOD AND OIL

(March 15, 2003)

"No blood for oil" goes the anti-war refrain, re-cycled from the 1991 Gulf War. That's what they cried back when the first President Bush assembled his coalition against Saddam Hussein in order to oust him from Kuwait, the little neighboring state he'd seized in a surprise blitzkrieg that caught the world off-guard. And now the anti-war groups have revived this tired slogan. What makes it so potent is that there is a kernel of truth in it.

Of course, oil is an issue in the present business. But it is a misunderstanding to think that means that George W. Bush and the U.S. want to seize and own the Iraqi oil fields. We could get the oil much more cheaply by just buying it and by lifting sanctions against Iraq, thereby enabling them to start selling more of their oil in the world market, thus bringing down prices for oil overall. In fact, if this was about stealing Iraqi oil why didn't the U.S do that back in 1991 when the same silly claim was leveled against the U.S by the same groups? Bush Sr. could have pursued the Republican Guard into Iraq and wiped them out and grabbed the oil fields. But he didn't. Instead he stopped short in order to keep the promise he'd made to his allies when he put the coalition together. And he caught hell for this from the same critics who had opposed the Gulf War in the first place!

The real problem is that Saddam has been trying to establish his dominance in the region so he can control not just Iraq's oil fields but all the others as well, either directly or through intimidation. If he succeeds, he will significantly alter the balance of power in the world (i.e., he will have Europe and much of East Asia under his thumb) because so much of the world's oil supply comes from that region. Moreover, the Middle East is an important transport nexus for seagoing commerce. Saddam can realize his dreams of establishing himself as a "major" power in time, if he can gain control over his region. This will substantially de-stabilize the world as we now know it.

Is it possible he could succeed? Yes. But it's really a long shot for him (although he is nothing if not a reckless risk-taker). The most likely scenario is that he would fail in this gambit because, in the end, he has neither the military power nor the national resources to pull this off, whether we deal with him preemptively now or wait until he comes out of his hole again (as he did against Iran and later against Kuwait). But if we let him get any farther down this road, he will be much harder to stop later on and, when we do have to deal with him, the conflict will be much more serious and risky since, by then, he will have better killing technologies under his belt and a network of other states in the region that owe him some kind of fealty. It will be a bigger, bloodier conflict in which we will have a lot more risk and will likely see many more casualties on both sides. In fact, allowing him to proceed along his current path is an invitation to something more akin to a traditional style world war than the current action is likely to be.

Of course, in any war there are risks and unforeseeables. Though none of us can predict the future, we can make reasoned judgments based on what we know and have seen in the past. In this case we know Saddam is a very bad guy. We know he fancies himself a conqueror and ruler of empire. We know he likes power and will do (and has done) whatever he thinks he needs to obtain and retain power. We know he is not averse to invading and conquering other states. We know he is seeking and has secured weapons of mass destruction. We know he has used them in war and on his own people. We know he is a brutal tyrant to his people. These are all good reasons to go to war with him if we have to. But our main reason is to prevent him from becoming a world class threat while we still can.

So yes, it is about oil. But not in the way those who fall back on that slogan mean. It is not about the U.S. coveting Iraqi oil. It is about geopolitical stability and the kind of world prosperity that comes with peace. If Saddam is allowed to have his way, the world we live in will be a very unpleasant place in a few years and yes, many people in the world will be a lot worse off than they are now.

If the West had dealt early on with Hitler, all the horrors of World War II might have been avoided. They didn't back then for many of the same reasons that people are giving now in urging that we avoid confrontation with Saddam Hussein.

They were wrong then.

We have a chance not to be wrong now.

THE FOG OF DEBATE

(April 19, 2003)

With the dramatic events of April 9th, 2003 in Baghdad, which saw the jubilant welcoming of U.S. troops and the destruction and defacement of monuments to the deposed dictator, Saddam Hussein, a stunned silence seemed to temporarily descend on the critics of the administration's policies. Unable to argue against the advisability of the U.S. led coalition's actions in Iraq in the face of the live shots pouring in from Baghdad of rejoicing Iraqis thumbing their noses at the symbols of Saddam's rule, rubbing the soles of their shoes on his broken visage, and shouting praises and thanks to America and Bush, many of the critics just seemed to shut up. It couldn't last of course.

By the following day, on April 10th, the Wall Street Journal carried a story headlined, in part, "Anti-War Groups Still Protest". Noting a shift in the strategy of these groups, the article reported that one critic, Ghada Razuki, a British protest leader, apparently recovering nicely from the initial images of joy in Baghdad, declared that the pictures we saw had been "stage-managed by the U.S. and don't necessarily mean anything." Ms. Razuki added that the people of Iraq may now "be happy Saddam is gone, but their euphoria will disappear as soon as they realize the Americans are in charge." Apparently in her mind this is a truly damning indictment.

One has to wonder what will happen to Ms. Razuki's own state of mind if the happiness of the freed Iraqis does not "disappear" as she predicts?[12] And what if the Americans do exactly as they have said they will do, i.e., secure the peace, assist in establishing a legitimate, democratic Iraqi government, and then go home?

Would Ms. Razuki's vehement opposition to the U.S. actions itself "disappear". You can bet it won't.

"The opposition movement is not going to disappear, and it's not going to shrink," Spanish Parliament member and New Left Coalition leader Diego Lopez Garrido assured the Journal's reporters in the same article. "It's going to be reconverted into a movement that keeps a vigilant eye on things to make sure that this doesn't happen again, with Syria, with Iran." But what is the "this" he has in mind? That we don't liberate any more populations from bloody dictators?

What, you have to ask yourself, are these people really against and how can they oppose the kinds of actions that brought the images we recently witnessed in Baghdad, as the realization that Saddam's horrid regime was finally gone sunk in?

"What concerns the anti-war movement seems to be a new American foreign policy which is a first-strike or preemptive doctrine by the Bush administration," Mary Lord, a leader in the American Friends Service Committee, told the Journal in the same article. But wait a moment: wasn't the anti-war movement against the President's proposed military intervention in Iraq even before his administration had crafted and announced the so-called preemptive doctrine, while it was still seeking U.N. agreement through yet another Security Council resolution, in fact?

"We're broadening our message," Bette Hoover, another critic, told the Journal. "Among other things we're going to be highlighting are those benefiting from the U.S.'s continued war on terrorism." Ms. Hoover is described in the article as an organizer of an upcoming Washington rally that hopes to give special attention to the Occidental Petroleum Corp. and the World Bank. A San Francisco human rights group, Global Exchange, according to the Journal article, "has begun to target companies and individuals it believes will benefit from the postwar reconstruction." Global Exchange leader Medea Benjamin emphatically told the Journal that "nobody should profit from this war." So maybe that's really what it's all about: a continuation of the now largely discredited war on capitalism that the Soviet Union once spearheaded?

Not to be outdone, on April 11th The New York Sun ran its own story on the anti-war critics, reporting that Maya Sen, a national organizer for the American peace group, Not in Our Name, noted that she was "appalled to see the footage and the coercion the U.S. and U.K. military have put on the people of Iraq. It's a little hard not to do what they tell you to do when they are armed with machine guns." One is tempted to ask Ms. Sen if she thought this past autumn's "election," orchestrated by the now departed Iraqi dictatorship, which resulted in a 100% vote for Saddam, was a better measure of the people's will?

In the same article The Sun also noted that City Councilman Charles Barron, a supporter of the Council resolution against the war said that "People died for hegemony over the Middle East area. Do you honestly believe Bush cares about the lives of Iraqi people? Please." Ms. Sen again: "We're dealing with something else now. The language that we're going to use is that this is straight up colonization."

So what is really going on here?

There seems to be a plethora of reasons for the opposition being expressed, not all of which have very much to do with freedom for oppressed peoples. The pre-war debate raged on maddeningly for months as politicians around the globe staked out their positions and anti-war protesters bestirred themselves from a long post-Vietnam War slumber. Sure they'd recently gotten it on over the twin matters of globalization and the environment. But these issues lacked real resonance. It took the rise of Middle Eastern terrorism, prompting an assertive American response, to finally warm the blood of those who see in America everything that is wrong with this world.

But when we strip away all the reasons these folks give, all the arguments which disregard the Iraqi population's craving for a free life, aren't we really left with just one thing: resentment of the U.S.? So is it power envy or fear of that power that motivates?

Well, even when we were bumbling about under Jimmy Carter in the seventies, the folks in the protest camp still hewed to this same line. In fact, this view has, since Vietnam, worked its way into our national psyche. Not only does a core of hard-line anti-establishment types hold to this vision but so, too, does a broad array of people in academia, in entertainment, in politics, in the professions, and in the media. Since Vietnam there has been a certain cachet to "protest," given that so many of today's adults cut their teeth on the anti-war movement of the sixties and seventies. It is the new received opinion. But is it right?

If you look closely at what drives the views of the protesters, you do not see rationality but rationalization. If the war was seen to be wrong because it was an infringement on the sovereign rights of an independent people, what happens when that same people rejoice at the war's results? Do the protesters stop to re-think their opposition in the face of the images of liberation beamed live from Baghdad? Hardly. Instead they scramble to cobble together new justifications for opposition, to keep the business of protest in business.

On April 9, 2003, we had a moment when the shrill cacophony of debate briefly stopped in deference to something real and memorable. We all stood still and many of us felt a flutter in our chests as freedom came to a long-oppressed people and as all the blood and sweat of the American-led coalition's efforts seemed to be vindicated. As elderly Iraqi men cried in the street and beat images of Saddam Hussein with their shoes, as crowds struggled to bring down a hideous statue of the dictator, as children pounded on the broken, Ozymandius-like head that other Iraqis drew triumphantly through the streets behind them, many of us felt tears well up in our eyes in unity with this long-suppressed, long-suffering people.

But the critics, the carpers, the leftovers of another era could not give up their raison d'etre. No amount of good news for the Iraqi people could possibly be enough to affect a world view that has been so deeply warped by the pain of bygone years. And so, disregarding what was right before their eyes, they began, almost immediately, the process of mental readjustment that would preserve their anti-American outrage. The debate and rancor ceased for a day as the world focused on liberation in Iraq. But soon it was again business as usual as the fog of debate once more replaced the fog of war.

WHY DO WE HATE US?

(April 26, 2003)

Since September 11th, 2001, we have been a different country. Initially recovering from the shock of a perfidious attack upon the homeland, we promptly struck back by unseating the rogue Taliban regime in Afghanistan, a regime that had given aid and comfort to (and made common cause with) the Middle Eastern terrorist entity, and avowed American enemy, al Qaeda. Riding an upsurge of international sympathy, the United States rigorously went about the business of extirpating the al Qaeda terrorist network and its sympathizers, winning an important victory with the overthrow of the Taliban's Mullah Omar. And yet, when the time came to turn our attention to another regime historically affiliated with Middle Eastern terror, Saddam Hussein's Iraq, everything seemed to fall apart before our eyes.

All over the world, populations on every continent turned against us and decried our expressed aim of dealing preemptively with Saddam or replacing him, if necessary, with a more stable, democratic and representative government. Those we had long thought our allies and friends were among the most vocal in opposition. Nations whose very independent existence in today's world we made possible (France, Germany, Belgium), and others we had thought new friends after decades of Cold War enmity, like China and Russia, led the charge to tie our hands and preserve the status quo. Even in countries whose leaders supported us, the polls showed marked popular opposition to America's expressed policy of dealing with Saddam. Tony Blair, for instance, still faces serious problems from within his own party because of the unpopularity, among the British populace, of his support for American policy.

It's not hard to see why the shift has occurred internationally, whether justified or not. There are all the usual suspects: fear and envy of another's apparent power; dislike of the American political, economic and cultural systems; competing geopolitical interests, etc. But what may have been the most surprising turn of all was why so much of this resonated inside the United States as well.

Although there was some national breast beating on the part of many media pundits after 9/11, Americans did not become deeply divided over the rightness of the Administration's expressed policies until Afghanistan was safely behind us and Iraq loomed ahead. With the lengthy delay that kicked in when President Bush acquiesced to advice that he seek and secure U.N. support before acting in the matter of Iraq, a powerful anti-war momentum took hold in this country, manifesting in a virtual re-birth of the old anti-war movement of Vietnam days. Many of the same crew of protesters "took to the streets", mostly older now but still sporting grotesque presidential masks and slogans (shades of the Johnson-Nixon years) and spouting the usual shrill denunciations of America's government and policies. Hollywood's intellectual policy elite swarmed into the fray, too, just like the old days, while the Old Left, which despises America's capitalist economic system on principle, turned up the volume on all its familiar complaints.

America, we were told, was arrogant and imperialistic, a threat to the rights and freedoms of other nations. Our expressed aim of freeing populations from a ruthless dictator was no more than a smokescreen. What we really lusted for was their oil and to reinstate colonial control! And it wasn't only the Old anti-American Left that bought into and promulgated this viewpoint. Liberal pundits could be heard across the broadcast spectrum calling down some of these same calumnies on the heads of Bush, his cabinet members and advisors, albeit leavened with the additional claims of diplomatic insensitivity, disregard for the international community, and a misdirection of American resources (away from Osama and to Saddam . . . or from the domestic economy to the military . . . take your pick).

Indeed, a whole basket of sometimes mutually exclusive reasons to avoid conflict were trotted out. Many of the trotters had their own agendas: the Old Left despises America's global primacy, of course; the Democrats despise the idea of Republicans in power; and much of the mainstream media just distrusts the government in principle (but especially when it's run by Republicans). And yet the surprise in all this is not that these various quarters have these views. It's that they found such a receptive audience among the American public. Throughout the period leading up to the present military action in Iraq, the polls showed a shifting and unsure American electorate with a core group of anti-war respondents, no matter what.

Back in the heady days after World War II and right up to the Vietnam debacle, Americans instinctively lined up with "their side" in matters of global policy. Not anymore. Vietnam's legacy and the Watergate scandal that followed have so soured Americans on their own government that many are ready, at the drop of the proverbial hat, to disbelieve their leaders and assume the worst. Our cultural manifestations reflect and reinforce this viewpoint with the ubiquity of anti-government paranoia that suffuses our television and film fare.

Indeed, this paranoid fear of our own government seems embedded in our very culture these days, along with the sense that we should feel embarrassed by American power or the occasional need to exercise it. We are all so politically correct now that many of us think it almost criminal to speak in terms of America's national interests or to imagine we have any right to act in the world without the consent of others. We are a Gulliver so sappy as to beg the Lilliputians to tie us up in knots lest they cease to like us! Somewhere between the trauma of Vietnam and the rise of al Qaeda's crazies, we forgot how to be the nation we once were.

Part of this, of course, is just reflective of the fact that we are such a diverse body politic, with so many cultures and national histories behind us, that we want to be all things to all people. But, in the end, we cannot be that. If we are to sustain and protect ourselves, we have to restore the sense of national cohesion we once had. Diversity is not an impediment if we are wise. It is an opportunity because it gives us such a rich pool of human resources on which to draw . . . and an instinctive understanding of, and cultural link with, all the far-flung lands that have contributed to making us what we are.

But we cannot remain free and prosperous in a world that is rife with unrestricted terror, where every two-bit rogue nation or group with a grudge can dream of attacking us with nuclear or "dirty" bombs . . . or infecting us with deadly biological agents . . . or flooding our subway systems with poisonous gases. We cannot be a nation if we do not act the part and behave on the global stage as though we have interests to protect . . . and will protect them.

We can surely be a better kind of world power than what has come before us, one whose aim is not conquest but world stability and prosperity in which all nations can share. But we cannot be anything at all if we abrogate what we are for fear of offending. Or if we forget that we have a common heritage, interests and lives to defend.

THE REASONS FOR WAR

(June 13, 2003)

I expended quite a few words in these pages during the period leading up to the war against Saddam Hussein's Iraqi regime, in defense of that action . . . and so I think it's appropriate to take stock now. There are still a number of open questions and the most vexing seems to be the matter of Saddam's alleged weapons of mass destruction (wmd). The Bush administration made this a cornerstone in its case for military action though it was certainly not the only justification. In fact the case seems to have stood on four distinct legs:

1. Saddam had, or was about to have, substantial (and dangerous) quantities of wmd and was concealing this;
2. Saddam was in league with (and supported) Middle East terrorists and so was linked to al Qaeda, the major Middle Eastern terrorist organization that had attacked the U.S.;
3. Saddam was a serial aggressor with designs on achieving hegemony in the Middle East, thereby threatening his neighbors and those dependent on Middle Eastern oil and transport via the Suez Canal;
4. Saddam was a brutal dictatorial thug who oppressed and slaughtered his own people.

All of these propositions were somewhat interrelated so the case did not depend on any one of them in particular but, rather, on the way each supported and fed into the others. Having wmd was an especially bad thing, for instance, if there was a link to al Qaeda and other terrorists. More, wmd would likely be used in any future aggressive actions by the regime (and could be used as a form of international blackmail). And his having this kind of weaponry increased the chance future aggressions would succeed. Also, Saddam was known to have used wmd on his own people during his various acts of oppression.

Those who opposed the war denied one or more of the above, as follows. They claimed that:

1. There was no evidence that Saddam still had wmd *but international inspections would be sufficient to control or eliminate them if he did have this stuff, in any case;*
2. There was no specific evidence that Saddam had any connection with al Qaeda and therefore no reason to assume he posed any near term threat to the U.S., while attacking him was likely to drive him into al Qaeda's camp for sure and further inflame the Middle East, increasing al Qaeda recruitment, thereby making things having to do with terrorism worse not better;
3. Saddam's aggression had been contained and was manageable in any case, should he somehow become an active threat in the region again;
4. Saddam was no worse than myriads of other dictators, some of whom we support or have supported and, moreover, Saddam himself was a dictator we had, ourselves, once supported, even while he was doing his worst. And besides, who were we to judge any other nation's form of government or "choice" of leaders?

Those opposed to the war went on to make the further claim that war entailed big risks and that many lives would be lost on both sides, including the lives of innocent civilians. Some of the opponents further asserted that the U.S. had ulterior motives (imperialism, worldwide hegemony, acquisition of Iraqi oil, furtherance of the interests of Israel over the Arabs, etc., etc.). Finally, many of the war's opponents held that no nation, including the

U.S., had the right to make what appeared to be preemptive war without international authorization which came to be defined as approval by the U.N. Security Council.

The war's opponents also vacillated between saying sanctions and inspections were adequate to contain Saddam and arguing that the sanctions had been too painful for the Iraqi people (more or less assuring that a future regime of sanctions would soon wither away, in any case, even if their continuation was offered by these critics as a near term alternative to war).

Needless to say, this is a very complex set of issues and they are still being debated. Of course, the U.S. acted anyway and the actual removal of Saddam was quicker and less bloody than anyone expected. But it was bloody enough. War, in the end, is war and not something to be lightly undertaken. But who was right?

In some sense, winners write history and, while the U.S. has not yet won its larger war on terror (so we are not yet sure how *that* will be written), the war on Saddam, a part of that larger war according to the Bush administration, has at least been won. Of course there is still its aftermath and any number of things can go wrong. But the questions obsessing public debate at this particular moment no longer seem to be about whether we had the reasons or the right to go to war against Saddam.[13]

Certainly, people of goodwill were arrayed on both sides. And there was a fairly clear divide: those who opposed war of almost any sort were aligned with those who opposed American power at almost any cost. Against these were those who believed the Middle East was a dangerous powder keg needing to be defused and those who just wanted to see Saddam overthrown. In the end it's all about how you view the world, isn't it?

Of the four reasons I cited above for favoring the war, few dispute today that Saddam was a brutal monster and that it is better for the people of Iraq that he is gone (though there are still many who think it wasn't worth the relatively modest cost in lives and treasure incurred at the time). As to Saddam's penchant for aggression, few can deny that he had given ample evidence of this in the years leading up to his ouster. More problematic, though, is the alleged connection with al Qaeda and the existence of wmd. While I think the overall situation warranted our action, I remain hopeful that the U.S. will find evidence of wmd and terrorist connections, even though I think the case was a good one without knock-down, drag-out proof of these two claims. But the fact is that we made such a point of claiming the wmd existed that our credibility is now on the line.[14]

Perhaps the U.S. could not have made as compelling a case for military action without the claims of wmd and terrorism since it is never easy to move a democracy toward war. In all likelihood, our government officials and intelligence experts had good reason to have believed the claims when they made them. But the U.S. must continue to operate on the world stage and it cannot do so effectively if its credibility is in question. That is exactly what happened in the Vietnam era when the American government was largely perceived to be deceptive and semi-competent at best. The residue of those years is still with us today in the cries of those who distrust everything America does or says.

Will these folks suddenly change their tune and say, yeah, I guess we should have gone to war, if the wmd and the al Qaeda connections are finally and definitively confirmed? Of course they won't because their minds are mired in the detritus of another era. But in order to avoid building on that, in order to avoid the further feeding of anti-American emotions, in order to avoid creating new generations of those who distrust us, it is imperative that the U.S. be shown to have acted intelligently and with goodwill in the Iraqi matter. This means we must find the wmd and the al Qaeda connections if they exist. But, if they don't we'd better be prepared to take a closer look at what we believe about ourselves and at the competence of our intelligence services and the men in Washington who relied on them.

BASHING BUSH

(June 20, 2003)

Watching President George W. Bush at the Arab peace summit in Sharm el Sheikh recently, I was struck by how different this man was from the bumbling, inarticulate candidate Bush who squeaked through in the 2000 election due to a narrow Florida vote and an American system that weights elections by states. Many Americans who voted for the other guy still have not accepted that outcome, blaming the Supreme Court for its decision to end the recounts while continuing to question Bush's legitimacy. This is unfair, of course, but they have hung onto the image of the bumbling neophyte as a means of bolstering their claim that the wrong guy won.

The early images we saw of Bush did not help matters any. Often appearing with a "deer in the headlights" expression and a silly, if somewhat timid, wise-guy smirk, the new president seemed out of his depth. The media piled on, as the media usually does, and we got image after image of presidential stumbling. A relatively poor public speaker, Bush's performance only seemed to confirm the perception that we had an amateur in the White House whose main claim to fame was a last name that recalled certain kinds of landscape shrubbery and a brief stint as owner of an undistinguished Texas baseball team.

Then came 9/11 and the ex-baseball man stepped up to the plate. Taking charge when that was most needed, the often awkward-seeming Bush reminded us of who we were and what we stood for. Rallying the administration and the country, George W. went after the terrorists where they lived and rooted out al Qaeda from its Taliban stronghold, took down its leaders and operatives from the Philippines to Pakistan to Yemen, and removed a rogue regime in Iraq that was a hotbed of Middle Eastern terror and anti-Americanism. In the process he showed the terrorists and the world that he, and we, meant business. Despite efforts by other, ostensibly more sophisticated, world leaders to hamstring us, Bush went ahead and did just what he said needed doing.

The rest of the world has noticed. In his recent European tour, the president reinforced the new vision of America as a state which needs to be taken seriously . . . and which expects to be. Now, pushing peace in the Middle East, he is building on the gains achieved by the removal of the dictator Saddam Hussein. The Arab prime ministers and potentates appear to be listening. As does the Israeli prime minister who knows full well that he owes a great deal to Bush and that Bush will expect cooperation as the price to be paid.

So the new Bush is a man who flies his own jets, sits confidently with seasoned European politicians and convenes and guides recalcitrant leaders down a road to new realities and peace in their region. How does this compare with the earlier Bush? Certainly those who are ideologically opposed to him will not see a difference. For the Sean Penns, the Molly Ivins and the Maureen Dowds of the world, Bush will always be the bumbling buffoon who must be evicted from the 'presidential palace' in favor of someone whose policies are more in keeping with their own preferences (which, thereby, legitimizes occupancy of that seat of power in their minds). Or, if he is not the class fool anymore, in their eyes, they will make him out to be something far worse, a purveyor of dangerous policies that threaten our economic well-being by favoring rich guys, that put costly government programs at risk by reducing taxes, and that make the rest of the world mad because he is willing to assert America's interests while threatening our liberties by his energetic pursuit of those who would terrorize us at home and abroad. Of course this is all poppycock!

For those of us whose main concern is competency and leadership in defense of our country, the sea change we have seen in Bush is telling. He has demonstrated that the American system did not misfire when the Electoral College vote overrode the "popular" results, just as it was meant to do by its designers. And he has demonstrated that eloquence and easy confidence before a camera are not the real measures of leadership. Bush is certainly no great intellectual, not the smartest guy on the planet. But, in truth, he's smart enough. He's a man who has grown in office while showing the world that Americans are not the pushovers that Osama bin Laden fantasized we were back when his Islamic fundamentalist fanatics foresaw an easy victory over America after the "tougher" Soviet Union was dispatched.

No, the struggle with those who hate us is not over yet. But so far, so good. And seeing Bush become a world leader right before our eyes is a good indication that we are on the right path.

Historical Note: As of this writing, Bush is again the object of ire and derision as Democrats vie with one another to portray him in the worst possible light. Alas, nothing of note came of his efforts to make a difference in the Mideast peace process. The Palestinian prime minister, appointed by Yasser Arafat in the aftermath of the removal of Saddam Hussein, resigned in protest over his political impotence and a new prime minister, Ahmed Qureia, subsequently took his place, a man who seems no more able to chart a new course today than his hapless predecessor had been. Recognizing the inevitable, that peace in the Middle East is unlikely to be accomplished so long as we lack leaders on both sides who are interested in, and capable of, moving toward, peace, Bush withdrew from engagement again. This only added fuel to the fire of criticism against him as his political opponents fondly recalled Bill Clinton's very active engagement during his two terms. What they forget, of course, is that Clinton was so eager to get an agreement that he pushed the two sides together before they were ready, hoping, apparently, to get a deal done before his second term expired. The result was the complete breakdown of the Oslo accords on which the peace process had been premised for nearly a decade previously. It also led to Arafat's decision to again unleash the violence of the "intifada" as a means of bringing pressure to bear on the Israelis to force a better deal. Of course,

Ehud Barak, Israeli Prime Minister at the time, had offered the best deal from the Israeli side for the Palestinians in the history of that very bloody conflict, only to have it rejected by Arafat when he abruptly walked away from the peace table. As a result Barak was swept from office in the next election and replaced by hardliner Ariel Sharon whom the Palestinians have particular reason to fear. So Bush tried to get the sides back together after Iraq, but there's an old Middle Eastern saying: "you can lead a camel to water, but you can't make him drink." Or is that about horses?

MESSAGES FROM THE INTERNET

(July 11, 2003)

Nothing promotes democracy like dialogue and nothing does dialogue quite like the Internet these days. But real dialogue in which the parties hear one another is hard to find and it's especially hard when the issue is politics. I have been astonished at the hard feeling manifested by so many against the current administration, both here and abroad. Recently someone posted some overseas articles on a website I frequent which attacked this country's actions and the administration. I responded by noting that most of the claims were half-truths and innuendo and that the real aim of the articles seemed to be to delegitimize Bush and his policies in one fell swoop. An avowed liberal on the site took me to task for this. I offer a sampling of our exchange here with some editing for brevity, of course (names deleted).

Him: The claim that Iraq had wmd and was linked to al Qaeda were the reasons used to sell the war.

Me: It was also about the threat posed by Saddam to the Middle Eastern region, a threat which was potentially destabilizing and dangerous to world peace. Moreover, Saddam was a very bad guy to his own people! It was always a combination of reasons . . .

Him: The (allegations of wmd) has turned out to be a con job.

Me: I don't think the facts are all in yet or that it's appropriate to jump the gun. As noted, this is not a simple question and always involved a lot of judgment by people in our government who get paid to make such judgments. We know Clinton lied about Monica. He said one thing on national TV and in a sworn deposition to a court of law. He then recanted publicly. So there's no question of falsehood on his part, though we can argue that it was over a minor transgression (although lying to the American public on national television and lying under oath may not, themselves, be minor). But Bush was repeating claims based on information gathered and believed by U.S. and other government sources since the early nineties and which Clinton, himself, and other Democratic leaders, said they believed at the time. Moreover Saddam continued to act as though he was hiding something. It's hard to make the case that Bush made it all up, even if it turns out to have been wrong!

Him: Note that Bush and gang sold this war on the premise of protecting this nation from attack.

Me: And they were. Saddam is out of power and he was clearly a nexus of terrorism.

Him: Not only that, we had to attack now, for the threat was immediate!

Me: The issue was more like we had to attack now because we'd probably never get another relatively low risk opportunity like the one we had. No one at the time was arguing Saddam was primed to attack the U.S. right then. The issue was that he posed a severe near term risk, in light of the events of 9/11.

Him: Then there was the alleged al Qaeda connection. Our great enemy, whom we have yet to smoke out, was out there ready to attack using those WMD Iraq had. To both reasons, I say horse puckey!

Me: There is clear evidence of contacts as well as of Saddam's sheltering al Qaeda operatives. It may never be that we'll find a smoking gun explicitly linking him with any al Qaeda actions. So what? Lots of Saddam's documents got "unaccountably" destroyed during the final days of the regime in Baghdad. Given that Saddam was a brutal thug and threat to his region (and thus to world stability and peace) and that he had contacts with al Qaeda and that he had pursued and used wmd in the past, there was every reason to address this problem now, before it got beyond our ability to handle easily and we were facing another 9/11 only this time involving release of chemical, biological or nuclear agents.

Him: Your third reason reminds me of the domino theory, and was concocted several years earlier by Pearl (sic), Wolfowitz, Cheney, Rumsfeld, and others. So we had to attack immediately to prevent the dominoes from falling? Again, horse puckey!

Me: It's not a question of dominoes but of real nations and people. When you're playing with fire, you're playing for keeps. No one "concocted" the scenario of Saddam taking over his region and thereby posing a global threat except, perhaps, Saddam in what he did and said.

Him: This pseudo reason is the one I think was sold to Bush and he had to use the first two pseudo reasons to sell this nation a pig in a poke. I cannot understand the lack of anger by the majority for being conned.

Me: Because they have the good sense to see that they weren't "conned" and are being served by good, solid, professionals who are doing the job they must in uncertain and dangerous times. Only those who are wedded to a view that is anti-Bush or anti-American (and I'll admit the two are not the same) seem willing to embrace this harebrained idea that Saddam was no threat and that the best thing to have done was to have allowed him to continue doing what he was doing and make nice to al Qaeda in hopes they'd go away.

Him: The idea that Saddam was a thug-like dictator as a reason to begin a war is laughable. Why, of all the brutal and vicious tyrants in this world, did we choose that particular one and ignore the rest? Gimme a break!

Me: Because of questions of national sovereignty, it is often hard to make a decision to remove a thuggish dictator. And since the lives of our own people are at stake in such wars and since one can never know outcomes, it is not easy to make decisions to fight to remove dictators in a society like ours where lives of citizens are valued. But when a really bad dictator arises who poses a growing threat to you, and you have a relatively low risk window of opportunity to act, then the smart thing to do is to do just that.

Him: From what you have written about those of us who reside on the left side of the aisle I can only conclude . . . that you are still calling us anti-Americans.

Me: I am not calling you anti-American though I am suggesting that you are allowing your hostility to the party and president in power to cloud your judgment to the detriment of American interests. Obviously, you can do that if you want to, but I'm entitled to call your attention to this if I think this is the case.

Him: You appear to be so Bush-bound that you would take my freedom away from me by requiring that I follow the "patriotic" line.

Me: Who's taking away your freedom? Aren't we debating this freely here with no one suggesting you should not be allowed to express your views? Nor would I ever dream of endorsing silencing you . . . or anyone. I am as much a democrat (small "d") as you are! No need to get hyperbolic about this.

Him: This line, by the way, was milked to the teat in the last election by Bush and gang in painting any who opposed him as giving aid and comfort to the enemy. Demonizing seems to be a common trait for your side of the aisle.

Me: This is silly. You are wrong and I have called that to your attention. There is no need to think anything more than that is going on here! Or would you rather restrict my freedom to criticize you?

Him: The great majority of the people in my circle express the same horror about what Bush is doing to OUR America (as shown in those articles from India). Claptrap and malarkey indeed! Where did you get the permission to say that being anti-Bush is being anti-American? This sounds much like the spin Bush and gang use to tar anyone who does not agree with them.

Me: No, you can be anti-Bush and not anti-American. But the articles that were posted merely gave a nod to being "for America", e.g., by claiming to like Walt Whitman, etc. It's easy to say that one is for America but not for the administration, its policies, etc. But when everything America does or says is subject to half-truth criticisms, then I count that as anti-American.

Of course, none of this is to say one cannot oppose the current administration. But it is patent baloney to say, for instance, that Bush wasn't really elected president and that he was installed via a coup by a right-wing Supreme Court, as was maintained in those articles. If you hold that view then you have bought into the same nonsense.

Bush did not win the popular vote (though he didn't lose it by much) but he won the electoral vote which is what counts. Sure Gore brought suit demanding recounts, but every recount still gave Florida to Bush. The Supreme Court made a decision to halt the recounts for legitimate reasons, at a certain point, despite the fact that many die-hards opposed this and still hoped that eventually some recount, at some point, would throw Florida to Gore. It was a tightly contested election and the system worked. The recounts had to stop some time and they had been going on for quite a while by the time the Supreme Court actually waded in (as a result of the legal actions initiated at the beginning by the Gore camp, since, of course, nothing can reach the Supreme Court unless it begins life as a lawsuit at some lower level).

It was within the U.S. Supreme Court's purview to make the decision to halt continuing recounts, just as it was within the Florida Supreme Court's jurisdiction to rule against Bush, and for Gore, when they did. If you will accept the Florida Supreme Court's ruling as legitimate, which enabled continuation of the recounts, why would you refuse to accept the legitimacy of the U.S. Supreme Court's later ruling? Isn't it just a matter of sour grapes and not getting the ruling you want?

For the record, I supported Clinton while he was in office (though I did not vote for him) because he was the duly elected president, even when he won less of the popular vote in his first run than Bush won in his. One of the things that characterizes a mature democracy is accepting electoral results. It's absurd to use the fact that this system enabled Bush's election as a basis for questioning his legitimacy. When people invoke such half-baked ideas in order to impugn American intentions and policies, I take offense. If they do this as part of an apparently larger strategy of castigating America, I do consider it anti-American. Bush may or may not be your idea of a good president. He may represent policies and a viewpoint that you are not comfortable with. In such a case, you or anyone are certainly free to criticize him and, if you an American, to vote against him. But he is our president, he was legitimately elected and he is acting to defend this country against some very real threats.

As to what you think Bush is doing to *your* America, I can only wonder. He has not eliminated freedoms (you certainly have plenty of opportunity to freely voice your views in open debate here!), he has not gutted social welfare programs, he has not even worked to eliminate abortion. Of course he *has* moved aggressively to defend this nation and to lower taxes and he is doing some things, in terms of Medicare, that many of his supporters are very troubled by . . . which, by the way, ought to please those like yourself who apparently favor greater government spending to provide more services.

I think what is at work here is that at least one part of the American electorate is very committed to a statist liberalism and bitterly resents loss of control of the government to that part that does not support those views. Apparently you identify with that portion of the electorate who resents loss of control to Bush and the Republicans. Well and good. Work for your positions and vote your way back into control of the instrumentalities of government if you can. If you are successful, I will probably try to overturn that in a subsequent election, but never by denying legitimacy to a legally elected president, or trying to tear him down. I will advocate for and vote for individuals who represent my viewpoint and against those who represent the views you seem to hold. Bush may not be a president after your own heart, but he is as legitimate as Clinton was and his intentions do not deserve to be impugned. Nor do America's.

Historical Note: This gentleman stopped corresponding with me shortly after this exchange. I have no reason to think that he altered any of his views as a result of our discussions.

THE BUSH "RESUME"

(August 1, 2003)

"Why can't we all just get along?" asked Rodney King after he was beaten senseless by a group of rogue white L.A. cops on the West Coast some years back. King, an African American, posed a good question and I thought the same thing the other day when I received an e-mail message, for the second time in a row, purporting to be the resume of President George W. Bush.

Of course, it isn't his resume at all but a laundry list of negatives about him in the guise of a resume.

Reading through it, I was struck by the fact that each item seemed so weighty and that, taken together, they created an overall picture of a foolish and failed second-rater who had sneaked into office when most Americans weren't looking. I did a point by point rebuttal and sent it back at once to those who had sent it to me, but I had little hope of their reading it. Why? Because this is not about facts anymore, except insofar as one can spin them to make a point. It's about pushing an agenda, making a case, and getting the other side out of power, by any means necessary. It reflects a real breakdown in a democratic point of view that tells us we should respect our political opponents and electoral outcomes.

Among the "facts" in the alleged resume used to discredit the president:

"I ran for Congress and lost."

This is actually presented as a serious claim intended to diminish Bush, as though losing an election were a disreputable outcome in itself. Indeed, more than 50% of the candidates in most races lose! Of course, many of these go on to win future political races, just as George W. Bush did.

"I bought an oil company but couldn't find any oil in Texas."

Here the entrepreneurial spirit is itself derided . . . without any recognition that most politicians, unlike George W. Bush, never even try to make a go of it in the private sector in the first place, spending their professional lives, instead, feeding at the public trough . . . hardly the way the founding generation of this country envisioned things. And then there's the little matter of not finding any oil in Texas, as though this, itself, was a demerit of note. In truth, most wildcatters come up dry and Texas is old hat, largely played out or already fully explored. But according to the writers of this "resume", it's a mark against Bush that his foray into free enterprise failed in the Texas oil patch.

"Company went bankrupt shortly after I sold my stock."

Well here's a good one. According to the writer of this particular screed, Bush should have held on to the stock of a failing company and gone down with the ship. But doesn't it make sense to sell out if you think the business you have shares in is going under? That's what markets and free enterprise are all about, though the writer of this diatribe seems to have missed *that* point. (At least Bush didn't play the futures market, like Hillary did in Arkansas, with no money down, parlaying a few thousand into a hundred thousand with the "guidance" of sophisticated market players the rest of us don't usually have access to!)

"I cut taxes and bankrupted the Texas government to the tune of billions of dollars in borrowed money."

Funny thing, Texas is not only still around, it's operating quite soundly thank you . . . and under a Republican governor. It certainly didn't file for bankruptcy while Bush was governor, or afterwards, and an argument can be made that cutting taxes there helped restore that state economically, just as it did the nation overall in the eighties under Reagan. Certainly no one can suggest Texas under Bush was in anything like the pickle big-spending Democratic governor Gray Davis has created for California where a statewide recall movement, reflecting that governor's bankrupting policies, which led to a $38 billion shortfall (larger than the entire budgets of most nations!), has prompted an off-season election to replace him in September.

The list of allegations like this goes on and on, with more of the same. So what's going on here? Obviously this is about spin, not substance. The "resume" is rife with charges like these, that seem to be damning but aren't on closer examination. But people tend to believe what they want and facts, when it comes to George W. Bush, rarely seem to matter much to some folks. It's about shaping the case to suit their pre-established views, not about what's really happening or what's best for this country.

We need to keep this in mind more and more as we are bombarded, almost daily, by attack-mode political diatribes like this one which purport to tell us the "facts". In the end, of course, it's not about the facts at all, but about shaping opinion and winning elections. If the recent spate of Democratic broadsides is any indication, we may already be well on the way toward becoming a nation of lawyers and spinners, while those who wish us ill, from Osama to the leftwing ideologues in Europe and elsewhere, gleefully join in to help us tear apart the social fabric which makes us us!

"Why can't we all just get along?" asked Mr. King.

Perhaps because we've lost sight of the importance of respecting opposing political views and their proponents in this country . . . and of the value of accepting the verdict of our own proven democratic processes?

WHEN FACTS DON'T COUNT!

(September 12, 2003)

A recent story in the New York Sun noted that the Riverside Church in Morningside Heights would be hosting an alternative symposium on September 11th for those "who doubt al Qaeda's role in the attacks of two years ago." Slated to speak include Cynthia McKinney, a former Georgia Congresswoman who lost her seat when her rather extravagant, and often colorful, allegations began to catch up with her. Among other things, Ms. McKinney "has suggested to a California radio station that President Bush knew about the attacks before they happened" the Sun article reports. Other conference participants and a church spokesman are also reported as pushing views along similar lines.

A "documentary filmmaker" who was present expressed doubts that Osama bin Laden really planned the attacks at all, questioning the authenticity of the November 2001 tape which showed the al Qaeda leader at a dinner party gloating over their results. According to The Sun the filmmaker is quoted as saying "it doesn't look like bin Laden to me." Church spokesman Tinoa Rodgers, said the paper, also echoed these sentiments, saying "I don't know if anyone knows who is behind the attacks on September 11th. There are a lot of theories going around and everybody draws their own conclusions."

He goes on: "I don't know what al Qaeda is, it's a name they throw around . . ."

Providentially, on the same day, the apparently metaphysically unknowable group, euphemistically known to some of us as "al Qaeda," released a new tape of bin Laden and his senior deputy,

Aymin al Zawahiry. In it the two leaders are depicted walking down a mountainside, rifles at the shoulder, walking sticks in hand. The voiceovers, said to be that of bin Laden and henchman Zawahiry, praise the 9/11 attacks, mention five of the suicide hijackers by name and call for more of the same, reiterating an ongoing claim that they are at war with the infidels (us) and will defeat our "crusade".

So what's a guy to do? Here we have all these denials that al Qaeda was really responsible for the attacks while these al Qaeda guys just can't seem to keep their mouths shut, publicly touting things their apologists want to exonerate them of.

Of course, tapes and such don't mean much to those who just want to believe. All sorts of absurd conspiracy theories get trotted out to account for bin Laden's self-incriminating pronouncements, just like the Pakistani "men in the street" who deny Osama's culpability, blaming the CIA, Israeli intelligence, etc. There's something peculiar about all this . . . as if facts aren't facts and that (as the Beatles might have put it) 'all you need is spin . . . la, la, la, la!'

But what makes this particularly troubling is the apparent entrenchment of this kind of thinking in the current American political landscape. Listening to this year's crop of Democratic contenders for the presidency, one begins to get the same sense of unreality. Maybe they haven't yet gone as far as asserting that Bush knew about 9/11 in advance or that Osama is the victim of a rightwing frame-up. But many of their supporters espouse just such views. And the presidential aspirants, themselves, fall all over one another to claim Bush lied, that he refused to work with some of our European "friends," that we are losing in Iraq and Afghanistan, etc., etc. These stories ring about as true as the claims of Osama's innocence. Asked at the recent Democratic debate about the success of the administration's policies in the war on terror, presidential hopeful Al Sharpton noted that Bush said he wanted bin Laden, dead or alive. Then Sharpton launched into an impassioned diatribe demanding to know "where is bin Laden?" as though our success or failure to get this one man was what our efforts to stop future 9/

11's and protect our nation hinged on! The applause that greeted his words was deafening.

Frontrunner Democratic hopeful Dr. Howard Dean began his run entirely on his opposition to the Bush policies that have taken us into Iraq. Of course, Dean's been all over the map, saying at one point we need to send in more troops, at another we need to withdraw them, etc. And while opposing the Iraqi intervention (notably unpopular with the political left), he favored intervention in Liberia for "humanitarian" reasons, something Bush was hesitant to pursue. Because Bush was cautious, opponents like Dean, who have raised the anti-war flag elsewhere, were eager to seize on it as something Bush should be doing. But imagine how they'd have reacted if he had committed us heavily to this as they demanded.

Dr. Dean says we could take the money Bush wants to apply to our continuing war on terror and fund health insurance and other social programs here at home instead. I guess we'll need plenty of that if the folks who brought us 9/11 find a way to breach our defenses again and manage to disperse some plague or smallpox in our major cities . . . or detonate a dirty bomb or nuclear device in midtown Manhattan. In Dr. Dean's view, Iraq "smells" like Vietnam. And, of course, with critics like him, it's starting to feel that way too. But that's just what Osama's doctor ordered isn't it? America withdraws, bleeding and whining, licking its wounds, so extremist Islam can revive its medieval "glories."

As we pass our second year since the dastardly attacks launched against us on September 11th, 2001, it pays to think about facts and what they really mean. In this country and, indeed, around the planet, we've been witness to the remarkable human propensity to tell stories. It may be the case that we don't yet have eyewitness testimony that Osama bin Laden and al Qaeda actually pulled the 9/11 trigger (and that we may never have it), but if their own testimony is not to be accepted, we might as well question whether American astronaut Neil Armstrong ever really walked on the moon (as some "alternative" theorists actually do). And, given the two years we've just gone through without any follow-on attacks here on our shores, might we not also be just the least bit justified in thinking the Bush policies, including proactive military action abroad, intensified counter-terrorist surveillance at home, and the linking of intelligence networks, have helped make us even a bit more secure?

Maybe presidential politics ought to be about something more than spinning our way back into that old Vietnam vortex?

THE COSTS OF POLITICAL DISCOURSE

(November 14, 2003)

Is there a cost to the harsh tilt of political rhetoric we're seeing in the latest election cycle? Sure politics is notoriously messy and can get pretty ugly, with candidates hurling vicious and often misleading accusations at one another in the heat of battle. And it's true that former President Bill Clinton was himself the recipient of what seemed like a barrage of endless carping and invective from conservative opponents . . . never mind all that ammunition he so obligingly provided them with. But the steady drumbeat of Bush bashing that has now become de rigueur in Washington, on the Democratic campaign trail, and in the media itself has pushed the level of political discourse to new lows. We need to think beyond its immediate political ramifications and ask what the real costs of this are to America.

When reporter Jonathan Chait can write in The New Republic that he "hates" George W. Bush, when Senator Edward Kennedy calls Bush a liar and accuses him of "bribing" foreign government leaders (without a shred of evidence), when Congressional Minority Leader Nancy Pelosi proclaims that Bush doesn't have a plan for post-war Iraq, has failed to work with international "partners" like Jacques Chirac of France and blames California Governor Gray Davis' recent defeat on Bush economic policies (despite nearly a decade of Democratic profligacy in California that drove that state's budget into the ground) it's time for a reality check. Something's going on here, and it's not just about the facts.

The latest set-to is over whether President Bush was telling us the war in Iraq was finished when he stood on the deck of the U.S.S. Lincoln under a banner saying "Mission Accomplished" to thank the troops. Never mind that the Lincoln was, indeed, done with its mission and heading home. Never mind that the president, in declaring an end to "major combat operations" in his speech, never claimed the hostilities were over and that he even insisted that the situation was still dangerous and represented only a single battle in the larger war on terror that was (and is) still far from ended. As far as the president's strident critics are concerned, what he actually said isn't really important . . . it's what they want to convince us he said. This is no different from when they accuse him of having taken us to war because of an "imminent threat" from Saddam Hussein when, in fact, he said, quite clearly, that the threat was *not* imminent and that the whole point of our acting when we did was to prevent it from becoming imminent, at which point, as he noted, it would be too late.

The president's critics have an ax to grind and this could not be clearer. If Bush says X, they will say Y. But if Bush says Y, they say X. Think of the current posturing about the decision to go to war in the first place. Senator Kerry inveighs against Bush's leadership while saying he didn't really vote to authorize the president to go to war in Iraq, when he voted for the resolution that did just that. Instead he claims he only voted to authorize the "threat of force". But that's NOT what the resolution he voted for said! It specifically gave the president the authority to act. Presumably the senator *read* the resolution before signing on to it. More, what kind of a threat would such a resolution be if it were just a bluff . . . which is all Kerry now wants to say he was supporting? So Kerry now votes against funding the troop costs and Iraqi reconstruction, which grew directly out of the resolution that Kerry initially voted for but says he didn't.

And then there's new Democratic hopeful and former general Wesley Clark. He supported the Bush administration's actions last year but not this year, now that he's decided his best shot at becoming president is to try to nab the Democratic nomination (not unlike Mayor Mike Bloomberg's becoming a Republican just in time to snag that party's nomination for mayor). Hey, in a crowded field you go where you can find that main chance. But Clark is particularly duplicitous in his efforts. Among his latest sound bites, he takes Bush to task for "prancing" around the U.S.S. Lincoln in a flight suit while suggesting Bush was somehow responsible for not preventing al Qaeda's attacks on 9/11!

Any port in a storm, I suppose, especially for a general desperate to make a splash in a crowded field. But it's getting pretty ugly out there. So is there a cost to all this? Well, besides the increasingly low tone of the debate dominating the political chorus this year, and the Democrats' obvious departure from the truth in favor of hyperbole and innuendo, and what all of this does to the quality of discourse, I would suggest that there is another, even more serious cost which we really do need to be concerned about.

On October 20th our friends at al Qaeda issued one of their now famous pronouncements, through that fair and balanced media outlet known as al Jazeera, in which Osama bin Laden accuses "Bush and his gang" of acts that "have encouraged hypocrisy, and spread vice and political bribes shamelessly at the level of heads of state." More, says Bush critic bin Laden:

> "this gang and their leader enjoy lying, war and looting to serve their own ambitions. The blood of the children of Vietnam, Somalia, Afghanistan, and Iraq is still dripping from their teeth. They have fooled you and deceived you into invading Iraq a second time. And they have lied to you and the whole world . . . Bush has sent your sons into the lion's den . . . claiming that this act was in defense of international peace and America's security, thus they are concealing the facts."

Sound like anyone we've heard before?

Setting aside the usual hyperbole and overwrought rhetoric that characterizes al Qaeda's pronouncements, it's hard not to notice a resonance here with what Bush's Democratic critics have been relentlessly shouting.

Does anyone think these terrorists who brought us 9/11 aren't listening to the merciless political debate the Democrats have initiated around the president's foreign policy and that they are not taking heart from it . . . or hoping to tap into it with their relentless messages of spite and hate that are intended to frighten us into withdrawing from the field?

If so, this latest missive from al Qaeda ought to put that notion to rest.

They are hearing the same stuff we are and have concluded that their main chance is to join the chorus of Democratic nay-sayers in order to convince Americans to throw in the towel. It's easy to understand why they're doing this. They can't beat us on the ground, despite their dastardly and foolish attacks on our cities and skyscrapers. But, if they can reignite Americans' fears of a Vietnam style imbroglio, they won't have to. We'll fold our tents and flee in the night, showing that the al Qaedas of the world can defeat the major Western democracy with nothing more than terrorism and bombast.

It's easy to see why al Qaeda says the things they say and what they hope to gain. What's not so easy is to figure out why the Democrats are doing it . . . or why they seem to have let partisan ambitions displace a genuine commitment to the security of the nation they say they want to serve.

GEORGE VS. GEORGE

(December 26, 2003)

In December's Atlantic Monthly, noted capital markets speculator and financier George Soros took George W. Bush to task for threatening world peace. According to Soros, Bush's reaction to the attacks of 9/11 was a radical departure from past U.S. policies, destabilizing and likely to separate us from the rest of the world at a time when we desperately need the world behind us. The financier, whose claims to fame include vast wealth accumulated through some very smart trading activity and a college stint with the late philosopher Karl Popper, sees this all as reflecting the ascendance of a problematic "neo-conservative" view of the world . . . a view that wants to proactively head off problems and push, with force if necessary, democratic change around the globe. Soros contrasts this sharply with his own Popperian idea that we can never hope to have the whole truth and so must avoid any actions or policies that reflect a belief in our own certainty.

Soros criticizes Bush administration policies for placing American power above the idea of law (as exemplified by Bush's willingness to go to war against Iraq without international sanction via the U.N.). Yet this is certainly the wrong take on what has occurred since 9/11. The Bush position is that we have played the diplomatic containment game for half a century and things have only gotten worse as manifested by the events leading up to and including 9/11. Thus a change in course is called for. Soros' own prescription, to replace the Bush policies with heightened, proactive internationalism including creation of international groups to pursue and try to head off terrorists, along with increased aid packages to different areas of the world in order to improve living conditions and change minds, are really nothing new. In fact, aid packages and international organizations already exist precisely because we have been developing and implementing them for the past 50 or so years. So Soros' solution is really just more of the same old medicine.

Still, he's convinced that the Bush willingness to undertake a go-it-alone strategy, if necessary, places us on the side of history's militarists. Perhaps it would be instructive, then, to look more closely at the Bush policies?

In Iran and Korea, Bush has not initiated military or other so-called unilateral action. Instead he is pursuing multilateral policies along with diplomacy at the U.N. More, even in the matter of Iraq, the Bush administration initially placed the question before the U.N. Security Council. That Bush could not get agreement there because of the self-interested vetoes of a few countries ought not to be construed as reason for America to fail to act if, in fact, a genuine threat existed. Contrary to the views of some Democratic presidential contenders (Howard Dean jumps to mind), it would be unconscionable for any American president to follow a policy of obtaining U.N. "permission" before acting in the interests of the nation he is charged with safeguarding.

Of course, Soros argues, with others, that there really wasn't a threat at all. In fact, given the failure to uncover the predicted wmd to date, it looks as though this expectation may have been based on misinformation. If so, Soros argues, the Bush administration must have either misled us or been foolishly misled itself. But this is to fail to look closely at the nature of the threat. Since his invasion of Kuwait and before, Saddam Hussein had been a danger in terms of his willful aggression, his manifest ambitions to overrun and dominate his part of the world, and his demonstrated interest in, and possession and use of, wmd against his own people and others. More, Saddam was a particularly brutal dictator (albeit not the only one of these around).

The idea that Saddam was a threat to the United States arises from all these factors together. After the Gulf War in 1991, Saddam was "contained" through a regime of U.N. imposed sanctions that were causing hardship and, if international relief organizations had it right, untold suffering to the people of Iraq. In fact, the will to maintain the sanctions was rapidly eroding in the years leading up to the events of 9/11/2001. Aside from the numerous violations of the sanctions that were going on over those years, more and more voices were being raised to remove the sanctions entirely and let Iraq return to normal. But, given Saddam's history and attitudes, it was very likely he was only laying low until he could return to his earlier dreams of conquest and dominance in his region.

Was this a threat to us? In light of the events of 9/11, President Bush and his administration concluded that it was. Why? Because Saddam was also a supporter of terrorism who funded terrorists in some parts of the world, implemented his own terrorist acts through his agents, and had high level dealings with al Qaeda operatives and affiliated terrorist groups. Sure we have not yet found a smoking gun showing Saddam was connected with 9/11 and we may never have that. But is one really needed? If the reason for going after Saddam was a claim that he was involved in the attacks of 9/11, then one would have to say "yes." But *that* is not the claim and never was. The issue was the threat he posed to us going forward, if allowed to continue to operate in the Middle East, particularly once the possibility of sanctions and ongoing inspections were taken off the table . . . which was fast becoming only a matter of time.

There is a right and a wrong, a good and a bad, even if we acknowledge, as Soros wants us to, that none of us has a lock on the truth. Indeed, just believing in the superiority of the Popperian notion of the "open society" implies that such societies are somehow right while tyrannical regimes are not. And if the "open society" is right, then it's surely wrong to try to shut such societies down . . . which is precisely the aim of terrorists like Osama bin Laden and tyrants like Saddam Hussein. Sometimes, in the real world, things are not as crystal clear as we'd like. But Soros' suggestion that Bush's policies are wrong because they offend and annoy others who would rather we consult with them on every action, giving them a veto over our decisions, fails to take account of the fact that there really is a right and a wrong and that sometimes even an American President can know it.

"HERD" ON THE STREET

(January 9, 2004)

It's getting nasty out there. The other day I was surfing the Net and came across a site with e-mailed comments concerning the current political contest. The bulk of the comments were hostile to Bush, conservatives and Republicans . . . in spite of the fact that the accompanying survey showed a 56% majority of respondents in favor of the current administration and its policies. Why the discrepancy? For one thing it seems that Bush opponents are just madder than anyone else. This is evident from the quality of contemporary political discourse as seen in the current crop of Democratic presidential hopefuls, their operatives and party leaders.

If Teddy Kennedy can say that Bush fraudulently cooked up the Iraqi campaign for political purposes and bribed world leaders to support him without a shred of supporting evidence, if Richard Gephardt can lambaste the president as a "miserable failure," if Howard Dean (and Wesley Clark before him) can suggest that the spurious allegation that Bush knew about the 9/11 attacks in advance and allowed them to happen is an "interesting theory," and former Clinton Secretary of State Madeleine Albright can aver that the Bush administration might just have Osama bin Laden under wraps somewhere until the politically opportune moment to reveal his capture, what can we expect of the Democratic rank and file?

But truthfully, I was flabbergasted by the level of unthinking hostility and pure vitriol these e-mails from self-avowed supporters of "anybody but Bush" revealed. Here are some of the choicer comments:

- "if everybody knew the entire dossier of 'Baghdad Bush' . . . ANY Democrat or ANY independent could beat Bush! Only the cover-up of all the failures, deceit, corruption and lying would keep Bush as the continuing 'current resident' of the White House!"

- "THE ONLY 'GOOD' REPUBLICAN ... IS A DEFEATED REPUBLICAN!"
- "Gore would not have let Bin Lauden (sic) get away. Gore has no business dealings with Bin Lauden. Gore would have let the UN attack Iraq thus saving American lives and money. Gore had no business dealings with Saddam either, nor did he want to steal any money! The minority that voted for Bush are little better than traitors to our great country!"
- "The stupid conservatives out there forget that bush did not win the popular vote!!!! DONT FORGET PEOPLE ... GORE WON BY HALF A MILLION VOTES!!!!!!!!!!!!!!!!!!!!"
- "IT APPEARS THAT 56% OF STUPID AMERICANS PREFER BUSH, A MAN WHOSE GOAL IS TO SACRIFICE AND KILL AS MANY OF THEIR YOUNG PEOPLE AS HE CAN IN ORDER TO ENRICH HIMSELF AND HIS FRIENDS ... AMERICANS ARE SICK PEOPLE!"
- "Most of you Bush lovers are so uneducated—you are incompetent to vote. You could not pass an 8th grade test on American Government .... Yet somehow you call yourselves 'patriots'. Your stupidity is astounding."
- "If you had told me two years ago that Osama bin Laden would still be at large in December of 2003, I would have never believed it. Bush has failed his most important mission ..."
- "ALL OF YOU ARE FOOLING YOURSELF IF YOU THINK BUSH IS GOING TO BE RE-ELECTED. HE SENT OUR TROOPS TO DIE .... FOR WHAT!!! FOR HIS OWN PERSONAL VENGENCE AND ITS NOT FAIR!! I WILL NOT VOTE FOR HIM .... HE WILL GO DOWN AS ONE THE MOST UNQUALIFIED PRESIDENTS IN HISTORY!!"
- "I HATE BUSH SOOOO MUCH I'm sorry but I do. I just can't stand him."

- "Name one person who could possibly be hated more than our own GWB? OBL? No f***ing way. Saddam? No f***ing way."
- "i'm sorry but anybody is better than bush. i'm so sick and tired of him pushing his 'christian values' down everybody's throat . . . . i feel that he's taking care of a lot of unfinished business from his daddy being in office at taxpayer's expense."
- "I respect most peoples decision, but ANYONE that supports George BUSH is a racist, ignorant, moron which lacks the character to help build this nation lead this world into prosperity in peace."
- "Bush spells only destruction and hatred."

Well that's a sampler of what I found and, I fear, an indication of what's happened to political discourse in this country today. Perhaps it tells more about the condition and state of mind of the people who typed these remarks than it does about the nature of the Bush presidency or Bush's real chances for re-election. But it also tells us something about the mindset and attitudes of the political opposition in this country and what the self-indulgent shift to leftwing extremism on the part of today's Democratic bigwigs is doing to this country's sense of civility and our precious democratic process.

Whatever the outcome in 2004, there is likely to be *still* more of this bitterly poisonous acrimony. If Bush wins, it will further polarize those who so resent their loss of the presidency in the last election that they have lost all sense of proportion and comity with their fellow Americans who supported Bush. And if he loses? Does anyone seriously think that a loss, in the face of this kind of vicious character assassination, will not embitter Republicans, too? Are we in for a cycle of greater and greater anger and polarization then? If so, it's clear who's to blame . . . those leaders who seem unable to step away from their own ambitions and prefer, instead, to fan these flames of bitterness to animate their political cadres in hopes of gaining entry to the Oval Office.

But then what?

THE CAUSES OF
WAR REVISITED

(January 27, 2004)

As the ongoing public debate continues to demonstrate, there are many who think President Bush went too far in taking the war on terrorism to Saddam Hussein—a brutal dictator who threatened world peace by posing a real and continuing threat to his neighbors. Most who think this now also thought it before the war, just as most supporters of the war find good reason to support that action today. Yet, with the failure to find the expected (and feared) wmd, the anti-war position seems reinforced and Bush somewhat weakened. Certainly the failure to find the dreaded weapons of mass destruction hurts America's, and this president's, credibility.

But the outrageous and over-the-top allegations that Bush lied, that he misrepresented the reasons for war to the American people, etc., are unsupported by the facts. The American and international intelligence communities were in general agreement that there were wmd in Iraq well before Bush was sworn into office. At worst, Bush believed the same things that Clinton had believed before him. Even John Kerry, already deep in his campaign for the Democratic nomination, was recently quoted as subscribing to this view while defending his own decision to vote for the Congressional resolution that President Bush ultimately acted on.

"From the moment that we kicked (Saddam) out of Kuwait in the early 1990's, all the way through 1998, we had an American team on the ground under (former U.N. weapons chief) Butler destroying weapons of mass destruction," Kerry recently told a questioner in New Hampshire, adding that for "seven and a half years we destroyed weapons of mass destruction . . . and you know what, we found he had more of them than we thought he had. And we found he was further down the road to the creation of nuclear weapons than we thought he was."

Kerry continued by noting that, after Saddam ceased cooperating in 1998 and former President Bill Clinton pulled the inspectors out, there were no follow-up inspections.

"Saddam Hussein is left alone," notes Kerry. "No inspectors go back in . . ." until four years later (with the resumption of inspections at the prodding of the Bush administration).

Says Kerry, continuing: "George Bush brings a legitimate security issue before the Congress (in 2002) . . . Am I supposed to turn away and ignore what I said in 1998, what I thought Clinton should have done? Do we ignore the fact that the last time we had inspectors there we had weapons that had not been destroyed? And our intelligence is telling us there are weapons there?"

So even Senator Kerry, no friend of the Bush administration, does not seem to doubt that the president relied on information that appeared convincing. The problem is that, with all the hullabaloo against Bush concerning our removal of the Saddam regime, the failure to find the wmd now looks awful. It wouldn't have been such a problem if people, going into the war, had recognized that the case for removing Saddam did not hinge on wmd alone. But the media and the American public like sound bytes and easy-to-swallow nuggets of information. So the argument the administration made seemed to many (who sometimes willfully ignored other, more complex parts of the argument) to boil down to a simple case of wmd use and proliferation. That threat surely existed, even if it was not accurately estimated by intelligence agencies and the U.S. government at the end. But it pays to remember that it was only a "threat" because of who Saddam was, i.e., a bloody and brutal tyrant with visions of conquest, like malignant sugar plums, dancing in his head. Lots of nations have wmd in their possession. We have them, too. The problem arises when their use and proliferation threaten to unleash the whirlwind.

Where other politicians, like former President Clinton, dithered, the present occupant of the White House acted. And what was the result? A brutal and vicious tyrant deposed; most Iraqis glad to have been set free (despite ongoing inter-ethnic friction and isolated elements of resistance); democracy given a chance to grow in fresh soil; and Iraq now able to return to the community of nations and develop economically for the betterment of all its people.

More than this, a message has now been clearly sent to those who would undermine world peace by behaving like international bandits and who imagine America is no more than a "paper tiger," a message that the world is not exactly as they'd fantasized it to be, free for the picking.

It's true that the war that was fought to achieve all this resulted in casualties, but they were far fewer than what any of us could have imagined going into it. War is always awful and casualties are unavoidable but America demonstrated, first in Afghanistan and then in Iraq, that it is the most humane military power in history as casualties were far below anything anyone ever expected. Sure we're still suffering casualties in Iraq because that country is now a magnet to those who want to prevent a new democratic state from arising there. Sure we want out. But everything has a price and the price of long term American security today depends on our willingness to see this through and plant the seeds of a new democratic stability in that part of the world.

Many on the left don't seem to see this and I'm not sure why. Do they think we can have a safe and prosperous nation and world if we are afraid to confront dictators and terrorists? I know, I know . . . the U.N. didn't say it was okay for us to remove Saddam! But they didn't say it was okay for us to remove the Taliban either. Or to remove Slobodan Milosevic when we bombed Kosovo under former President Clinton.

Oh right, President Bush just didn't try hard enough to get U.N. "permission" we're told. Well, did President Clinton try hard enough with Kosovo? (He used NATO, not the U.N., for cover.) Or did the French turn to the U.N. before going into the Ivory

Coast as they recently did? It takes two to tango, as the saying goes, and I'm not sure how Bush, or anyone else, could have gotten the French out on the dance floor in the Iraqi matter when they were so determined to sit that one out.

In the end, Bush acted on information others had (or thought they had) and did the right thing for Iraqis and the world . . . and that's the right thing for America, too. The failure to uncover the expected wmd is a problem, to be sure. But it's largely a problem if you start out from the position that it was wrong to intervene in the first place, either because intervention is always wrong (a la Dennis Kucinich) or intervention without U.N. permission is wrong (as Dr. Dean likes to put it). But the first claim is untenable if we are to have a peaceful world and the second is disingenuous because it is not a standard that others follow, either now or historically.

If the possession of copious amounts of wmd was the stand-alone reason for intervention, and that intervention was not appropriately sanctioned by moral or international authority, then failing to find the wmd after the fact certainly undercuts the justification for this action. But the reasons we acted against Saddam Hussein were bigger than the wmd he was thought to have. They spanned decades of misrule, cruelty, support for terrorism, aggression and skulking in the shadows of international intrigue and schemes. It's too bad you can't say all this in one simple, politically correct sound byte, though.

POLITICS AND DISCOURSE

(February 15, 2004)

Right after the horrendous events of 9/11, this country came together in a way we had rarely seen before. Reeling in shock from an attack on all Americans, no matter who or where we were, expressions of concern and support poured into New York from around the country. In my former capacity as Assistant Commissioner for Operations in a New York City mayoral agency, I personally fielded calls from all over the nation, calls from concerned citizens and companies who just wanted to help us out. They volunteered time, money, and physical space in which to site our displaced offices (since most city agencies were blown out of the downtown Manhattan area due to airborne pollutants from the ongoing fire then raging in the bowels of what had been the Trade Center).

Politicians, too, came together in support of the national administration in Washington. And the airwaves were filled with pundits declaring their shock and disgust with the vicious, unprovoked attacks that left a gaping hole in lower Manhattan, drove people from their homes and places of business, and, worst of all, took the lives of nearly 3,000 innocent human beings in the hellish conflagration of the two towers, driving some to leap to their deaths to avoid the inferno that was engulfing them. Bush and his team acted decisively, once they were convinced they knew who had been behind the unprecedented destruction we had endured. And Americans came together behind them.

But then something happened. As the horror of the immediate events receded, as the president began to pursue his policy of proactive engagement with the world's terrorists, many Americans began to remember their political affiliations. It wouldn't do for a president, who these people felt was part of that "other" party, to get too strong. How could you win an election against a popular wartime president? So, very quickly, the narrative began to change, even as our memories of the horrors of 9/11 grew cold. One after another, political pundits and leaders from the other side of the aisle began to find reasons to carp, reasons that only grew with time, particularly as the Bush administration turned its attention to the terror fraught regime in the Middle East of our old enemy Saddam Hussein.

For many who had opposed Saddam throughout the nineties, he suddenly became the touchstone of opposition to a president perceived as becoming too popular because of his resolute actions after 9/11. Saddam wasn't Osama after all. Why was Bush bothering with a rogue like him, a man whose main crime of the moment seemed to be the torture and oppression of his own people? And so the opposition grew, rolling into an election year that was to be punctuated with repeated jabs at the president for allegedly telling us lies, getting it wrong, taking away our civil liberties, failing to revive the economy, etc., etc. The president's opponents in the media and the political world relentlessly tore at him in order to break down that mantle of authority and respectability he'd won in the public's mind after 9/11.

But were these criticisms on the money? One can't help having the feeling that, had George W. Bush waffled and been timid in his response to the terrorists after 9/11, Democrats like Kerry and Dean (not to mention Daschle, Pelosi, Kennedy, et al) would have castigated him for *having failed to show the necessary leadership and resolve*. And had Bush failed to go after Saddam and focused entirely on Osama instead, wouldn't the Democrats have said, 'sure he's fixated on the al Qaeda leader but look how he's forgotten the real threat to this country, Saddam Hussein, that Iraqi dictator who funds and supports terrorism, has invaded his neighbors, pursued wmd and even tried to assassinate an American president'!

On the matter of the economy, when the indicators were still in recession mode, the knock on Bush was that he was presiding over a failing economy and his only solution, tax breaks, would just make things worse. Of course, as the economy came roaring back, they cried that the tax breaks had nothing to do with *that*, and that, besides, jobs haven't come back yet (time will still have to tell on that score!), and that our current deficit is now the worst in history which bodes ill for the future if not the present! (By the way, this deficit's hardly the worst in history in relation to the size of our current economy, but most people don't pay close attention to little nuances like that.)

So the narrative, which has been changing since the Democrats realized the problem they'd be facing in trying to unseat a sitting, wartime president, has become ever more shrill and harsh. Why? Well, there's resentment out there, of course, resentment at having lost the White House to the "other" party, the party that doesn't represent the Northeastern and West Coast establishments, the party that doesn't trace its roots back to Roosevelt's New Deal (never mind that current scholarly opinion is beginning to note that Roosevelt's policies *failed to end* the Great Depression and that it really took a World War to do that).

And so in the end it's all about narrative. With the relentless pounding of political punditry, the story about this president is being slowly and inexorably changed. Did Bush respond firmly and swiftly to defend this nation after 9/11? Well, they tell us, maybe he really should have prevented those attacks in the first place. (Bet Clinton and Gore would have, right?) And look how Bush has gone and made everyone mad at us, including our beloved friends, the French. And now he's meddled in the affairs of sovereign Iraq, removing a revered and honored leader who was the legitimate ruler of his country (we know he was legitimate, of course, because he told us so).

When you look at these arguments, listen to the claims, what are you left with? Is it facts we're hearing? Is it information about the way things really are? Or is it something else? Isn't it really just the usual spin any group will put on a narrative to shape it? Bush was in the National Guard and distinguished himself as a bright young pilot. Oh yeah, well let him prove it, they say. Where's that "band of brothers" our guy, Kerry, has at his back? Sure when the Democratic candidate was Clinton, who famously failed to show up at his promised ROTC rendezvous and took off for England instead, what you did back then didn't seem to matter to these critics. But now the Democrats have got themselves a candidate who wears his war service on his inflated chest, just like one of those medals he said he threw away on the steps of the Capitol building during a protest back in the seventies . . . but really didn't.

Let Bush compete with Kerry's heroism, they cry, as they revive the war service issue. And if Bush responds to all this? He's on the defensive, they tell us . . . or, worse, he's "going negative" against poor, brave John Kerry. Say what? What have the Democrats been doing all this time to Bush, as 9/11 faded from our collective consciousness?

NOW WE KNOW

(March 5, 2004)

Reacting to a charge of ideological imbalance at North Carolina's Duke University, Robert Brandon, the chair of that University's philosophy department was recently quoted as follows:

> "If, as John Stuart Mill said, stupid people are generally conservative, then there are lots of conservatives we will never hire. Mill's analysis may go a long way towards explaining the power of the Republican Party in our society and the relative scarcity of Republicans in academia. Players in the NBA tend to be taller than average. There is good reason for this. Members of academia tend to be a bit smarter than average. There is good reason for this too."

If anyone was wondering what the current presidential election cycle is all about, I respectfully suggest that this line of thinking goes a long way towards explaining it. An entire group of people in this country today identifies itself with a philosophy of liberalism, a philosophy that goes back to John Stuart Mill and other English thinkers of his day and before (back, indeed, to the French Enlightenment). But what is it that lies at the heart of liberalism and that is driving the current debate?

In Mill's time, liberalism had two important strands: 1) a concern for social justice; and 2) opposition to statist interference in the lives of individual citizens. The connection between these two strands was natural enough. The institutions of aristocratic England, controlled and operated by a moneyed elite, callously oppressed England's working class. Liberal opposition to such institutions via a doctrine that demanded smaller, less intrusive government served to help the broader population which suffered from the abuse and indifference of such institutional elitism.

In our own time, though, a divergence has occurred between these two strands of classical liberalism. The idea of individual liberty (non-intrusive government) has fallen by the wayside among modern liberals in favor of a belief that the state has a duty to do good. While not abandoning notions of individual liberty, modern liberals think the first order of any government's business is to protect us, even from ourselves. And so they support increased spending on bigger and more numerous programs, more intrusive laws and increased taxes to enable all this.

However, a breakaway group of old-fashioned liberals, who place the emphasis on individual liberty, have redefined themselves as libertarians. This group tends to gravitate toward conservatism because individual liberty was one of the founding principles of this nation. While modern liberalism and libertarianism are not always in disagreement (most proponents of individual liberty care about others as deeply as any statist, while most proponents of larger and more involved government also cherish individual liberty), they really do represent a clear divide in today's American politics.

Americans of the modern liberal bent viewed with horror the ascension of George W. Bush to the presidency. Bush achieved the presidency by bringing together social conservatives (who favor a restoration of old-fashioned American moralism in national life) with libertarian conservatives who loathe and fear big, intrusive government. Of course there is an inherent tension in this alliance since libertarians are suspicious of any effort to impose morality while social conservatives tend to favor this. But, with the cooptation of mainstream liberalism by a modern elitist culture that visibly disdains old-fashioned mores and values, the conservative alliance that brought Reagan, and Bush after him, to the presidency, became possible. Libertarians who spurned big government found it easy to make common cause with their socially conservative peers who feared the liberal-dominated big government's efforts to demolish old and cherished social values. George W. Bush recognized and rekindled this connection and squeaked his way into the White House in a closely contested race as a result.

But the forces of elitism, which dominate the liberal agenda today, have never been able to get over this perceived "disaster." Expecting to extend the Clinton years via the election of his anointed successor, Al Gore, they were visibly shaken by Gore's narrow loss. To this day they haven't been able to throw off the feeling of having been cheated by fate . . . or by the imagined ill-doings of a Republican cabal of conservative dullards, people who clearly, on their view, didn't deserve to win the White House and so could only have done so by skullduggery.

Bush, himself, is the lightning rod for this kind of thinking. A plain man with a mediocre history, in the liberal mind he epitomizes all they disdain in their conservative opponents. He does not speak particularly well off-the-cuff, and frequently seems at a loss for words. How could someone so ordinary, on this view, have beaten the handsomely credentialed Democratic candidate? How could such a seemingly simple fellow have taken the White House away from the smart folks, the ones who really know what's good for this country?

This is the real reason for the level of anger and nastiness the current presidential campaign seems to be descending into. It's become a crusade, on the liberal side, to take back what they view as their birthright. Why? Because they believe they're the smart ones, the ones who really know what's right for this nation, and that they have been denied their right to lead by a mean trick of fate, abetted by fantasized Republican dirty tricks. But who is really guilty of dirty tricks? Who has brought the current election cycle into the gutter by making all sorts of outrageous claims and propagating falsehoods? Who has demeaned the man they oppose by name-calling and, as White House Press Secretary Scott McClellan recently put it, "trolling for trash" on the president? Who has politicized a war that, in prior incarnations (during the Clinton years), they were quick to advocate for? Who has been inconsistent, in word and deed, regarding dealing with the terrorist threats that face this country?

The election this year reflects a deep divide between groups in this nation, between those who feel that national power is their birthright, to be reclaimed at any cost, and those who feel America needed to be re-directed back toward self-reliance and strong national defense . . . and who rose to the occasion, in demonstration of this, after the cataclysmic events of September 11th, 2001. If the good Professor Brandon is to be believed, conservatives are generally dummies compared to the best and the brightest in the liberal ranks. Personally I have a problem with this kind of thinking. But, I fear, most liberals really do subscribe to it. And it is this deep-seated feeling that makes them so livid and shrill when faced with a plain-talking, average George sitting in a White House they thought reserved for one of their own.

DECONSTRUCTING KERRY

(April 2, 2004)

So what do we know about the Democrats' presumptive nominee for president, Massachusetts Senator John Kerry, so far? Well, he's been in the public spotlight for a long time now, beginning with his very public anti-war activities, undertaken after his return from a brief stint of combat in the coastal waters of Vietnam. He went on to get a law degree and then to make a career for himself in politics. He went from public prosecutor to Lieutenant Governor of Massachusetts under Michael Dukakis and then, in the mid-eighties, he won a seat in the United States Senate. There he quickly established himself on the left side of the political aisle, opposing the policies of Ronald Reagan and the first President Bush, favoring cuts in defense spending and increases in social spending. Fair enough . . . that, after all, is the Democratic position.

Of course, Senator Kerry is also a shrewd and, as his supporters like to say, nuanced politician. And so he managed to take many sides of issues, to find ways to avoid offending critical constituencies or of risking his political capital, during his senate years. He voted against the first Gulf War though, famously, he wrote two contradictory letters to the same constituent, saying he both opposed and supported it! Of course that may just have been a staffer's blunder since office holders rarely write their own constituent correspondence. On the other hand, you have to wonder how his staffers could have been so wrong re: Kerry's actual position because, surely, at least one of them would have had to be wrong . . . right?

This is the same John Kerry who flaunted his Irish sounding name in front of a Boston Irish audience, saying he was proud to be one of them, but who hasn't any Irish in his ancestry to speak of. In fact, John Forbes Kerry can trace his ancestry back to English colonists who came over on the Mayflower (he's a real Boston Brahmin) though one of his grandfathers was Jewish, from Eastern Europe. And he has cousins in France. Nothing wrong with any of that . . . unless you're trying to convey to people that you're something you're not.

What about his heroic war record? No one wants to challenge that and, in truth, it does seem kind of an unlikely place to go, given his military decorations and the testimony of his "band of brothers." But a little history is in order here, too. It seems that Kerry in his college days was actually anti-war. So why enlist? Well, like many of us, he was in danger of being drafted. Here's a young guy with political ambitions facing a stint in the military, fighting a war he opposed. Well you can't simply refuse to go. That won't look very good in some future political campaign. And you can't run off somewhere, like to Canada, and figure everyone will forget some day. Ever the nuanced strategist, John Kerry chose, instead, to enlist in the Navy where the risks were presumably more limited since Vietnam was manifestly a land war.

He got himself a lieutenancy on a coastal boat and for four months led patrols and demonstrated valor in the face of the enemy. Repeatedly he raced his boat onto the shore and led aggressive landing operations against the VC. He was decorated at least four times for his boldness and wounded three times. Then what? Well he invoked a military rule that, if a combatant were wounded three times, he had to be taken out of the fight. And so Lieutenant John Forbes Kerry demanded from his superiors, and after some negotiation, got, reassignment from the combat zone, leaving his men after only four months in action.

What did his superiors have to say about his service? Apparently, Lieutenant Kerry was dressed down for recklessness in beaching his boat and unnecessarily risking his men, at least once. And there are some stories of his chasing wounded VC behind hooches and killing them out of sight of his crewmen. But he got his decorations and his reassignment stateside and, as soon as he could, he joined the anti-war movement as a disgruntled anti-war veteran . . . never mind that he'd been against the war before enlisting! At subsequent hearings, he told stories of so-called war crimes by American troops, claiming these were commonplace, not exceptions, and angering many of his fellow Vietnam vets at the time. Now his staff tell us he was young and eager to end the war back then so we shouldn't hold him accountable for his past excursions into hyperbole.

So John Kerry presents himself to us as a genuine war hero who just happens to oppose war, including the one we fought in Vietnam and the 1991 Gulf War, which he subsequently told at least one constituent he really supported. He's also the guy who threw his Vietnam era medals away in protest . . . except he really didn't, since it turns out he still had them years later . . . apparently he threw someone else's away!

Kerry, of course, did vote for the Congressional resolution authorizing President George W. Bush to take military action against Saddam Hussein. But then, when he saw the traction Howard Dean's anti-war stance was getting, he reversed course and told Democratic primary voters he didn't really mean what the resolution he voted for said! And then, when it came time to vote funds to support the military action, he dutifully voted against those. (Imagine how a vote "for" would have gone over by then with the vituperative Democratic base already baying for Bush's political blood?)

Of course, Senator Kerry and his supporters would have us believe all this is somehow "off-limits" in debate. While it's fine on their view to call George W. Bush a liar, a deserter, a betrayer of his country, etc., and to suggest that Bush knew about 9/11 in advance but let it happen, or that he cooked up the removal of Saddam to gain political points (*that's* rich since it's clearly Bush's political albatross and any half-savvy politician, especially John Kerry, must know the risks American politicians run in supporting wars), still they want to tell us Kerry's own history is out of bounds. Indeed, "the Republican attack squad," Kerry recently told us, is already gearing up to get him, even while he mutters, off camera, about Republicans being "crooks" and "liars," presumably letting us know how he really feels but offering no evidence to support such inflammatory allegations. For Bush to make his case via a muted television commercial with fleeting images of the remains of the World Trade Center is somehow an affront to decency, the Kerryites tell us. But Kerry's invocation of his "heroic" history in Vietnam is just fine; his "patriotism" beyond discussion. Kerry's the "patriot," Bush the "betrayer of his country."

Of course, this is typical of the tenor of the opposition to Bush since he first became president. It's always been about demeaning and negatively characterizing the current occupant of the White House. So Kerry is just following his own historic practice and grabbing the main chance, jumping onto the Bush-bashing bandwagon first driven out of the station by Howard Dean et al and amply supported by the likes of Michael Moore, Maureen Dowd, Molly Ivins and nearly every other left-leaning liberal pundit you can imagine.

But maybe Kerry's latest potshots are really just about preemption, no matter how nasty it all smells? Maybe Kerry is just hoping to keep the Republicans so off-balance and on the defensive that his own history will never emerge as a real campaign issue, not even his numerous votes against defense spending . . . but *for* higher domestic spending, with increased taxes to support that.

Still, you have to wonder about a guy who had political ambitions from his earliest days and somehow figured to get his ticket punched in Vietnam quickly, to get in and get out, with his resume suitably enhanced, while limiting the risks to himself by getting it over with, so to speak. Sure he chose a bold course and demonstrated bravery over there, even while recklessly charging ashore with his men against standing orders from his superiors. But what else was going on in Kerry's mind back then? John Fitzgerald Kennedy famously benefited from his war-hero status on a P.T. boat in World War II. Why shouldn't John Forbes Kerry do so as well?

THE TIDES OF POLITICS

(April 30, 2004)

I recently finished reading a novel, *Tides of War* by Steven Pressfield, recalling the events of the 27-year conflict between ancient Athens and Sparta for dominance of the fifth century Hellenic world. Based largely on the account of a contemporary ancient Greek historian, Thucydides (*The History of the Peloponnesian War*), it tells the tale of the rise and fall of the Athenian leader Alcibiades, a brilliant orator and general who never lost a battle but who had a somewhat harder time hanging onto his command. Alcibiades was the best Athens had to offer in his time, a man of vision and profound intelligence, a brilliant strategist . . . though, if Pressfield has it right, he was also somewhat self-serving. What brought him down was the "democratic" dynamic of his city-state, since the Athenian citizenry was given to constant bickering, incessant litigation, and intense investigation and prosecution of its officials, reflecting the different factions and individuals within the state jockeying for power.

In Alcibiades' case, he was initially called home on charges of sacrilege, brought by his political enemies, just as he was successfully kicking off Athens' war against Syracuse in the west. Rather than face charges that could result in his death, Alcibiades bolted and fled to Sparta where he joined the Spartan cause, to the Athenians' great discomfort. Without Alcibiades at the head of its armies in the west, the Syracusan campaign collapsed. Athens' army was routed and most of its troops were slaughtered, with the remainder condemned to a living death in the mines of Syracuse.

Eventually Alcibiades left Sparta and, after a brief sojourn in the Persian Empire, made his way back to Athens where he was welcomed contritely by his countrymen who were tired of losing to Sparta. They gave him control of their forces again and, in a series of brilliant campaigns, Alcibiades turned the tables on the Spartans and restored Athenian supremacy on the Aegean Sea. But, while he was at work on the field of battle, his old enemies in the Athenian democracy renewed their struggle for power with him and brought a series of lawsuits against him, charging him and those around him with all kinds of perfidy, eventually succeeding in convincing the Athenian democracy to cut his funding. Without money for supplies or to pay his troops, Alcibiades' forces slowly began to wither on the vine and, in one last bid to finish things quickly, he struck at the Spartans at a place called Ephesus in Asia Minor (today's Turkey). Although he again succeeded in destroying the Spartan forces, he was unable to dislodge them from their stronghold and, as they stubbornly hung on, Alcibiades, Pressfield tells us, recognized his ultimate defeat. He could not win a final victory in time to stave off the work of his opposition at home since his own forces were weakening each day, even as the Spartans were digging in, aided by unlimited amounts of Persian gold. In the end Alcibiades fled again, rather than lose a war which he expected his ungrateful fellow citizens would then blame and execute him for.

But the crowning stupidity of the ancient Athenians, having allowed their fickle minds to be turned against their most effective leader, came afterwards. To replace Alcibiades, they sent out a committee of ten generals (to make sure none could become pre-eminent as Alcibiades had been). This committee, despite shrinking resources in the face of the inexhaustible funding the Spartans were able to secure from Persia, managed, through superior seamanship, to win battles . . . though not with the panache and consistency of Alcibiades. But after one successful battle against the clumsier Spartan navy, a fierce and unexpected storm came up, making it impossible for the leaders of the Athenian expedition to rescue many thousands of their own seamen who had been swept into the sea.

Despite heroic efforts, these sailors were drowned. Returning to Athens, the generals were not hailed for their victories but indicted by the populace instead, for failing to save their brethren . . . even though all evidence pointed to the fact that the storm had made this impossible. Six of the ten generals fled, but four were caught in the Athenians' political fury and forced to stand trial for their lives. In the heated recriminations that ensued, these men were condemned to death and slaughtered ignominiously by the Athenian democrats intent on consuming their own. Athens never recovered, having executed or driven out its best military leaders. Its subsequent leaders proved too timid to take further risks or to think clearly when confronting the Spartans. They were rapidly destroyed on the field of battle and Sparta ultimately marched into Athens. It demolished Athenian democracy, set up a reign of terror run by 30 Spartan-appointed despots, demolished Athens' walls and other defenses, and crushed all opposition. The Spartans could not have been more delighted with the work the self-destructive Athenian democracy had done for them.

Why is this important today? I'm reminded of these events every time I turn on the news and read about the incessant clamor against the Bush administration over who was at fault for 9/11. The media, hungry for excitement or just dead set against the current administration (or both), fall all over themselves to find new nails for this president's political coffin, seeking to blame George W. Bush for events that none of us could have envisioned . . . right up to the very moment they occurred. As the political opposition takes every opportunity to fan the flames of suspicion concerning Bush and his staff, the American public increasingly doubts the administration that produced the first al Qaeda reverses in that terrorist organization's decades long history.

Never mind that the Bush administration responded to the vicious sneak attacks by al Qaeda in an unprecedentedly forceful and effective way. Never mind that Bush and his people did what no American president before him had done, taking the war the terrorists had declared on us *back to them* and unseating a dangerous monster in the Middle East who had made it his mission to secure dominance for himself in that critical region. Instead the political opposition and its ratings-hungry media abettors want to tell us that Bush erred for failing to stop attacks no one before him had managed to deal effectively with either. They want to hold Bush accountable for not doing what Bill Clinton also had not done. This despite the fact that contentious political lawsuits, originally initiated by the Democrats over Florida back in 2000, had drastically delayed the usual transfer of power between administrations, while testy congressional hearings had slowed approval of Bush appointees into the critical summer before 9/11, thereby adversely affecting the new administration's efforts to put its government in place.

What's changed since ancient times? Certainly, democracy and politics still seem to be about bringing down the guy in charge for the benefit of those who are temporarily out of power. Bush may be no Alcibiades, and that's no bad thing since Alcibiades, for all his brilliance, was a somewhat self-serving egoist, convinced of his own superiority to ordinary men. But Americans have certainly set themselves up as modern day Athenians, allowing democratic principles to be used to undermine their own interests and institutions. In fanning the flames of the current witch-hunt to somehow blame the Bush administration for a storm it could not have controlled and was not in a position to prevent, we present day "Athenians" are seeking to exile or eliminate the very generals who have brought us our first victories and who have turned the tables on those Spartan-like elements who want to destroy our nation and culture. How can we be so foolish? Are Osama and his ilk right, that Americans have no stomach for real conflict? Is democracy's greatest flaw that it contains, within itself, the seeds of its own demise?

RIGHT VS. LEFT[15]

(May 14, 2004)

Since I began writing this column for The Wave (I actually used to write it for another paper back in the early nineties), I've been interested in what seems to be driving the current level of political animosity. Anyone following my comments will note that I return, again and again, to the amazingly harsh level of rhetoric so often leveled against President Bush, his administration and Republicans in general.

In fact I'm perplexed by the way this debate has gone. It isn't enough for opponents of this administration to disagree with its policies, to argue for a different approach to governing. Instead they have repeatedly invoked claims of illegitimacy (the Florida vote in 2000, Bush's family connections) and castigated this president for his apparent lack of intellectual heft (since he frequently gets tongue-tied in public and is certainly no policy wonk a la Bill Clinton or Al Gore). Nor does it stop there. Bush is routinely accused of being a shirker, AWOL from his military obligations, unengaged, a liar, a fraud, a substance abuser, a religious fanatic, a dictator wannabe seeking to abrogate our civil liberties, etc., etc. Why is this happening and is there anything that justifies such claims?

I've offered a number of explanations in these pages, including what I take to be an anti-conservative bias within certain groups and the sense that many liberals have that they've somehow been cheated out of their "right" to govern in Washington by those dastardly, underhanded Republicans. Some of my comments have prompted reader responses and, as if in answer to what I've been saying, The Wave recently introduced a new column, The

Progressive, to give voice to the other side in the current political debate. Now I think this is a good thing since debate is what democracy is all about and I want to welcome John Paul Culotta to these pages. However, after reading his first column and some recent letters-to-the-editor, I'm convinced more and more that this debate is not about facts and never was, i.e., no amount of facts presented will serve to resolve the differences that now seem to divide us.

Mr. Culotta began his inaugural column by taking me to task for an earlier piece I'd written, called *Politics and Discourse*,[16] in which I argued that current political charges against President Bush have fallen off the curb and into the gutter. My fellow columnist correctly pointed out that criticism of sitting presidents, even during wartime, has a long (if not necessarily glorious) history in this country. He said I was wrong in thinking I could shut down debate. But, of course, that was not what I'd said in my column at all. I was not arguing that people should not be free to criticize the president or that there might not be merit in some of the criticisms. I was saying, rather, that the current criticism has literally curdled, like old milk, and that Democrats now seem to spend all their time trying to besmirch the president via various and sundry forms of character assassination. My claim was, and is, that this criticism is not about the facts but about tearing Bush down in order to restore the White House to Democratic control. I suppose in a competitive political environment we must expect some of this. But my point is that this has gotten way out of hand.

As if on cue, along come two recent letters-to-the-editor from readers of The Wave, letters which make my case better than I ever could myself. If Democratic opposition to Bush is mainly about taking back power . . . and resentment at having lost it . . . it may be expected to manifest as anger rather than reasoned argument. And that's exactly what we get in these letters. Here's the first letter writer on my recent article concerning John Kerry's war record[17]:

"Behold a smear job," he writes indignantly, "under the guise of pseudo-scholarship, with much hearsay, unworthy evidence and a lot of irrelevant personal musings . . . A more inept, unprofessional piece of words without meaning is hard to imagine."

Of course, our correspondent doesn't bother to reply to my points in a targeted, itemized way. He goes, instead, right for the verbal jugular. But, in so doing, isn't he doing exactly the same thing to me that Bush's critics habitually do to him, i.e., resorting to verbal tar-and-feathering? In relation to Kerry's role in Vietnam, this gentleman goes on to note that "Mr. Kerry actually enlisted which again," he claims, "makes Mirsky angry."

But where in my article did I suggest that I was either angry at Kerry or at the fact he enlisted? On the other hand, what better bespeaks anger than this letter writer's own somewhat overheated locutions?

I won't go into the full litany of his charges. Suffice it to note that he accuses me of "inordinate guile and chutzpah," as though my criticisms of the presumptive Democratic candidate for president are somehow unacceptable, even while the Republican incumbent remains, in his mind, fair game. For him, his own point of view seems perfectly reasonable and acceptable. But those disagreeing with him must be, he tells us, "seeing events through the filter of (their) own fervid imagination," and be guilty of "convoluted rhetorical flourishes, indicative of a bankrupt political agenda, pushing (our) great country into chaos and despair."

Who is indulging here in "rhetorical flourishes"?

And what about the second letter writer?

He, too, fails to deal directly with my points though he is not quite so furious in his denunciations: "Mirsky questions Kerry's diverse ethnic background," says our correspondent, despite the fact that I didn't "question" it at all but merely noted its failure to match what Kerry, himself, is reported to have said about it at a political meeting he attended.

Then our second correspondent goes on to re-run the usual anti-Bush charges (Clarke said this, Joe Wilson said that) and concludes by grandly allowing that, in fact, "there is a role for conservatives in this election. They can remind us of the need for a balanced budget," and that government should be "truthful and constrained."

But, he seems to be saying, how dare they presume to defend a sitting president or argue against a liberal challenge to that presidency? His message seems to be that conservatives should just keep their mouths shut unless they have something as nasty to say about the president as the president's recent critics in the Democratic Party have offered.

Well thanks, but no thanks. We conservatives (and there are many different kinds of conservative, by the way), can decide quite nicely as to what we should be talking about and advocating. We don't need help from those whose idea of debate is to muzzle the opposition by resorting to rhetorical indignation.

What else need I say than to offer more of their own words as evidence that political debate in the current election cycle has taken a harshly wrong turn . . . and that it is those on the left who are leading this charge?

"As for Mirsky," says our first correspondent again, "his vituperation abounds right off in his diatribe."

And: " . . . is it reasonable to dignify such tripe with an answer? Or perhaps to leave its distortions to rot in its own overheated rhetorical nonsense?"

Is *this* what my new colleague, Mr. Culotta, had in mind when he wrongly suggested that I was somehow trying to muzzle dissent?

THE ANGRY LEFT

(June 11, 2004)

Recently someone sent me an e-mail containing the usual diatribes against the Bush administration. And, as usual, I couldn't help myself; I had to offer a response. The individual who wrote the anti-Bush screed excerpted below offered a few choice remarks as follows (name excluded to protect the guilty):

"Don't you know," said the lady, "that George Liar Bush and almost all his cabinet members are egotistic, selfish, liars, and disinterested in peace and justice? Additionally that they don't care about human rights and our planet! The truth about all the lies will hopefully be coming out gradually as we approach November. We have already seen one liar resign, George Tenet, CIA Director. Dummy Rums will most likely be next. Then Powell and Con-artist Rice. Afterwards, Ashie. They will be followed by Dick "Holliburton" Channey (sic) and finally George King Liar Bush . . . . Who was the CEO of Holliburton (sic) from 1995 to 2000? . . . make the connection of Bush's order to invade and destroy Iraq so that Holliburton (sic) could be given the right to RECONSTRUCT/REBUILD it without following the legal bidding procedure. Then look into the relationship of Conartist Rice to CITGO. Finally, find out what relationship exists between the rulers of Saudi-Arabia (The Binladen Dynasty) and the Bushes. You'll freak out and reconsider voting for George LIAR Bush . . . vote for Kerry."

Appalled at this kind of thinking, though no longer surprised to find it in my in-box, I tried to offer a measured, albeit, somewhat educational response:

Dear so-and-so:

Apparently the plethora of anti-Bush books that have been spawned in recent months (testimony to the power of capitalism!) has convinced you that this is all about lies, conspiracies, etc. Of course, the fact that Vice President Cheney was CEO of Halliburton, before signing on to run for the nation's second top job, is no big secret; nor is it any reason to imagine a conspiracy. Halliburton had what is sometimes called a requirements contract [18] with the U.S. government before the Iraq action. This kind of contract (which is won by open bid, by the way, in advance of actual need) allows the government to call on a company to perform services, based on previously agreed upon costs, during those times when going through the usual 4-6 months' bidding process would be too cumbersome and time-consuming to meet a critical need. In addition, Halliburton obtained a no-bid contract for restoration of Iraq's oil field services systems based on its demonstrated past performance in this area. Of course, it stood to reason that we needed to begin addressing Iraqi infrastructure issues pronto after the quick war, rather than delay for lengthy bidding and re-bidding (since initial bid processes often collapse over technicalities). Imagine how angry you'd be today if the Bush administration had, in fact, delayed addressing critical Iraqi infrastructure needs in order to go through such a lengthy, attenuated process. I'll bet you'd have been the first to accuse them of incompetence because of unseemly bureaucratic delays!

Like many who are desperate to restore Democratic control in Washington, you are among those who will latch onto anything and everything to buttress their case. Needless to say, the fact that Cheney once ran Halliburton is no reason to claim that the Iraqi action was undertaken to serve Halliburton. But you imagine that such a link exists, merely because of the man's resume. Although there's no basis for such claims, this is typical of the current extreme anti-Bush/ anti-Republican partisanship of the moment. The fact that this level of rhetoric is countenanced, even encouraged, by Democratic Party leaders and officials because it serves their ends is more troubling though. It's hurting the political discourse in this country and creates an atmosphere of irrationality verging on paranoia. But I guess that is not something that concerns you . . . or that, perhaps, you have even noticed. That's too bad, the more so since such flames of anger and hatred, once fanned, can be hard to extinguish.

Besides misinterpreting facts like Cheney's history with Halliburton, people like yourself seem unable to distinguish between lies and errors of fact. You say Bush "lied" but what do we really know about these alleged "lies"? We know that Bush and a whole host of others, both within and outside his administration and within and outside this country, appear to have gotten certain facts wrong. Getting facts wrong is not necessarily lying. But you either cannot see the difference or deliberately attempt to blur that distinction. I'm not sure which is worse . . . though inflammatory allegations of "lies," while they may be emotionally satisfying for some, only add to the fire now being fanned which threatens to consume our political house.

Some people think the best way to make their case is by name calling, as you have done above. But that is not to make any kind of rational argument. It's just emoting. "Dummy Rums" (he's anything but dumb, by the way!), "Con-artist Rice," "George King Liar Bush," are all just examples of this irrational and despicable tendency. As to your allegation about "liar" George Tenet, who recently resigned from his post as CIA Director, perhaps you should bear in mind that he was a Democratic appointee, a holdover from the Clinton administration, and not brought in by Bush and his folks.

What about your claim regarding the Bush family and the Saudis? (I note you confuse the Saudi ruling family with the bin Laden clan, but I won't go into that one here.) There is certainly no one denying that George Bush Sr. had a relationship with the Saudis. Why shouldn't he? He is and was a businessman and investor. Nevertheless, neither of the Bushes who served as president has ever been shown to have cut the Saudis any special slack where the interests of this country were at stake. The most obvious example is that, after 9/11, George W. Bush correctly went after Saudi money streams and put pressure on the Saudi leadership to start rolling up al Qaeda networks in their own country. Of course, this is a complex world. We need a stable Saudi Arabia and we need the continued accessibility of Mideast oil so it's in our interest to work with an oil rich country like Saudi Arabia.

Is that a bad thing? Well, it's a fact of our economic life, however much we might wish to hide behind our two oceans or find less problematic energy sources. Take the oil away and it's virtually guaranteed the U.S. would encounter some very hard economic times. The consequent loss of national prosperity would hurt all of us, especially those who are part of the usual Democratic constituency. I can just imagine your response if Bush's policies were to cause the Saudis to become radicalized or result in de-stabilizing their state, perhaps because he decided to unilaterally replace the autocratic rulers of that land. The same people who today allude to nefarious "conspiracies" between Bush and the Saudis or Bush and the bin Ladens would be the first to start screaming about how Bush doesn't know how to get along with our critical friends in the Middle East (just as they now decry his lack of success in pleasing "friends" like France and Germany). Or they'd be shouting from the rooftops, or other venue of protest, that this only proved Bush was a bully and an imperialist.

Remember Kerry's claim that it was "outrageous" that Bush was alleged to have had a deal with the Saudis to keep oil prices low (as reported in Bob Woodward's latest book)? Of course it has now turned out that, whether he had such a deal or not, oil prices *aren't* low. So what do Kerry and the Democrats have to say about that? Why they castigate Bush for *not* having a deal with the Saudis that would keep oil prices low! Can you honestly imagine that there is anything Bush could do that would win him the plaudits of Kerry and the Democrats? Or even yourself?

I must confess, I am mystified at this deep-seated antipathy for Bush. I suppose it's because of what he represents: conservative government instead of government by the liberal intelligentsia. Somehow, his occupancy of the White House has become a cultural cause celebre for the partisan left, a virtual war of those who hold liberal views (not always bad, in themselves, by the way) against those who hold more conservative ones. I guess the liberals (like yourself?), who dominate the two coasts and the national media, fear the religious right and see current conservative dominance at the federal level as the ascendance of such religious thinking in the body politic.

Certainly Bush has made clear that he holds religious beliefs. But so what? What's wrong with religious people winning elections and running things at times? They have as much right to be politically involved as any and certainly as much as those whose "religion" is an unabashed secular liberalism that finds traditional religious beliefs somehow frightening and abhorrent. Our country was built to withstand the winds of democratic change. What's got me worried, though, is whether, in this critical time of national testing, it will be able to withstand the windbags of hatred and innuendo.

Yours in truth,
SWM

UNDERSTANDING BUSH

(July 9, 2004)

The news these days isn't great for those of us who appreciate the presidency of George W. Bush. Slipping in the polls, beset on every side by negative naysayers in the media, Bush's chances of winning re-election are looking less and less likely. You can't count him out yet since his presumed Democratic opponent, John Kerry, still has to catch fire and Bush has a history of being "mis-underestimated," both for his penchant for malapropisms and the silly smirks he often flashes at inopportune moments. But Kerry is showing growing strength, as a steady drum-beat of bad news besieges the man whose job he has targeted.

Recently Wall Street Journal reporter John Harwood detailed the growing confidence of liberals as they see a White House restoration in their future, coming off a recent off-year election, in which they narrowly edged out a Republican, in what was once thought to be Bush country: South Dakota. Harwood interviewed Robert Borosage as he hosted the "Take Back America Conference" in downtown Washington, D.C.

Notes Mr. Borosage, a former top aide to Democrat Jesse Jackson, the Republicans "have left us weaker, more indebted, more isolated and far less secure." Borosage went on to tell Harwood that most liberals can be expected to give Kerry plenty of maneuvering room in this election year because they're so keen to oust George W. Bush from the White House. Given that, it would be unwise to expect a replay of Nader's relatively strong showing in 2000 in key battleground states.

As liberals are heartened, conservatives appear to be correspondingly disheartened. On the same day as Harwood's article appeared in the Journal, conservative journalist Bruce Bartlett, writing in the New York Sun, recited a litany of reasons why conservatives are also down on Bush. According to Bartlett, not only do many conservatives tend towards isolationism, disliking foreign entanglements like Iraq, they are dismayed and embarrassed over the poor intelligence concerning the missing WMD, the prime casus belli in Iraq, and fault President Bush for not sticking to conservative principles across a host of issues. Bush's slogan of "compassionate conservatism," says Bartlett, annoys some conservatives because it implies conservatism usually isn't.

Bartlett also notes that the president "rammed through Congress an education bill written by Senator Kennedy that did almost nothing to improve education (except) throw money at the problem. And now liberals are complaining he didn't throw enough."

According to Bartlett, Bush also waffled on free trade (with on-again/off-again tariffs, among other things), signed a campaign finance law most conservatives deemed unconstitutional, supported "vast increases in domestic spending, including . . . unjustified pork barrel spending," and has done little or nothing in fighting for his conservative judicial nominees.

Not long before reading Bartlett, I had the chance to speak with Queens County Conservative Party leader Tom Long who echoed these very sentiments. Bush is wrong on immigration, Long told me, and on spending. But Conservatives like Long and Bartlett aren't prepared to give up on the president just yet, for all their misgivings. Where else, asks Bartlett, can conservatives go? "Mr. Kerry," he notes, "is worse on every one of these issues. Imprisoned by the left wing of his party . . ."

So how did we get to this stage after the record approval ratings Bush had been garnering roughly a year ago? Certainly the problems in Iraq have worked against the president and will continue to be a sore point until Americans start to think we are turning the corner over there. But the truth is, most of the big complaints leveled against Bush actually ring false when you examine the facts. Critics slammed the president for his tax cuts, saying they were likely to harm the economy. Instead the economy is now roaring back, exactly as predicted by the tax cuts' supporters. The critics said the deficit would only get worse and bankrupt the country but improving government tax receipts, reflecting the economic momentum enabled by the Bush tax cuts, have already begun to reduce deficit estimates, just like tax cut supporters had predicted. Critics said the jobs just wouldn't come back, either. But instead, here they are, a trifle late but within the expected window, just as Bush supporters predicted.

Still, Americans, according to recent polls, now believe the economy really is worse, not better, though they were far more upbeat many months ago when the economy was, in fact, really worse.

Of course some of this is about lagged perceptions. But there's another dynamic at work, too. In the first half of the twentieth century Hitler's minister of propaganda, one Josef Goebbels, enunciated his "big lie" principle. The gist of it was that you don't have to worry about the facts when talking to the public, that if you say something often enough and loudly enough, the ideas you are trying to convey will take hold. People tend to believe the last thing they've heard if it sounds authoritative to them, all other things being equal. And when the media amplifies and reinforces every negative claim, it's hard to keep your wits about you and recognize partisan spinning when you hear it.

Since Bush was elected in 2000, there has been a relentless effort on the part of his political opponents to undermine his credibility, an effort that halted only briefly after the shock of 9/11, but that has been renewed with a vengeance since. Aspersions and demeaning name-calling, directed at the president and his administration, have reached new lows in the public forum. Nor has this effort been confined to partisans in the opposing political factions alone. The bulk of the mainstream media, both subtly and with the proverbial blunt instrument, have acted like the political opposition they are ostensibly reporting on, magnifying every fault and problem, while downplaying or ignoring what might be considered positive. The New York Times, for instance, prefers to focus on Iraqi problems like Abu Ghraib and Ahmed

Chalabi, with a few thrown-in mea culpas declaring that they, themselves, were had by the administration concerning claims about WMD. They have very little interest in depicting a resurgent economy which Bush might take credit for. Indeed, it's sometimes hard to see how anything positive about Bush's efforts ever manages to make its way through the partisan noise that passes for journalism in America today.

But this isn't the first time this has happened, though it's certainly louder and more overwhelming now than in past years, as liberal partisans, smelling blood, go in for the kill.

Teddy Kennedy declares the president a liar and a fraud while Nancy Pelosi, frozen-faced before the cameras, solemnly pronounces the president "incompetent." Back when the senior Bush was president, this same kind of stuff happened, too. The fact that former president George H. W. Bush successfully dealt with a Latin American debt crisis and a U.S. Savings & Loan crisis which together threatened to tip us into a worldwide financial debacle, even as he smoothly managed the Soviet implosion and ousted a swaggering Saddam Hussein from a neighboring nation he had invaded, carried no weight with the American electorate when Bush pere campaigned for a second term.

George H. W. Bush became the recipient of what was (until now) an unprecedented campaign of disinformation and partisan assault as Bill Clinton brazenly alleged that Bush was presiding over "the worst downturn since the Great Depression" despite manifest evidence to the contrary. Clinton's attack was supported and abetted by most of the mainstream media at the time, who steadfastly refused to report the already marked economic recovery that was then under way . . . refused to report it, that is, until Clinton had been safely elected. (One day after the election, the New York Times carried its first lead story about the economic recovery that had been going on, at that point, for most of the preceding year.)

Even as every bit of bad news was being blown up to heroic proportions by a less and less circumspect partisan media, former President George H. W. Bush was being attacked, in his re-election bid, for allegedly being disengaged, for not feeling America's pain, and for signing off on a tax increase rammed through by a Democratic Congress as a condition for their support in the Gulf War. Almost as soon as the ink was dry on the pen with which the senior Bush had signed the Congressional tax increase, the partisan sniping began as then Democratic Senate Majority Leader George Mitchell led the charge, accusing him of breaking his campaign promise about "no new taxes." So Bush Sr. allowed himself to be snookered and trapped by Democrats who, with the tacit aid of a biased media, drew him deeper and deeper into a situation where he would break a specific promise he had made to the American public when it elected him to the presidency. He thought he could work with the Democrats for a broader purpose. But he misjudged the nature and intensity of his opposition.

All of this goes a long way towards explaining the actions and policies of the current President Bush. Witness to the strategic errors his father made in facing the partisan Democratic opposition, George W. seems intent on avoiding the same pitfalls. His father blundered in breaking a "no new taxes" pledge, thereby handing his opportunistic opposition a bat with which to beat him relentlessly over the head in the subsequent campaign. So Bush Jr. kept his own word on the promised tax cuts, not only getting them passed twice in his first term, but actually seeing them do precisely what they were expected to do in re-booting a faltering economy left over from the bursting of the dot.com bubble and the aftershocks of 9/11.

Bush's father appeared unsympathetic to the average guy?

Well, Bush Jr. *is the average guy.*

His father had no aggressive domestic agenda?

Bush Jr., the compassionate conservative, does, giving us more Medicare, more school spending, and protection for steel workers. But Bush Jr. ought to have known none of this could possibly be enough for Democrats.

George W. Bush came into office promising to change the tone in Washington, but it takes two to tango as the saying goes. So the tone has gotten worse, not better . . . and the Democrats slam him for that, too.

And George W., trying to be what his father wasn't, has now managed to alienate some of his own natural base, without pleasing those left-leaning factions who want only one thing, their own return to power.

Most conservatives aren't likely to desert Bush in this election year but they clearly are not as enthused as they ought to be at this point in the presidential cycle, especially considering the alternative.

Meanwhile Bush keeps trying, keeps making nice, no doubt concerned that the first time he says something as cutting about Kerry as Kerry and company routinely say about him, he will be attacked from all sides for embodying the still missing-in-action and now mythic "Republican attack machine."

But things are not looking good for this president and he's going to need to get proactive soon, to start giving as good as he gets . . . or else he's likely to follow in his father's footsteps, ousted by the sturm und drang of partisan politics-as-usual.

WHO'S LYING NOW?

(July 19, 2004)[19]

So former Ambassador Joe Wilson told us a few fibs about President Bush and his administration! That's the obvious conclusion from the recent reports by the Senate Intelligence Committee and Lord Butler's report to the British Parliament issued in mid-July. Last year Mr. Wilson told us that his foray into Niger for the CIA had debunked the claim, made by President Bush in his State of the Union Address, that the British government had learned Saddam Hussein was attempting to buy uranium in Africa. Wilson said he had learned otherwise on his trip and that there was no basis for the Bush claim except a forged document, and that he had enlightened the CIA on these very points well before the President's speech. Wilson also asserted at the time that his role in the whole matter had had nothing whatever to do with his wife's position inside the CIA. Well it looks like he misstated across the board.

According to the reports just out, Wilson actually reported to the CIA that his contact in Niger did believe Iraq was after "yellowcake" (weaponizable uranium), the primary export of that African nation, and that Saddam had sent his emissaries to Niger. This confirmed other information the CIA had from British and European intelligence agencies and is what the CIA told the President in the briefings that preceded his State of the Union Address. And Wilson's wife, it seems, wrote a memo of her own, taking credit for Mr. Wilson's appointment as special CIA envoy to Niger concerning the Saddam-yellowcake question. So Mr. Wilson told us a fib about what he found in Niger, about what he told the CIA when he got back, and about his wife's role in his getting the Niger junket in the first place. Whoops.

Joe Wilson's attacks on the President's case for a Saddam-yellowcake connection was one of the opening salvos in a relentless assault by establishment types, since the removal of Saddam Hussein, against Bush's credibility. So much has been said so loudly by so many for so long, as amplified by a sympathetic media, that it's become virtually gospel by now that Saddam really wasn't a threat to anyone, contra the administration's pre-war claims. The obvious conclusion we have been asked to draw from this is that Bush wrongly took us to war, whether purposefully or not. And the most vituperative of his critics, of course, tell us Bush and his people did all this knowingly, i.e., they lied. Joe Wilson said so, himself, when he called Bush and Cheney liars at a campaign rally for John Kerry.

The media gobbled it all up and made Wilson a household name in interview after interview. Democratic political leaders, from Teddy Kennedy and Nancy Pelosi to Howard Dean and, finally, John Kerry, made political hay of the Wilson allegations, using these to hammer the president and drive home the mantra to the American people that Bush was a liar. Pseudo-documentarian Michael Moore is only the latest, if perhaps one of the most vicious and disingenuous, to jump on this crowded "Bush lied" bandwagon.

Only now it turns out that Wilson, himself, wasn't telling us the truth. Well, was *he* lying? Since we can presume he knew the facts we now know, back when he was making his claims, what else are we to conclude? Bush may have gotten incorrect information in some cases from his intelligence briefers (though it doesn't look like they were wrong about Saddam's search for yellowcake anymore). Still, unless he knew more than his briefers knew at the time, unless he knew they were wrong on this or that issue, he can't be said to have been lying when he relied on their information to make his decisions. But knowingly speaking falsely? Well that, by any definition is lying. And Joe Wilson's oft-repeated claims clearly fit that bill.

But what's behind this mad rush we have witnessed to accuse the president of lying as Wilson and his spiritual fellow, Michael Moore, have done? What's going on in the media and with the political opposition that they seem to have lost their moral compass like this? It's one thing to criticize someone on the facts. But it's quite another to create or misrepresent facts in order to make your case. And yet we've seen this repeatedly in an unprecedented outpouring of hostility and vituperation against this administration from the academy, the media and from the Democratic Party itself. In fact, we have witnessed a virtual tidal wave of charges and allegations against this president since the removal of Saddam in '03 even as the national media, like the New York Times and CNN, remain reticent in correcting the record when claims like Wilson's start to collapse in the face of the facts.

In past periods in this country, going back to the Cold War and earlier, there has been a certain unanimity among the majority of Americans on international matters. Whatever differences divided us on the domestic front, we left our partisan baggage at the door and went out to face the world with common purpose. But no more. So ferocious has the contest for power at home become that there no longer seem to be any inhibitions, on the part of those in pursuit of it, concerning damage to U.S. interests abroad. If flagrant and unsupportable allegations of lies are what it takes to bring down an administration, then that, these partisans seem to be saying, is what they will do. So determined are they to reclaim the levers of power in Washington, they have lost their bearings.

Well now the facts are in on the Wilson matter, but the question at hand is whether anyone will pay attention at this point . . . and whether those who alleged the worst of this president will step forward and retract the lies they, themselves, helped promulgate. And whether the truth will even matter in the electoral calculations of the American people, now that the damage has been done.

STAYING OUT OF
THE "DRAFT"

(June 14, 2004)

If anyone is wondering why I find the Democratic attacks on Bush's integrity so disingenuous, perhaps a small example may be helpful. I recently received an e-mail from a concerned individual who had gotten a message via the internet asserting that the Bush administration was "quietly" planning to bring back the draft while the rest of us were paying attention to other things and that the administration intended to reinstitute it soon after the 2004 presidential election. The clear implication was that the Bush administration was trying to pull the wool over the eyes of the American people. Here's the relevant portion of the e-mail message:

"There is pending legislation in the House and Senate (twin bills: S 89 and HR 163) which will time the program's initiation so the draft can begin as early as Spring 2005—just after the 2004 presidential election. The administration is quietly trying to get these bills passed now, while the public's attention is on the elections, so our action on this is needed immediately."

So, asked my correspondent, who wanted to support the president but definitely didn't want to see the draft reinstated, how true is this? I turned to my son, an eminently draftable soon-to-be twenty year old, and a skilled navigator of the World Wide Web, and asked him to check it out.

Jumping right on this (since his age gives him a real stake in the question!) he quickly got back to me with his findings. Turns out both bills referenced in the internet message were introduced by Democrats and had no administration support at all! The House bill was the contribution of New York Democratic Representative Charles Rangel while the Senate bill was put on the floor of that august body by Senate Democrat Fritz Hollings of South Carolina. In fact, the Republican majority in Congress opposed both bills, as did the Bush administration. As a result of this opposition, the two bills have languished for over a year now with no action being taken to bring them to a vote. So what gives?

Says Parrish Baker's Kansas City Independent blog (to which my son directed me): "despite all the abrupt panicked clamor in blogs, from the Democratic underground all the way to Warren Ellis and halfway back, there is not going to be a draft." Baker, a blogger with no particular love for the Bush administration, goes on to note that: "The record shows that S. 89 was introduced on 1/7/2003 and was referred to the Committee on Armed Services the same day. H.R. 163 was also introduced on 1/7/2003 and was referred to the Subcommittee on Total Force on 2/3/2003. There has been absolutely no action on either bill since they were referred to committee."

According to California Representative Pete Stark, who co-sponsored the House version of the bill, this is about opposition to the Bush administration's actions in Iraq. Said Stark in a statement to Congress on January 8, 2003: "Reinstituting the draft may seem unnecessary to some. But, it will ensure all Americans share in the cost and sacrifice of war. Without a universal draft, this burden weighs disproportionately on the shoulders of the poor, the disadvantaged and minority populations . . . . Maybe some of you in this Congress would think twice about voting for war in Iraq if you knew your child may be sent to fight in the streets of Baghdad?"

So this is not the Bush administration at work but those who opposed the administration and its policies. But why send the e-mail around now and why suggest, as the text of the message clearly does, that this is a surreptitious attempt on Bush's part to sneak the draft back into our national life? Blogger Baker asks the same thing and offers his own suspicions: "So why the sudden panic? Hmmmmmm . . . frightening college aged kids into voting for Kerry, perhaps?"

It certainly looks like the posters of the e-mail message referenced above were not being entirely honest with us, doesn't it? But of course, as they keep telling us, it's Bush and the Republicans who are the liars not the Democrats and their supporters. Still, it ought to make us all wonder whether those who are so continuously and loudly accusing others of lying have any credibility left at all when they are themselves caught in such boldfaced dissembling. It's certainly not as difficult to believe that Bush and his administration were misled or misinterpreted intelligence data about Saddam Hussein's possession of wmd as it is to assume that they were lying about it. On the other hand, the above e-mail, sent to my correspondent by a Kerry supporter, deliberately misstates the facts about the case to suggest a false conclusion. If that ain't lying, I don't know what is.

Oh, and by the way, in answer to the reader of these pages who recently demanded my response to his question of whether I'd be willing to send my own son off to war in Iraq if I were called on to do so (and who doubted I'd offer him an answer "any time soon"), the answer is yes, I would. While no more happy about the prospect than anyone else who loves his children, if my son enlisted and then got deployed to Iraq, I would have to accept that since that is what comes of joining the armed forces. Sometimes you have to actually use the training they give you in real combat and you always have to follow lawful orders concerning when and where.

If the draft were ever reinstituted (as the spurious e-mail referenced above falsely reported it was about to be), I would also have to accept this. My son, who supports the war in Iraq by the way, feels the same way. Still, he has no plans to enlist in the military at this time nor is he required to do so, absent a draft. On the other hand, he is required to be honest with others and himself all the time. That's how I raised him. Apparently many of today's partisans of the left don't feel bound by the same constraints.

MAKING THE CITY
BETTER

INCREASED PROPERTY TAXES OR GOVERNMENTAL EFFICIENCY?

(December 7, 2002)

Mayor Bloomberg's recent push for increased property taxes (a prelude to even more taxes in other areas?) poses a special problem to Rockawayites. Home ownership is substantial on the peninsula and even renters stand to have tax increases passed along to them, though they may be among those least able to afford these. This all comes as something of a disappointment to many who supported Bloomberg in his race for the mayoralty since he presented himself as a Republican, someone in Rudy Giuliani's image (a mayor who lowered taxes and reined in parts of government during his years in office).

The fear, of course, is that our current Mayor "bought" his nomination from a party without any substantive contenders of its own, in a Democratic town, and so has no real commitment to the historic platform of that party: less government through lower taxes and strict accountability of government agencies. Now that he has responded to a major fiscal crisis as a Democrat would have, by calling for increased taxes in lieu of painful spending cuts, many feel let down at best and betrayed at worst. But is this the end of the story?

The truth is, as a businessman, Mayor Mike has extensive experience with the need to control costs and to innovate. Although he clearly came to City Hall with a desire to change the tone set by his combative predecessor, and has gone out of his way to establish better relations with the various interest groups that dominate City politics, it's highly unlikely that he has forgotten what he learned during his years in the private sector. True, he has taken the lead on tax increases in order to avoid painful service cuts. But it's not yet clear what he means to do beyond this.

The first thing he *should* do, of course, is make clear that he is not wedded to the tax and spend policies of the discredited seventies, even if he must push for increased taxes to keep city services operating at their current levels. He needs to clearly state that tax increases today are not necessarily tax increases forever and that he is as keen to lower them as raise them . . . when the environment is right for it. And that means that he needs to be looking at the workings of city government now, if the environment is to be made right again!

If New York City is not to simply slide back into the stagnation of the seventies, the Mayor has to use this present crisis to reshape city government. If he can successfully do that, then the time for lowering taxes again will not be far off, since he will have made New York City a more viable "business" than it was when he found it. Can this be done and, if so, where to start? A few modest suggestions:

City agencies annually rent many millions of dollars worth of privately owned space while city-owned space goes begging or is underutilized. And, while city agencies are paying market rates, or more, for their rented space (often renting more space than they actually need!), city-owned space gets "rented" out to non-city organizations for a pittance compared to actual costs . . . or for no payment at all. The difference between operating costs and the rentals paid by non-city agencies are sometimes as great as ten to one ($1 in "rent" paid for every $10 of city expenditures to maintain the rented space). Such cheap or non-existent rents amount to subsidies paid for by each of us through our taxes.

Another area with opportunities to obtain savings in order to offset the need for new taxes is the city's capital process. City-run capital jobs routinely incur construction costs of $300-$500 a square foot (or greater) against comparable costs in the private sector of between $150-$200 a square foot. Why the big discrepancy? The reasons include an attenuated and inefficient bidding and contracting process, inadequate agency monitoring of work done and failure to monitor actual costs. But the main reason is probably that the city agency charged with management of capital work obtains a substantial portion of its annual operating budget based on the value of the projects it manages for other city agencies. Thus, it has a built-in incentive to countenance higher costs.

Where else can the city find needed savings in lieu of tax cuts? Telephone costs have risen dramatically in recent years across city agencies, reflecting an inability to track agencies' usage or to impose a system of accountability on such usage. As a result, city agencies maintain far too many phones for the number of staff requiring them. Many city agencies also operate independent fleets where a substantial percentage of their vehicles may be underutilized. Costs here reflect excessive purchasing outlays and increased maintenance for the vehicles in question, along with garage space rentals.

City personnel management and hiring processes also foster inefficiency in the workforce, reducing worker output and causing managers to over-hire to compensate for the reduced output. At the same time, the structure of the city's budgeting process actually encourages spending rather than saving since it rewards excess spending at year-end rather than frugality and the efficient use of funds because city managers have every incentive to spend down their budgets, rather than conserving the funds against future need. This leads to mad, inefficient scrambling to make year-end purchases . . . frequently of things for which the operation in question has no real identified need.

The point here is that there are many areas which offer an opportunity to reduce city operating costs without resorting to endlessly raising our taxes, areas which the Mayor ought now to be addressing. Increasing taxes only feeds the inefficiency monster while damaging the long-term viability of our communities. Granted that finding and fixing these problems is not something that can be done quickly enough to stave off the current crisis in the short term. Still, the Mayor should demonstrate now that he is seriously interested in addressing the problem of government inefficiency, even while he is pushing new taxes at us. If he wants to win back the confidence of Rockawayites and all New Yorkers, he needs to undertake a serious and focused restructuring review of where our taxes are really going. If he misses this historic opportunity, it's hard to see how New Yorkers will forgive him in the next election cycle . . . or how we will avoid another 1970's style municipal depression as a legacy of the Bloomberg years.

DUMPING THE WASTE ALONG WITH THE TRASH

(April 12, 2003)

The other day (actually it was the other night) I was awakened from a sound sleep by the rumbling of heavy trucks outside my window.

Slowly rising to consciousness, I gradually recognized the familiar, if irritating, sound of idling compaction trucks and banging garbage cans in the dark street below. It was the Sanitation Department crew making one of its not infrequent nightly runs. There was no snow on the ground or in the offing so I started wondering why they were on night duty once again!

I knew, of course, that very often the city must alter crew shifts to meet various weather-related emergencies, the most common being snow storms. But the night in question was clear and warm with no snow forecasted. Why put the guys on overtime, then, especially in this period of fiscal crisis when the Mayor says there is no waste to cut; only taxes to be raised?

And why disturb the sleep of the neighborhood?

Well, of course the answer was pretty simple and I knew it from my days in the Sanitation Department. Overtime is considered by many city workers, however unofficially, to be a regular part of their annual pay package, i.e., they believe they are entitled to it. I remember during those long snowless years that we endured back in the nineties, how Sanitation management would worry about finding enough snow-related activity to justify spending out its snow budget before year-end! But why? Surely that is not the best way to manage a budget . . . or a department.

Well, most of the Department of Sanitation's management came up through the ranks. They supplemented their pay by overtime in their day, just like the guys on the ground are doing today. Moreover, many of those in so-called "managerial" positions in the Department are actually still in "line" titles, which means, of course, that they continue to be represented by the same unions that represent the crews.

Even more telling, because of their job titles, these "managers" are eligible to earn overtime along with the guys! Of course this inflates their annual salaries and results in a double whammy for the city: increased pay in the year it was earned, along with a higher base when their pensions are finally calculated. Holy conflict of interest, Batman!

So the city's Sanitation Department does its darnedest to spend its overtime budget, whether they need to or not. Of course, even when it's needed, how do we, the taxpayers and recipients of this essential service, know that it's being spent in the most cost/efficient manner, given the modus operandi which determines its use? The answer, of course, is that we don't. So we get those late night pick-ups that are often loud enough to wake the dead, let alone the lighter sleepers among us, and garbage that often sits for days on end at the curb, awaiting the Department of Sanitation's kindly ministrations. Never mind the near total abandon many of the crews exhibit when they pick the stuff up!

I'm thinking here of garbage that falls out of the cans and ends up on the street after the trucks have passed through. And of cans tossed cavalierly about, ending up in the gutter or in front of our neighbors' houses instead of our own. (I've lost more cans that way than I care to count.) Sometimes, too, the crews won't even deign to take what we leave, if it looks too heavy or like it might be too much! And there have been many times that I've found some paper goods taken and some left behind, without any obvious rhyme or reason to the selection process. I guess we just ought to count ourselves lucky that they don't also come out and give us tickets when garbage gets left like this, since they are also empowered to do that! (Fines for this might even help pay for some of those overtime costs after all . . . . now there's an idea.)

Excess overtime expenditures and delayed pick-ups, with garbage sitting on the streets, sometimes for days on end, attracting rodents and other foraging beasts to rifle through the cans and scatter the "goods" to the four winds! And increases to our property taxes and maybe other increases soon to come?

What was it that Mayor Bloomberg said back on November 14, 2002 when he was so busy justifying the tax increases he was proposing to close the gargantuan budget gap the city was facing: "You can't just say let's go cut corruption, waste and meaningless programs. Because fundamentally they don't exist."

Sez who?

SMOKESCREEN FOR SPENDING?

(May 2, 2003)

Despite the looming budget crisis, the New York City Health Commissioner recently announced a $2.5 million campaign to aid smokers to kick the habit by offering a free quit-smoking packet to the public on a first-come, first-serve basis. Like Mayor Bloomberg, himself a reformed smoker, the Commissioner is a strong anti-smoking advocate. But some have raised questions as to the advisability of such costly new programs when the city is facing continuing budget cuts that will need to be addressed by tax increases, service reductions and/or layoffs. Sure the amount allocated for this new program is a drop in the proverbial bucket, but couldn't it be put to better use in the current crisis? Is this really the time for this kind of service expansion?

Personally, I've never been a smoker and don't particularly like the habit so I have no problem with strong advocacy against it. On the other hand, I'm not very comfortable with the idea of the nanny state, of government that is always telling us what we can and cannot do. I know this is not a highly popular view these days but I never liked New York State's seatbelt laws (although I happen to wear a seatbelt for my own safety) and am not in favor now of the draconian ban on smoking in commercial establishments that has become the law, courtesy of this Mayor and his Health Commissioner.

But the issue is not merely one of government overexpansion and intrusiveness (although it is that too). It is a matter of how government itself functions. The nanny state means big and growing government, as those in power find more and newer ways to intervene in our lives. Of course you can't do that without growing the various organs of government and for that you need funds. The present anti-smoking program by the city's Health Department, for instance, involves hiring additional inspectors, to enforce the new citywide ban, as well as paying for the freebies that must first be purchased, packaged and mailed to those who are inspired by the public outreach to request them. Naturally, it also includes costs for back-office staff to perform the necessary "outreach" and to respond to the anticipated requests for the "free" packages. Although I have no access to the agency's budget for all this, I will bet you that the true costs will turn out to be well in excess of the quoted amount.

And this is really the crux of the problem when city government grows to the sky like this. Costs are never really known or properly accounted for. For every dollar publicly reported, a significant multiple of that is buried in ancillary costs and, precisely because it is "buried," it is wasted more often than not. It is wasted in salaries for employees who don't operate at full capacity or in a top-loaded management structure. It is wasted in the purchase of unnecessary goods and services. It is wasted in an inefficient purchasing process that does nothing to incentivize cost-effectiveness beyond forcing group buys that may involve poorly negotiated "requirements contracts" and/or the acquisition of substandard goods.[20]

There are always innumerable hidden costs. One "hidden" item, in particular, involves the actual set-up of the offices needed to accommodate new programs like this anti-smoking initiative. Many City agencies, in fact, actually seem to spend nearly as much time moving their staffs and programs around as they spend performing their mandated programmatic functions. The dislocation and relocations involved are costly since they involve disruptions to the programs, outlays for moving personnel, renovations to the new (and, not infrequently, the vacated) space, and purchases of brand new (and often expensive) furniture when the old stuff is deemed too drab or "old-fashioned" to be retained.

More often than not, in moves like this, there are also added costs for unnecessary rentals of privately owned space along with operating costs and lost revenue for the city-owned space left vacant or underutilized in favor of rentals.

If agencies moved their staff once every five years or so, this might not be such a big deal. But some agencies play what looks like an annual game of musical chairs with their organizations and so the costs continually mount up as this year's space is vacated and reconfigured for new occupants, while the old occupants move on to next year's space. Frequently, ancillary funds get tapped to support these various relocations, but sometimes actual programmatic funds, which could be better spent to directly support the services they're earmarked for, are used. But you would never see these added costs reflected in the programs' reported figures. Thus, true program costs are never really tracked or fully accounted for.

The problem is not just that the nanny state is intrusive but that it results in inflated government which, given the lack of accountability within the system, leads to frivolous use of taxpayer dollars. And this means overspending in both fat and lean times, leading to the inevitable budget deficits and the consequent demands for raising taxes.

Anti-smoking as an information initiative is a good thing although it should not become the new Prohibition (which is where it now seems to be going). But, as an example of government getting beyond itself, it is merely the tip of a very problematic iceberg, the beginnings of another new and growing government initiative which will not only butt its nose into our personal lives, but will charge us for doing this at a rate whose true cost no one in this city can really monitor . . . or seems willing to even think about.

WHO "LOST" THE CITY?

(May 9, 2003)

In a recent column in The New York Sun, J. P. Avlon, a Sun columnist and former staffer in the Giuliani administration, compared the former Mayor's record to his successor's and suggested that it's unfair to blame Rudy for the problems Mayor Mike has inherited. While noting that overall city headcount did rise during the Giuliani years, this was offset, he said, by many other administrative reductions. And the increases, he noted, were mainly focused in the uniformed services, specifically the Police and Fire Departments. These increases, said Avlon, were essential to improving the quality of life in the city, for which Giuliani has rightly been credited. Finally, he noted that Giuliani's cost-cutting and tax reductions, in contradistinction to the present Mayor's performance, were a spur to business and the city's economy.

Well there's truth to all this, of course, but it's not the whole story. Mayor Giuliani did lower taxes and do away with a lot of business-impeding red tape. And he did make the city more habitable, pushing his agencies to do more. Moreover, it is clear that the events of 9/11, which have played a big part in the city's current economic malaise (and City Hall's deficit), were not the fault of then Mayor Giuliani. But the fact remains that Rudy missed a chance to deal structurally with many of the city's problems and that, when 9/11 hit, the city under Mayor Giuliani, rightly or wrongly, was forced to pull out all the stops causing spending to blow through the roof. There may not have been much choice as to how we responded in the face of the unprecedented disaster but, in the context of a still-bloated and inefficient administration, it was a one-way ticket to budgetary palookaville for the city.

Bloomberg inherited the oversized and inefficient government his predecessor left us with.

How did it get that way and why? Well, like Avlon, I was also part of the last administration though not as close to the top as he was. I did a ten-month stint in City Hall as a senior policy analyst for one of Giuliani's Deputy Mayors in the latter part of his first term and later served for nearly seven years as an Assistant Commissioner in one of the mayoral agencies. While I never hobnobbed with the Mayor and his inner circle, I did run into him a few times . . . he even tripped over me once as he was rushing into a meeting while I was coming out. He's a good deal taller than I am and was in a bit of a hurry so it was perfectly understandable. And besides, he was a perfect gentleman about it.

My job in those days was to work with the Deputy Mayor who was my boss to represent the administration to various community and advocacy groups. What we were really doing, of course, was making sure that the budgetary pie got shared out to the various groups in such a way as to ensure these groups perceived that the Mayor was in their corner. We were building constituency . . . or trying to win it. This could get hairy sometimes as we occasionally stumbled into various hornets' nests and had to backpedal as quickly as we could. Of course, we tried to be balanced in making financial support available to the various community groups but it was evident that some groups had more claim on us than others and we often took great pains to include groups with apparent clout in order to cement their loyalty to the Mayor.

Although this sometimes made me feel uncomfortable, since it wasn't about efficiency or better management, I figured it was a necessary activity in order to keep the Mayor's administration in power so that it could do the many right things it was doing. In a democracy you depend on votes . . . and voters are often guided by their community leaders. Such leaders, of course, maintain their leadership by securing the goodies for their constituents in the form of more programs and services. And so it goes. Giuliani had squeaked through in that first term and was already doing good things, reining government in, etc., so I figured that we were serving a greater purpose.

But lots of the money we were in the business of spending could certainly, in an ideal world, have been better directed to more essential things. Later, when I moved over to the Health Department, after my ten months at City Hall, my new job involved reviving what was then perceived to be a moribund division that most in the Health Department preferred to disregard and work around. I met a lot of resistance from my new staff, who wrongly considered me a political appointee, and had to work hard to prove to them that I wasn't. In my first year I reorganized the bureau and effected a plan designed to secure annual savings of more than half a million dollars while tripling service levels. The top administration of the Health Department loved it and the savings occurred, just as predicted, in the first year of implementation.

But a funny thing happened on the way to the bank. As the Mayor's re-election campaign geared up, the interest in saving money and being efficient that had previously galvanized us seemed to disappear. Suddenly the mandate to be frugal evaporated and the issue reverted to one of getting those services out there, just like it had been during my time at City Hall. In one egregious case, a large rat was reputed to have run across the Mayor's front steps at Gracie Mansion and was seen by reporters in all its glory. Suddenly, as we moved into the electoral season that year, the public focus shifted to the Health Department's anti-rat initiative, the Pest Control Program. The newspapers were full of stories about rats and City Hall told us to solve the problem fast.

Top management in the Health Department put their heads together and came up with a new plan and took it to City Hall. Playing the usual game, they grossly overstated their need, figuring they'd be cut back by the bureaucrats in the Mayor's office. But in this case they weren't. In fact, they got all the resources they asked for and more.

The only problem was that they hadn't thought through the program model they were proposing. They had dreamed up something on paper which focused on pre-selected multi-block sections of the city, to be chosen by discussion with local community leaders. In other words, rather than focusing on where the rats actually were, they had decided to follow the usual political prescription and spread their resources evenly to all constituencies . . . whether the communities had a real rat problem or just a perceived one. The idea was to keep all parts of the city, and a broad range of community leaders, happy. But the program they had dreamed up was based on revenue-raising, at its core, rather than rat eradication and so, once an area was singled out, the practice was to do blanket inspections, house to house or building to building. Whenever evidence of rats was found, tickets were issued to the property owners. Failure to resolve a problem led to fines. And, needless to say, irate owners.

Because the program had made no provision for discovering and dealing with actual sources of infestation, if they were outside the surveyed areas or premises, property owners were often ticketed for having rats when the rats really came from nearby construction sites, parks or highways. So the owners would have to pay up but could not, even if they tried, eradicate the problem on their own. And, of course, because so many of the selected areas had no serious rat problem at all, much activity was often expended with very little return . . . while areas with real rat problems languished unaddressed. So the program spent a lot of time antagonizing the public, either by issuing fines to property owners who could not resolve their problem or by ignoring whole communities where serious rat infestations did exist but which were not on the calendar until much later in the politically driven process.

This was all compounded by the fact that other city agencies were, themselves, often the sources of the rat infestations (e.g., poorly maintained parks, city housing, or other city-owned properties). But, since the focus of the program was on generating enough revenue to pay for itself (this was how it had been sold to City Hall, after all), and the Health Department could not issue summonses to, or collect fines from, other city agencies, the Department could not act to ameliorate these clearly identified sources. Nor could it force the other responsible city agencies to spend their own funds to do this either.

Of course the Health Department could continue to ticket and bill private property owners onto whose lands or buildings the rats had migrated. And this is exactly what was done.

Needless to say, the rat problem did not go away although much in the way of resources was being expended to deal with it. And, while the rats persisted and the public screamed and the newspapers trumpeted the problem far and wide, the program, itself, proved unable to generate the revenue envisioned for it at the outset.

Much of the problem for all this lay with those who were then in charge because they didn't take the problem seriously. In fact, they didn't really believe the Department could actually have an impact on the rat population at all (though they hadn't bothered to tell *that* to City Hall for fear of jeopardizing the substantial budgetary infusion the program was bringing into the Department). So top management structured the program for public visibility and revenue generation, rather than for actual pest control purposes. It failed on all counts.

Other systemic problems also added to this program's woes, of course, including a dysfunctionally fragmented bureaucracy steeped in a culture of resource pilferage, internecine infighting and an apparently congenital aversion to truth-telling . . . without any serious top-down leadership to knock the necessary heads together to overcome these obstacles. But this is the stuff of other tales and would only take us too far afield at this point. Suffice it to say here that, in the final analysis, City Hall ultimately lost faith in the program they had once pushed for and funded. They angrily rolled some heads (though not the ones who had created the mess in the first place) and everyone moved on.[21]

Why do I offer this cautionary tale now? Because it is indicative of what began to happen as Mayor Giuliani went into his second term. In the first term he'd had his eye on the ball, despite a necessary penchant for playing the political game. But by the time he was moving into the election and after he began his second term, something had changed. The Mayor began opening the spending sluice gates and allowing the agencies to grow fatter and sloppier. By the time we got a new Commissioner at the Health Department in the Mayor's new term, the whole culture in the Department was changing. Instead of striving to save and be efficient, as we had been expected to do in the past, we were suddenly driven by a new imperative: to provide more services, costs be damned. And this new focus was not just directed at the various communities in the city. It involved our own management as well. Salary increases for senior staff soon became relatively easy to secure, with little regard for actual performance, and hiring constraints were eased as new monies were infused into the system to support a policy of "spreading the wealth" around the city. Of course demands for service sky-rocketed as this became known, both among the communities themselves and among agency managers who suddenly wanted nicer office space, more and fancier vehicles, personal chauffeur services, etc.

But what had not happened was the real structural reform that might have served to make the city more efficient at providing these kinds of things. We were left with the same clumsy, bureaucratic hiring process, the same ridiculously inefficient procurement systems, the same inability to hold staff accountable for incompetence or worse, the same budgetary system that encouraged wasteful overspending without any real accountability. On top of all of this the message from City Hall was that perquisites, once frowned on, were now okay, that fattening up after the lean times was acceptable. The Mayor had his eye on a U.S. Senate run by this time, was encountering health and marital problems, and no longer seemed to have his heart in managing a tighter city ship.

And then came 9/11 and everything changed. Certainly Mayor Giuliani could not have predicted that, nor avoided its serious and costly consequences. But he had already missed a real opportunity to achieve genuine and lasting reform in city government. And that was the legacy he left for our current Mayor. I do not think Bloomberg is right to keep pushing tax increases while avoiding serious agency restructuring but at least you have to admit that the problems are not of his making. And that they might have been avoided if his predecessor had kept a keener eye on the ball in the outgoing innings of his now fabled administration.

THEIR BAAAAAACK!

(May 16, 2003)

Since the discovery of the West Nile Virus in northern Queens a number of years ago, New York City's Health Department has geared up annually, at about this time, to combat this health risk. Compared to issues like bio-terrorism and other recent threats from abroad, of course, this seems relatively insignificant these days. Yet to many—particularly in places like Rockaway—the presence of potentially disease carrying mosquitoes can be a very real concern.

To deal with the problem citywide, the Health Department developed a comprehensive and proactive program (after decades of outright, and hard to justify, mosquito neglect). The program monitors dead bird reports (since the virus strikes birds first) and samples mosquitoes citywide for signs of the virus. It also comprehensively inspects for standing water pools where mosquitoes can breed. Additionally, it monitors medical provider reports to determine if and when symptoms of the disease are showing up in the human population. And it initiates a program of preventive larviciding, in the spring, to reduce mosquito populations in areas where standing water cannot be eliminated (e.g., ponds, sewers and catch basins).

When signs of the virus are noted, the Department has also responded, in recent years, by spraying chemicals intended to suppress the adult mosquito population. This part of the program, however, has been somewhat controversial since some feel spraying may be more hazardous than the relatively low risk of actual viral infection, given that West Nile, which can sometimes be fatal, usually isn't. Risks from the virus increase dramatically, of course, for the very young or very old and for those with compromised immune systems.

Proactive and aggressive standing water inspections and larviciding are two ways to reduce the need for spraying and, in truth, the Department has sprayed less and less each year, partly reflecting its learning curve and partly its increased ability to be preemptive and focused. But there are other ways of addressing the mosquito problem in certain areas that can also dramatically reduce the need for spraying. One of these has been tried by the Department in Rockaway for the past couple of years: mosquito magnets.

These are powerful traps that combine heat and the production of carbon dioxide (given off by mammals when they breathe) with use of a proprietary "bait" that acts as an added draw for mosquitoes "on the make". These magnets are roughly the size of small barbecue grills and, like the grills, require a tank of propane gas to operate (producing the heat and CO_2 that draw in the flying pests). But the magnets are not equally effective everywhere.

They're fairly costly and need to be deployed in very particular configurations to get the best out of them, ideally as a barrier between the places where the mosquitoes breed and where they feed. In Rockaway, at the urging of the local community, the Health Department introduced magnets at a place called Dubos Point some years ago, an area where an environmentally protected wetland abuts a small community of homes with a paved road between. Using the road as a natural border, the Department set up a line of magnets to form the requisite barrier between breeding ground and feeding ground. A second site, ringing a local ball field in Broad Channel, was also established.

Did this effort work? Community residents actually reported that it did at both locations. But no effort was ever made at the Department level to determine if this initiative was anything more than a placebo, a sop to angry residents, or if there were, perhaps, other ancillary factors that may have explained the reported reductions in mosquitoes (e.g., a one-time Parks Department clean-up of Dubos, intensified area larviciding, changes in weather patterns, etc.).

Because the magnets are costly to purchase, install and maintain (traps must be emptied weekly by staff assigned to this function and gas tanks must be refilled every twenty days), they are not suitable for use everywhere. Larger areas like the nearby Edgemere or Bayswater parks, which also suffer extensively from annual mosquito infestations, would require far more magnets than the nine the Department has dedicated in past years to Dubos or the five placed in Broad Channel. But, absent any scientific determination of the efficacy of these magnets, we cannot know if they would be a good investment for other areas.

In order to make such a determination, the Department would need to establish a baseline of mosquito activity against which to judge changes once the magnets are in place and operating. Additionally, some clear indicators would need to be established including systematic trap counts, resident complaint levels, and on-site observations. (In my former capacity with the Department, I used to make periodic impromptu visits to Dubos and other sites, myself, just to anecdotally gauge levels of activity, though it did not fall within my purview to initiate or pursue anything more systematic than this.) Finally, the Department would need to ensure a program of consistent servicing of the magnets once they are in operation since, in past years, there has been a great deal of omission of this kind of follow-up and support, e.g., gas tanks allowed to run on empty and trap bags allowed to become overfilled for weeks at a time. For some inexplicable reason, the Department has failed to do all these things, despite installing these very costly devices for the past couple of years.[22]

A systematic review of the efficacy of these magnets should now be undertaken since this might enable a real determination of cost/benefit and a decision to use more of these in more places, thereby reducing the need for potentially harmful spraying. Edgemere and Bayswater Parks could both be beneficiaries, if the magnets proved genuinely effective, as could other areas throughout the city. Certainly it makes sense to be proactive here, rather than merely reactive or haphazard, and to pay attention to the magnets when they are deployed. Otherwise they become little more than an expensive tool for quieting angry residents . . . and another obvious waste of taxpayer dollars.

PATTERNS

(June 27, 2003)

Is there a pattern forming in city governance lately? First we had a draconian smoking ban in public establishments and then enforcement of old out-of-date laws concerning how much (and what kind of) information commercial establishments could display on their street awnings. Following hard on those two heels, we've learned that the city has decided to impose and enforce curfews on community beaches. This last, at least, seems still to be under discussion. Local politicians like Councilman Addabbo have taken the issue under advisement . . . so we may yet see some change to the policy. But now comes a piece in Wednesday's New York Sun by Manhattan-based writer Julia Vitullo-Martin concerning the city's increased enforcement of old strictures on dancing in restaurants! Is there no end to it all?

It seems, as Ms. Vitullo-Martin tells us, that the City's Department of Consumer Affairs is enforcing vintage 1926 cabaret laws that may have been passed to "regulate" Harlem jazz. Citing information provided by NYU professor Paul Chevigny, author of Gigs: Jazz and the Cabaret Laws in New York City, she notes that "some local legislators viewed 'social mixing' as a growing problem as jazz moved south through the city." The resultant laws, she goes on, "restrained jazz by requiring that any restaurant with live music hold a hard-to-get cabaret license." Although a New York State Supreme Court decision ultimately struck down some of the more onerous provisions of this law involving use of live musicians in 1986, it left in place the regulation on dancing which restricts a restaurant's ability to offer this as part of its regular fare if the restaurant is not zoned correctly.

According to Ms. Vitullo-Martin, this restriction was largely unenforced in the Dinkins years, but Rudy Giuliani revived enforcement to go after "huge, noisy, drug-infested nightclubs." Although Giuliani's administration is remembered now for its restoration of peace and civic order to New York's streets, and this enforcement was certainly part of that, the city's abrupt lurch toward nannyism under Giuliani's successor, Mayor Bloomberg, which has seen increased emphasis on just these kinds of issues, has to give us pause.

Per Ms. Vitullo-Martin, the problem is really one of governmental efficiency and business-friendliness. She notes that the restaurant industry is a major economic draw for the city and that dancing is a big piece of that. Under the law, she explains, restaurants must deal with the City Planning Commission on zoning issues, the Department of Buildings re: certificates of occupancy, and Consumer Affairs for appropriate licensing. Given the need to grow the city's economy, Ms. Vitullo-Martin notes that this works against that by creating a "triple barrier to business."

Certainly this is a concern . . . but it's only the tip of what now looks to be a growing iceberg. Instead of improving things by streamlining government functions and reducing the high costs of bureaucracy, our mayor has moved in what seems to be the opposite direction: going after the very public he was elected to serve by creating or reviving new laws that can be used to squeeze added revenues from "violators".

'Enforce and collect' may have become the order of the day, replacing the call to make the hard choices involved in reinventing government. If you can't tax 'em anymore, then, by golly, summons 'em! Raise fines and issue more tickets for everything. No smoking, no leisurely walks on the beaches or boardwalks after hours and, by golly, no dancing! What kind of city are we becoming? There is a pattern forming here and it's a disturbing one, especially with an ostensibly Republican mayor in office who, presumably, believes in more accountable and businesslike government. Aren't the Democrats supposed to be the ones who call for higher taxes and more government involvement in our lives? And isn't it the Republicans who stand for smaller government and less busybody interference? I must have missed something back in '01 when I pulled the lever for a Republican mayor. Maybe there ought to be stricter enforcement of the truth in labeling laws?

ARNOLD AND MIKE

(October 17, 2003)

With the dramatic Schwarzenegger win in California, Democratic critics, who have been relentlessly pummeling President Bush as they fall all over themselves in the race to the White House, have had to take a moment to re-orient. Sure Arnold's a moderate and Gray Davis was uniquely disliked by large segments of his constituency, but the fact remains that roughly 60% of Californians who voted (and it *was* a big turnout!) put their money on a Republican. What's a Democrat to do?

Democratic Congresswoman Nancy Pelosi, Minority Leader in the House, put the usual spin on things and told us Arnold's win means only one thing: that George W. Bush better watch out! Huh? Voters sweep a leading Democratic governor resoundingly out of office, in a long time Democratic state, replacing him with a Republican, and Bush is in trouble? But wait, it gets worse. According to indefatigable Democratic presidential candidate, Howard Dean, Gray Davis was rejected by California voters because of the failure of the economy on Bush's watch. So, of course, the rejection of Davis is really a rejection of Bush, never mind that California's Democratic executive and legislative branches jointly ran up their budget by 40% during the boom years of the 90's with no thought of a rainy day! In Dean's view it's Bush who's responsible for their profligacy.

The new Republican Governor of California is going to have his hands full in this environment and with a Democratic establishment still firmly in control of the other branches of California's government. Obviously any success Arnold achieves will not be seen as a positive thing by Democratic fantasists. Arnold was voted in with a largely Republican agenda (avoid tax increases, roll back some taxes and cut waste wherever he can find it, while shrinking excessive government programs and removing anti-business legislation). Any success he attains will cause countless sleepless nights for the Democratic dreamsters and work against their playbook for the presidential election in '04. Arnold has his work cut out for him, indeed.

Like our own Mayor Bloomberg, Arnold is facing a huge budget deficit the first day he walks through the door of his new office, a deficit whose scope he cannot even be sure of at this writing. All that's known is that California's operating budget for this year could be anywhere from 8 to 20 billion dollars in the hole. But unlike Mayor Mike, Arnold is not faced with a legal requirement to balance the books. Indeed, he can run the state in the red, as Gray Davis was doing, if he has to. But, of course, that's not why he was elected and it won't do him any good if he were to fall into that mode. So what's to be done?

First, of course, he needs to nail down the size and scope of the problem (which he's already begun to do). But more important, he needs to immediately start reining it in. And he can't do this by raising taxes since that would make him no better than his predecessor who was thought to have lied to the public about the problems in Sacramento when he ran for re-election! Our own Mayor Mike raised taxes shortly after walking in the door though you can make an argument that he had no choice in the short term since New York City was under a legal obligation to operate in the black. And now Mayor Mike's talking about rolling the property tax back, if he can get the operating budget under control. He's already asked for an across-the-board 3% cut in most of his agencies' budgets so that's a start.

Arnold, too, needs to make a start. Because he *can* run a deficit in the short term, he can delay closing his state's budgetary gap for a year (though it would be unwise politically to let it go longer) and phase in some of his more painful cuts over the remaining three years of Davis' term which are now allotted to him. Mayor Mike did not have that luxury. But at a minimum,

Arnold needs to quickly develop and disseminate a plan that shows
what's to be cut and relates these items to future tax reductions so
the public will see he means business. Voters will tolerate a lot
from a politician if they believe he's leveling with them (the reverse
of what they saw in Gray Davis).

Also, while it's true Arnold gave his word to Californians that
he would not raise taxes except in the direst of emergencies, he
might want to consider creating a "rainy day fund" for his state.
Many wealthy Californians are quite liberal (think Barbara
Streisand, Martin Sheen, Lou Asner, Tim Robbins, Susan
Sarandon and Sean Penn, to name a few). They have made no secret
of their support for higher taxes. So maybe it's time they put their
money where their mouths are and demonstrate just how
committed they really are to the public weal by making voluntary
contributions to help keep California's services afloat in the short
term? In fact, this seems like a good idea to institutionalize by
creating a special account for such monies (and to which the state
could also contribute in boom times). Such funds would collect
interest when not needed but would be available to cushion
downturns, thereby avoiding some of the cyclical budgetary disasters
we are continuously witness to. Is it so unreasonable, after all, to
expect politicians not to spend every cent that flows
into government coffers as soon as they get it?

Arnold has also begun gathering experts and professionals
around him who have an interest in righting the states' finances
and improving economic conditions and these are not just the
usual suspects but a wide range of interested private citizens from
many walks of life including famous investor Warren Buffett, ex-
baseball Commissioner Peter Ueberoth, former government officials
like George Schultz and even a local sheriff from Arnold's
community. Such individuals bring commitment, interest and fresh
perspectives to the effort to fix a broken administrative machine.

Come to think of it, these are all good ideas for New York
City, too, i.e., laying out a multi-year plan that matches proposed
operational improvements with planned tax reductions so voters
can start to see what they're getting for their money, recruiting

voluntary civic-minded donors to build a special fund for special purposes, and setting up a task force of civic-minded experts to look at the problems in governmental operations with a fresh eye. Indeed, I happen to know of a few former city managers with real first-hand experience in city government who would be invaluable in rooting out and fixing the endemic structural problems that make city operations intrinsically more costly than they should be and who would be delighted to share what they know with this administration. Maybe Mayor Mike should start watching the West Coast to see how it's done?

IF ARNOLD CAN, WHY CAN'T MIKE?

(January 2, 2004)

The news out of California gets interestinger and interestinger! Newly elected Governor Arnold Schwarzenegger is making headway. After setting up a panel of outside experts to review his options, he has convinced the legislature to place proposals on the ballot, come March, designed to address the structural and budgetary problems now plaguing the Golden State. Among other things, they will seek voter authorization of a new bond issue to cover the current deficit while, at the same time, instituting a "rainy day fund" to set some state monies aside for the inevitable cyclical downturns that seem to persistently bedevil local governments and politicians. (Hmmmm, that seems like an idea I've heard somewhere else!)

Cuts to government services, of course, will be much harder but the new governor of California has declared a fiscal emergency, giving him six months of executive level discretion in the matter. It's not yet clear if he'll get the kind of spending increase caps he's also asked for, the kind already in place in nearby Arizona, but his term's not over yet. Arnold still has a lot of personal capital to draw on, reflecting his lopsided win over Gray Davis et al in the California free-for-all.

What about our own Mayor Bloomberg who has a two-year head start on Governor Schwarzenegger? He also ran on a pledge not to raise taxes, but turned around and did just that, after walking in the door in the wake of 9/11 and the national economic downturn that began in the last year of the Clinton presidency. Unlike Arnold, Mayor

Mike was legally obliged to balance his budget or lose control of the city to a state oversight board, a legacy of past city profligacy. Unable to get the cost reductions he needed to close a humongous budget gap, Mayor Bloomberg made his case to the citizenry for increased taxes. It was pretty clear to anyone who was fair-minded that the Mayor didn't have much choice, however unpalatable the tax increases.

But now, midway through the Mayor's initial term, City Comptroller William Thompson notes that things are better, for the short term at least. And, of course, the economy seems to be reviving. The Mayor has even begun talking about rolling back taxes. "We have to find ways to balance the budget and not continue to do it on the backs of the taxpayers," he said recently. Sounds good, but where's the beef? Even the City Comptroller is not sanguine, suggesting that significant structural deficits will return by 2004-2007.

Of course, there's only one way. The Mayor has to cut expenses. He has to reduce what it costs to run the city. But massive layoffs don't seem to be an option if the Mayor wants to get re-elected. At over 250,000 city workers on the payroll (not counting staff working for the city under the auspices of non-mayoral agencies like the Health and Hospitals Corporation), with most having immediate family and other relatives living within the five boroughs, there are an awful lot of voters a Mayor, up for re-election, just can't afford to annoy.

But there are other ways. The Mayor could take a leaf from Arnold's playbook and set up a non-partisan (he seems to like that word!) task force of experts, staffed by former city managers, representatives and consultants from the private sector, and even folks from local think tanks. He could then charge this group with ferreting through the dark alleyways of city business practices to identify structural inefficiencies. This is a road to real cost savings that is long overdue which does not presume massive employee layoffs.

Are there such opportunities? I recently undertook a review of certain city processes to identify waste and opportunities for savings, using relatively recent data from one city agency. With roughly a million square feet of city-owned space in this agency's real estate portfolio, it turned out that about 10% (103,294 square feet) was actually sitting unoccupied and had been unoccupied for years. At least another 38% (380,145 square feet) was seriously to significantly underutilized. At the same time, this agency was renting space from private sector landlords, sometimes at premium prices. So what's going on?

In 14 of this agency's 26 city-owned facilities, there were actually 18 non-city tenants in occupancy. What were they paying for the space they were using? In six of the facilities, seven renters were actually *paying nothing at all*, though the average annual operating cost to the city to run these facilities was reported at $12.07 per square foot.

Of those non-city tenants *who were paying something*, eight tenants paid an average of only $5.10 per square foot per annum against an average annual reported city operating cost of $12.51 a square foot. At one facility the city was only collecting about 10% of actual operating costs ($1.05 vs. costs of $10.94 a square foot). In only two sites was the city collecting anywhere near what it actually cost it to maintain and operate the facilities in question.

Three of the facilities I looked at were basically rented out in total. The agency reported no presence in them and no incurred costs for operating and maintaining them at all. The average rental returned to the city by the tenants at these facilities, however, was only $3.46 per square foot per annum. Though there were no reported operating costs, it's highly questionable that this rental amount comes anywhere near approximating real market rates in the areas where these facilities are situated. Where, after all, can you find annual square foot charges in today's New York City market that are anything like $3.46 per square foot? And what private landlord would countenance letting his space go for such an absurdly low amount?

Of course, while all this space goes wanting or brings back only a pittance to the city, compared to its true value and/or the costs to maintain it, city agencies routinely pay substantially higher rentals for office and other types of space to landlords in the private sector. The agency holding the space referred to here actually rents office and program space in over 17 locations throughout the city at an average annual rental (excluding ancillary costs) of $19.43 per square foot, well above the city's own operating costs in space this agency controls . . . and considerably higher than the amounts the city recoups in rents at these locations from its non-city tenants.

Of these 17 rented locations, I was actually able to assess six for utilization levels. In five of them (over 80%), serious underutilization was apparent, meaning more space was rented by the agency in question at these locations than it actually required.

As noted, these results only reflect the activities of a single city agency. But what if someone looked at this for *all* city agencies? Think of the potential savings if the city actually kept track of its "owned" square footage under the auspices of all its agencies throughout the five boroughs in this fashion . . . and monitored real costs to maintain and operate, just like a private landlord would. Savings could be substantial, once each agency was obliged to make better use of the space under its control and/or to share its unutilized or underutilized locations with other city agencies in the same communities.

And think of the payback to the city if currently unutilized space *was actually rented out in a manner designed to recapture costs and market values!*

The city suffers from chronic inefficiency throughout a broad array of its business practices . . . from the way it manages its property (as noted above), to its management of capital project activity (where it actually incentivizes higher costs while failing to control for overruns), to the way it handles personnel (leading to over-hiring and employee non-accountability). Indeed, the litany of inefficiencies could fill a good sized book and maybe someday someone will write it. But for now the key is for our Mayor to remember his background in the private sector and, like that other multimillionaire entrepreneur-turned-politician over on the West Coast, start addressing these issues. That's why we sometimes elect businessmen instead of career politicians, after all.

BUSINESS PRACTICES INSTEAD OF BUREAUCRACY?

(July 2, 2004)[23]

The city has recently come out of its economic tailspin along with the rest of the country (reflecting the improved conditions arising from the Bush tax cuts and other economic strategies). In recognition of its better financial condition New York Mayor Michael Bloomberg is seeking to offer residential property owners up to $400 in one-time rebates on their recently increased property taxes. And he's talking about allowing other tax increases he had previously pushed through in order to balance a painfully listing city budget to phase out as well. His new budget also contains a number of programmatic restorations, making city agencies happier than they've been in a long time.

But city taxpayers may not be happier in the long run if the mayor doesn't make serious structural changes to city operations now, given the fact that city inefficiencies contribute to the need to keep taxes high ... and to raise them every time we get the inevitable cyclical pullback. So far, the mayor has not put any real tax cuts on the table. But a city government dependent on high relative taxation remains absurdly vulnerable to reversals in the economy.

Even though he's now going into the final year of his four year term, it's not too late for Mayor Bloomberg, an experienced business hand, to apply many of the tried and true practices used in the private sector to running this city. This is not an easy thing to do because governments, unlike businesses, don't have a bottom line. They are service-oriented, not profit making, and so have no

underlying reason to pay attention to costs. Still, there's an awful
lot to be learned from the private sector and who better to teach
the city's agencies than the consummate businessman who now
serves as its mayor?

The place to start is at the agency level and the way is by
identifying structural factors responsible for increased costs. Bring
these costs down and the need for more revenue and perpetually
high taxes can at last be ameliorated. One area to look at is how
the city manages its capital expenditures. Under the Giuliani
administration the city combined the architectural and engineering
resources of most of its agencies into a single organization, the
Department of Design and Construction (DDC), and made it
responsible for brokering and managing capital activity for other
city agencies with a need for capital investment. Such city agencies
may have buildings on their portfolio which need to be maintained,
upgraded, etc., or they may be responsible for other kinds of
construction activity (such as street cutting and restoration).
These jobs are generally scoped by the city's capital agency, in
concert with the "owner" agencies, and then put out to bid. The
selected vendors are then managed by DDC for the "owners".

What's wrong with this picture? Nothing on the face of it as
there are clear benefits to be gained through economies of scale
and by centralizing the capital functions. However, there are also
drawbacks that have been allowed to become part of the system
which bear closer scrutiny. For one thing, DDC has a monopoly
on most city capital jobs and so "owner" agencies do not have a lot
of choice when they need to get their capital work accomplished.
This means there is no competition and, thus, no incentive for
DDC to provide superior service to its "customers."

More seriously, DDC secures a significant portion of its funding
based on the value of the projects it manages. Like the vendors
that bid on these projects, DDC stands to benefit financially if
the projects it manages are more costly. So the inherent bias of the
system can cause this agency to prefer larger projects to smaller
and, in certain cases, to "spec" projects at a level that may very well
exceed need.

There is also little or no incentive in this system to more tightly manage capital job vendors since DDC doesn't have a profit-driven bottom line to attend to. This can lead to huge cost overruns, on-the-job errors and omissions. At the same time, there are insufficient systems in place to track and identify cost overruns within the various "trades," to monitor milestone slippages, and to ensure adequate contractor performance. These kinds of omissions, of course, add significantly to city costs because jobs end up taking too long, exceed their budgeted funding and frequently require extensive post-completion work to remedy defects left over from the initial work.

In a number of multi-million dollar jobs throughout the five boroughs, for instance, critical air handling systems were inadequately designed or installed in the mid-nineties, leading to extensive and costly retrofitting after the fact, when the systems failed to perform to specifications. This led to costly facility shut-downs and/or extensive delays in actually opening long completed facilities, as well as unplanned additional costs to rectify the unsuccessful initial work.

Often, too, substandard materials are used by the vendors when no one is looking, leading to deficiencies that are only discovered after DDC's contractual one-year post completion warranty period has expired. When this occurs, the agency and the city must eat the costs for additional projects to rectify the past errors. In one site in Brooklyn, an alert "owner" agency site manager recently caught just such a deficiency. Discovering continued leakage into his building, after a costly roofing and re-pointing job had been completed and accepted by his agency and DDC, he raised the alarm. When DDC came back to review the situation, they decided to send samples of the mortar material for testing. The resultant report indicated the material was sub-standard. Because the warranty period hadn't yet expired, the vendor had to re-do this work.

But too many project failures like this routinely get past less-than-vigilant city personnel who are often inadequately trained or just too thinly stretched to monitor the work as it's being performed.

Once such work is completed, of course, it's often hard, and far more costly, to pinpoint the problems since they may be buried behind closed walls or ceilings.

An obvious solution to all this is to improve DDC's on-the-job monitoring capacity so that vendor shortcuts or errors like this can be caught before they are sealed behind new walls and ceilings . . . not after. (Since DDC was formed by taking substantial technical resources from many "owner" agencies, it's DDC's job to perform this critical on-the-job monitoring function, given that its "customers" have long since ceased to be equipped for this role.) At the same time, it would be wise to contractually extend post-completion warranty periods and enhance DDC's own post-completion monitoring efforts. Routine sampling and testing of materials used, during the course of projects, would also appear to be in order.

Of course, deficiencies in the capital process are not limited to vendor oversight problems alone. The project funding process that the city relies on is, itself, often highly politicized and dependent on extensive negotiations between "owner" agencies, DDC and the city's Office of Management and Budget. Since no project can be initiated without sufficient funds in place, jobs often languish for years as city officials engage in an intricate minuet regarding need and available funding. The resultant prolonged delays and uncertainties adversely affect the ability to plan and "spec" the jobs going into each project. Failure to plan adequately, of course, also leads to extensive mid-project adjustments, which further adds significantly to costs.

The upshot here is that the city's capital jobs generally cost two or three times what they run in the private sector and take considerably longer than comparable private work to be initiated and completed. But why should the city, which is a major employer and purchaser of capital construction services, not benefit from the immense buying power it commands? To realize such benefits the city needs to take a look at the current structure and strategies it relies on for getting capital work done. A complete review of the capital function should be undertaken and current deficiencies and disincentives for optimal performance identified and wrung out of the system.

At the least, it certainly makes no sense to reward an agency for higher costs as the current system does. In a nation that values competition and the benefits of the marketplace, there is no good reason for New York City to suffer from a lack of competition and marketplace efficiencies in the way it does its business.

WHITHER
ROCKAWAY?

BULL MARKET IN ROCKAWAY?

(December 7, 1993)

What do gold bullion and the Rockaways have in common? Answer: Both have recently experienced extended, multi-year bear markets. But while gold apparently ended its 13 year downturn in late 1992, Rockaway may only be bottoming now, after more than two decades of deterioration, with the upset victory of Republican Al Stabile in the recent race for the local City Council seat.

Just as gold was a terrible investment for most of the eighties, our peninsula has been a dismal bust for businesses and residents alike, with business districts shrinking and becoming progressively shabbier, while the quality of life in most of our communities has steadily declined.

Not long ago, my wife and I took a trip to Cape Cod. I went along under duress, arguing that we already lived in a beachfront community, so Massachusetts couldn't possibly offer us anything we didn't already have right here. After a whirlwind tour of Martha's Vineyard (we just missed the Clintons), Provincetown and other points of interest, we came back home, only to be greeted by the dreary Rockaway "skyline," slung low along the horizon. In place of the lush, unspoiled greenery of the New England coast, with its quaint fishing villages and picturesque artists' colonies, we saw vacant, overgrown lots, ramshackle buildings that could have been left over from the Industrial Revolution, and massive, rust-streaked concrete pillars carrying the elevated train from one end of our community to another. I didn't remember Rockaway ever being as scenic as the Massachusetts resort area we had just returned from, but I had to admit it hadn't always been this rundown, either.

And when you're talking about a community, that's the equivalent of a bear market—a time when nearly every investment, whether for a home or a business, tends to go sour. When stores shut down and streets grow shabby and people stop feeling safe in their own neighborhoods. Houses may go up in value along with the wider real estate market (and tank when that market tanks), but overall you know you're in a bear market when you look around and see more and more vacant lots, commercial stagnation, and the loss of those qualities that once made your community special. Once we had an amusement park and a vibrant honky-tonk night life on our boardwalks which, while admittedly a trifle crass and commercial, at least were part of Rockaway's own special character. And we had beaches that people came from miles around to use.

Today our peninsula lies prostrate and abandoned, from that grim relic of a business district we once called "town" in Far Rockaway, through the scarred landscape that follows the train tracks west to B. 116th Street where a few stubborn merchants boldly make their stand against an encroaching urban blight that has already swallowed nearly half the street,

But now there's a whiff of change in the air blowing in from the sea. People, who for decades have chosen to remain isolated in their own little communities, who have opposed any sort of development as inimical to their interests as residents of this out-of-the-way pocket of New York City, have suddenly looked up and asked "what's become of our community?" Even the residents of some of our tonier neighborhoods seem to have paused for a moment to watch the red tide of neglect, as it laps against their bulkheads in their own little enclaves, bringing, in its wake, that deterioration which already has B. 116th Street in its jaws.

In a move that surprised many of us, residents of Rockaway's west end recently voted out the old guard this election year, and the supporters of the status quo, in favor of a candidate who is an unabashed advocate of development. The incoming City Councilman, Al Stabile, is a businessman who sees the possibilities in Rockaway and wants to help us realize them. He looks at our peninsula and sees Martha's Vineyard. He sees restaurants and hotels and brightly colored buildings. He's even spoken of getting our rundown train trestle painted in bright pastels a la Florida. Where Rockaway residents used to run from one another, into their own little communities, there is now a dawning recognition that we're all in this boat together and that keeping vast parts of the peninsula underdeveloped may not serve anyone's interest. The lack of jobs reinforces local poverty which leads to more neighborhood deterioration and increased street crime. Thus Rockawayites voted for change, this time around, and invited in a man who wants to make the peninsula we call home a metropolitan oasis.

Stabile promises us development and many now believe it's long overdue. And that's the sea change which signals an end to our own, long-running bear market. How do you play it? Well, if you're a resident out here, you enjoy it. But there's no reason to let outsiders reap all the benefits. When bear markets end, bull markets generally follow. So local people ought to participate by buying property (with commercial potential, primarily) and opening businesses. That's where the impact is going to be felt, with residential properties going along for the ride. If you don't have big money to invest, and many of us don't, then maybe it wouldn't hurt to form Rockaway investment pools, where a lot of little guys can join forces to invest in a number of local ventures. There's still room on the ground floor, but the bull market elevator is notorious for leaving the crowd behind.

Historical Note (August 6, 2004): As it happens, I was a bit early on this one and the new Councilman, after an energetic start, settled into a more prosaic pace. Aside from a revitalization of B. 116th Street, which he did push, none of his other economic initiatives came to fruition. However, in time the city's long term Arverne renewal project (to build new, affordable homes on abandoned properties in central Rockaway in the old Arverne area), along with the surging national real estate market of the late nineties (reflecting boom times and historically low interest rates), boosted the price of Rockaway property (residential in particular) into the stratosphere. In fact, the peninsula is now set to get an influx of new residents in its restored central areas, even as property values in key national markets appear to be peaking. Recent activity on B. 116th Street suggests some new development in the offing, as well. Meanwhile, the gold market, which had prompted my musings in this article in the first place, actually tanked and went lower after I wrote the piece and after gold's brief, dramatic up-tick back in 1992. Indeed, gold did not raise its head in any significant way again until around 2002. So, on balance, gold proved to be a lousy investment for the decade . . . even though it's turned out otherwise with Rockaway. Well, I never claimed to be a particularly astute prognosticator of markets.

GOING IT ALONE?

(December 14, 2002)

All this talk of tax increases, service cuts and a city government that is inefficient in extremis, suggests that we need to start thinking out of the proverbial box if we're going to improve our situation in Rockaway. And what could be more "out of the box" than the idea proposed in the past by John Baxter, Rockaway's local curmudgeon par excellence and leader of its Independence Party, that we ought to just secede from New York City and start over?

It seems that John stumbled on some rather interesting information about a year or so back: in 1915, Rockaway was actually designated as an independent municipality by the State Legislature. Although the actual steps involved in creating the new city were never taken, the law setting all this up seems never to have been formally rescinded. An opportunity here?

Given the current hullabaloo about budget deficits for New York City and the mayor's emphasis on addressing this by raising property taxes (a big deal out here in Rockaway where there is a growing body of homeowners), what better way to send a message to City Hall than to demonstrate that we are seriously looking at other options? Who says, after all, that Rockaway can only achieve economic and political viability as part of a larger city, one that not only has a history of ignoring us but can't even seem to keep its own house in order?

There are implications in exploring this route, of course. Most notably the fact that an independent Rockaway would have to take over paying for and running all those services we currently get from City Hall. Could we fund our own local services on the thin tax base represented by the folks living out here alone? Well, that depends on whether we're getting more back now from City Hall, or less, relative to what we pay in. Given the low level of services we often see out here and the general inattention to Rockaway's needs, it's probably a good bet that we get less back than we actually pay for with our taxes . . . and this is before the planned property tax (and other) increases!

Of course, funding our own municipal services could actually be more costly since we'd have to replicate an administrative structure now covered by the existing citywide one. But some folks might argue that the citywide structure is so bloated we'd actually save money by funding our own, scale-appropriate administration right here on the peninsula. These things would all have to be looked at as part of a feasibility review.

Still another issue would be affiliation. A township has to be part of a county. We're now part of Queens County, which is wholly enrolled in New York City's municipal structure. But if we left New York City, we'd no longer be able to remain part of Queens. Since we're probably too small to be our own county, the only other alternative would be alignment with nearby Nassau. Now that's a radical thought. We'd be Long Islanders rather than New Yorkers. Of course, Nassau has one of the highest tax rates in the country so this doesn't sound all that tempting, especially given their property taxes. On the other hand, Nassau is famous for the higher level of services it provides its residents while New York's tax rates look like they're on the upswing anyway.

Moreover, there's room for creativity here. If this were to be viable, a City of Rockaway would have to be attractive to its citizenry, the future taxpayers of the new municipality, so taxes would either have to be lower than we now pay to New York City or, at the least, the ratio of return to pay-out would need to be significantly better. We'd need our own Departments of Sanitation, Parks, Health, Schools, etc. And all of this costs money. But this might also give us an opportunity to experiment with better models than the top heavy, labor intensive New York City approach we now suffer from. We could do this by contracting out to local businesses or nearby townships for many basic municipal services.

Perhaps we could even let New York City, itself, bid against the others for our business.

But how you do all this without unduly dunning your tax base is critical. Fortunately, Rockaway does have one thing most other parts of New York City lack: its beach, a highly underutilized resource though it was not always so. As many never tire of pointing out, at the turn of the century Rockaway was, in fact, a classy resort. Now one of the things that distinguishes resort areas is that they usually have a real recreation orientation. Besides beaches and nice weather, for instance, Florida has its bevy of theme parks (begun with Disney World many years ago). Places like Cape Cod in Massachusetts not only have beaches but pristine scenic vistas and historic sites around which attractive tourist areas have been created. In Rockaway we have lots of overgrown vacant lots and rundown stores and housing projects, but not much else worth looking at.

But what if we also had a theme park and if that park had a real historic aspect to it? Does Rockaway have a history? I submit that we do: the turn of the century beach culture that was Rockaway in its heyday . . . a time when Coney Island was king and Rockaway was the exclusive preserve of the classier elements of society. So why not build a theme park around a restoration of that ambience, the turn of the century beach world that was Rockaway? Within that, we could also have various sub-themes including a restoration of a mid-eighteenth century "old town", a "Rekouwacky" Indian village,[24] and a pirate's cove (since it's rumored that Captain Kidd himself often used our beaches as a landing base and may have even hid some of his treasure here). We may not have whaling ships and a sea-going culture, like Cape Cod and Martha's Vineyard, or an arts colony like Provincetown, but we have our own little history, waiting to be developed.

How does this contribute toward a City of Rockaway? Simple. It helps make us financially independent. We could look at restoring Rockaway's dream of township by combining it with a plan to build a visitor's center and theme park, somewhere on the peninsula, to be financed through joint government-private development. But, and here's the key, the government would be a Rockaway-only government. Financially, it could be structured in three parts: one third for a small group of high-rolling private investors, one third for any Rockaway residents willing to buy shares, and one third set aside for Rockaway's new municipality, in trust for all its citizens. The two thirds of privately held shares could eventually be traded on one of the stock exchanges, enabling value to be recognized in the marketplace, while one third of all profits would always accrue to the municipality to fund services on the peninsula.

There would still be a need for a tax base, but it would hopefully be less onerous than might otherwise be the case. And we'd gain a free hand with our own resources, to develop and use them as we see fit. The resulting boom, which would occur because of Rockaway's restoration, would increase the value of shares in the enterprise while fueling overall improvement on the peninsula.

This wouldn't solve all the problems, of course, but it gives us a chance to make our own decisions and stop living off the "largess" of a distant and often distracted City Hall. At the least, a serious effort to look at this option can't help but send a message to the current political powers-that-be and might even get them to re-examine what they have to offer us . . . and, perhaps, try a little harder! It's worth a serious look and I, for one, think a Mayor John Baxter might not be the worst thing that could happen to this community. On the other hand, I'm betting he'd have plenty of competition.

A TRESTLE'S TALE

(January 11, 2003)

Has anyone looked closely at the elevated trestle that runs down Rockaway's spine lately? Recently driving along Rockaway Beach Boulevard, I happened to look up at what usually just fades into a kind of featureless background for me . . . when I'm busy focusing on other things, that is. What I saw caused me to do a kind of double take and, later, to drive along beneath the trestle a couple more times just to take a series of closer looks.

The long steel and concrete elevated tracks that unite the east and west ends of our peninsula, and join both to mainland Queens and the rest of the city, are in a state of fairly advanced deterioration at many locations. I noted exposed steel girders all along the track line, where the concrete had delaminated, as well as plenty of spalling and weather induced efflorescence and exposed, corroded rebar where large pieces of concrete have come away in chunks. This is not only an eyesore, it's an outright hazard to drivers, pedestrians and, eventually, to the passengers on the trains which make their way along these tracks.

According to Vincent Seyfried and William Asadorian, authors of OLD ROCKAWAY, NEW YORK IN EARLY PHOTOGRAPHS, the railway "viaduct" that is today used by the Far Rockaway and Rockaway Park subway lines was completed around 1942 and was intended to increase safety for pedestrians and vehicular traffic by eliminating dangerous grade crossings like those we still see in nearby parts of Long Island. No longer having to wait for trains to pass by, or worry about switches and signals, the traveling public in Rockaway benefited enormously by the conversion of ground level tracks to the current elevated trestle.

But 1942 was a long time ago and, except for the apparent removal of obviously loose and dangerously delaminated concrete (evidenced by large areas where the concrete has been systematically stripped away to expose the steel girders underneath), there is not much indication that upkeep has been ongoing since the forties. Back in the early nineties, when Al Stabile was first running for City Councilman from our area (ages ago it now seems), one of his platforms was to upgrade and paint the trestle a lively pastel color in keeping with our beachfront ambience. Similar things had been done in Howard Beach where Stabile hailed from. But, despite his two terms as our Councilman, this seems to have been an idea whose time never came.

Today, we'd be grateful, I suppose, just to get the upkeep part. But Stabile aside, where has the city itself been and what is the MTA planning to do to address the obviously extensive deterioration that is eroding the old elevated structure that serves as the very backbone of the peninsula? During the nearly seven years I spent as Assistant Commissioner for Operations at the New York City Department of Health, I shut down facilities and cordoned off areas for far less cause than the problems that are now manifesting along the length of these elevated tracks. It always seemed better to me to act preemptively than to wait until a chunk of concrete fell on someone's head. But hey, that's just me.

Now it's certainly clear that the city is at least aware of the problem or there would not be so many areas that have been sculled clean of loose and deteriorating concrete, as I saw when I did a closer inspection. But there are still plenty of areas where the situation does not appear to have been addressed at all and where weather-eroded material continues to pose an imminent hazard to those underneath. One gets the sense that the city is not being sufficiently systematic, comprehensive or proactive here in finding and addressing areas of concern. At the least, they are not keeping pace with the extent of the deterioration that is occurring.

More, while it is important, on a short-term basis, to strip away all loosened materials before they fall onto those below, it is just as critical to develop and implement a capital restoration project as soon as possible in order to arrest further deterioration and return the trestle to acceptable condition. Given the city's current budget crisis (even capital projects are being cut back) and the long and complex city capital initiation process, we may be sure that if this is not already underway, we will not be looking at any substantial remediation of this problem for the next five years . . . at the earliest.

City capital jobs, of course, are not only lengthy to initiate, they are generally a good deal more costly than their private sector equivalents (because the city bureaucracy kicks up the costs of doing business, all the way around, while adversely affecting market competition). But even current costs may pale by comparison to what this could cost us in the future. The longer this is delayed, the more costly it will get. Left long enough, the only solution will be to tear large sections of the trestle down and rebuild (as happened with the city's old West Side Highway which was allowed to deteriorate until it began to fall, literally in pieces, onto the road below).

But surely, this would be an unconscionable situation in today's world here in Rockaway, given that we pay what seem to be ever increasing taxes annually, expecting, in exchange, that our local needs will be handled expeditiously and effectively. All of this, of course, is a result of our having ceded the right of home rule to so-called Greater New York City back in 1898, along with other non-Manhattan locations. But what have we gotten in return: a city government that is too big and too cumbersome to pay close attention to the needs of this area or, when they do this, to do it with a reasonable level of efficiency?

How great, in the end, can that arrangement that made us a cog in the wheel of "Greater New York" really have been if Rockawayites must today watch their community and its critical infrastructure fall apart around them each year, worrying all the while about the day they'll have to start dodging falling debris from a trestle that was once the pride of this peninsula? It's time for city officials to open their eyes and take another look at what they've wrought . . . before communities like ours and others in the outer boroughs do it for them.

ROCKAWAY CITY REDUX

(January 18, 2003)

Since I wrote in this column about the Rockaway City initiative being spearheaded by John Baxter and the Independence Party some time back, there appears to have actually been some movement on this front. For those who missed it, John found an old bit of state legislation from the period between 1915 and 1917 when reformist John Purroy Mitchel, the anti-Tammany Hall candidate who briefly won a single term as New York City Mayor, was in office. (Mitchel Field on Long Island is named after this guy who was known, in his time, as the Boy Mayor of New York because of his youth and brashness; he died in a World War I airplane accident during a training exercise after he lost his bid for re-election to his Tammany Hall opponent.)

As John Baxter tells it, Mayor Mitchel was engaged in a pitched battle with the Tammany bosses over his reformist agenda and Rockaway was one of the plums. This all took place beginning in 1914 when Mitchel entered office and about sixteen years after the consolidation of the various outlying townships and villages, with Manhattan and Brooklyn, into the city of Greater New York. It seems that many of the residents of the Rockaways at that time felt they had been railroaded into the merger with New York City and wanted out. Mitchel's accession to the mayoralty seems to have coincided with the movement to separate Rockaway from the city that had swallowed it.

According to a Resolution adopted by the Civic Federation of the Rockaways around 1914, Rockaway was then paying close to a million dollars in annual taxes to City Hall . . . but only getting back about 75% of that in actual services. Despite this apparent under-spending on Rockaway (or was it over-taxing?), the Civic Federation found that an equivalent, stand-alone community could do better for itself on its own. When the Federation compared what was being purchased for Rockaway to what the town of Utica in upstate New York spent for services (then of roughly comparable size in population and square miles), they concluded that Rockaway was not getting as much for its dollars as Utica was. The Civic Federation went on to report a litany of deficiencies in services to Rockaway, including inadequate infrastructure (roads, water, sewage, lighting, parks and boardwalks), poor street sanitation and refuse disposal, and difficult-to-obtain permits for building and other things requiring permits.

The feeling that Rockaway was being short-changed like this resulted in a movement to break the area off from Greater New York and establish it as a separate municipality dedicated to the development of its beachfront for recreational purposes. The Rockaway town fathers felt inadequately represented and serviced by the City of New York and believed that Rockaway could do better managing its own affairs, using every dollar it generated as it saw fit, rather than remitting these funds to a distant and apparently disinterested City Hall.

They took this pretty far it seems, as the bills to separate Rockaway into a freestanding municipality passed the State Assembly and the State Senate in 1915 and again in 1917 (after apparently being initially rejected by Mayor Mitchel in 1915). A "home rule" provision seems to have given New York City's mayor "veto" power over state legislation affecting the city though the legislature was certainly empowered to establish separate municipalities elsewhere in the state.

Interestingly, John notes that his research so far has been unable to turn up a definitive record that Mayor Mitchel actually exercised his power to outright reject the legislation. There is indication that Mitchel returned the 1915 bills to the state legislature as "not approved" but as late as April 6, 1917 they were still alive and kicking since John found a letter from Thomas A. McWhinney, who appears to have been the bill's sponsor in the Assembly, to

Mayor Mitchel, seeking his agreement to certain alterations in the "financial provision" in order to get him to accept the legislation. There is no record, so far, of Mitchel's response, but it does appear that he was out of town for part of this period. More, this was the final year of his mayoralty and he was in a tough and ultimately losing battle for a second term.

Although continuing to hunt for indication that the mayor did or did not definitively reject the bills, John thinks, with the tough campaign that was then underway, there is a real chance Mitchel just let the matter lie, in order to avoid alienating Rockaway's voters while effecting what was, in essence, a kind of "pocket veto". After Mitchel was succeeded by Mayor James J. Hylan, the Tammany candidate who unseated him, the Rockaway secession movement seems to fade from the history books. What happened?

It looks like the residents of Rockaway were convinced by the electoral outcome that things would get better under the new administration. But John notes that if Mitchel never formally rejected the bill in its final incarnation, it may still be on the books. That means that Rockaway may officially still have a stand-alone city charter. John let me have a look at the charter itself and it's quite interesting. It lays out a proposed city government for Rockaway along with various parameters for governing including a 2% ceiling on real estate taxes! The question, of course, is would such a stand-alone municipality be feasible in today's Rockaway?

We have been integrated in Greater New York for over a century now and probably wouldn't know how to govern ourselves anymore if we tried. Or would we? Could a self-governing Rockaway City actually be formed today and could it operate effectively enough to improve conditions out here on the relatively thin tax base we have? Well, one thing's for sure, we have certainly had no real development of our beachfront (our one real resource) in the past century. Developing that alone could have a very significant impact on the new city's tax base. But, under the present structure we continue to be forgotten. As John notes, we are barely included in the city's plans for Olympic development though, he points out, those plans call for development of beach volleyball facilities in Williamsburg, Brooklyn, of all places, while seeming to take no notice of Rockaway's longstanding undeveloped beachfront!

John wants to know if we're getting our fair share today, in light of all the deterioration we see around us and the slowness of the city's responses to our needs. He notes that while specifics may have changed over the past hundred years, Rockaway's grievances against City Hall today haven't really altered all that much since the Civic Federation drafted its resolution calling for secession from a city they never wanted to join back in 1914.

John indicates he is continuing his research and is setting up an ad hoc committee to review Rockaway's options in light of the city charter the state granted it back in 1915 and again in 1917. He's invited me to sit in and I've agreed. There are some very interesting possibilities here and we owe it to ourselves to see where they lead.

SECEDING TO CUT COSTS?

(May 30, 2003)

Bad news folks: John Baxter, Rockaway's Independence Party leader, reports that his operatives have now confirmed that the Rockaway City charter, passed in 1915 and again in 1917 by the State legislature in Albany, which broke the peninsula off from New York City as a separate municipality, was definitively rejected by then-mayor John Purroy Mitchel. Under the state constitution's "home rule" provision, the legislature cannot implement laws affecting the internal prerogatives of a legally constituted local municipality without that municipality's agreement. Since Rockaway was then (as it still is) a sub-division of New York City, local government agreement was required before the charter could take effect. In 1917 this appears to have meant mayoral acquiescence. Apparently Mayor Mitchel did not acquiesce, in spite of a majority of Rockawayites being in favor of this in those days, and so the charter is now a moot issue.

Why is this important to us today? Given our current Mayor Bloomberg's penchant for tax increases, combined with his inability to seriously restructure city government and rein in spending (think of new spending for things like an anti-smoking program, the ongoing waste in various city agencies involving things like cooping on the job and overtime abuse, top-heavy management, continued demand for the perqs of power, etc.), it is clear that having an existing city charter to enable a quick getaway for Rockaway would have been a godsend. But even if we never implemented it, the mere threat that we might would have sent a strong message to a City Hall that has spent more than a century pretending we don't exist.

Of course, setting up a stand-alone municipality would have been a challenge with the usual attendant risks. But nothing comes free as we all know. On the other hand, it would have given us a real chance to explore whether or not there is a better way to run our own town, one that would create a model for other localities as well. More, an economically viable model for a Rockaway City would certainly have sent a strong message to our Manhattan-based leaders that there *is another way to run things*, that it doesn't always have to be about top-heavy bureaucracies and red tape and the added costs and problems you get with over-centralization of power.

Indeed, a recent Wall Street Journal article, entitled Save Our City and signed by a high-powered team (Hugh Carey, Richard Gilder, H. Dale Hemmerdinger, Roger Hertog, Felix G. Rohatyn and Walter B. Wriston) on May 9, 2003, took Mayor Bloomberg to task for missing a whole slew of cost reduction opportunities while pushing tax rates up nearly everywhere, making New York a less hospitable town for its residents and businesspeople. In the same edition of the paper, an editorial compared Mayor Mike to the infamous John V. Lindsay whose tax and spend ways pushed New York City to the brink of ruin back in the 70's.

According to the Save Our City authors, our city currently "spends more money, and employs more public workers per capita than most American cities" but is "proceeding as if the private economy existed solely to preserve as many government jobs as possible . . . Bolstered by projected revenues from the new tax increases, the city is only seeking minimal job cuts, amounting to less than 2% of what is the largest municipal workforce in America." Failing to win "any significant concessions from its unions," the writers note, the city is focused, instead, on increasing revenue by ramping up taxes despite the long history of adverse consequences such policies have on overall economic conditions. Do we want a re-play of the Lindsay years? That, says the Wall Street Journal editorial writer, is where we're headed.

What has any of this to do with the hypothetical secession of Rockaway? According to Messrs. Carey et al, the Mayor has "rejected, or simply not explored, a host of potential cost savings advocated by budget watchdogs, such as private contracting of services, from filling potholes to providing school lunches. Privatizing trash services alone could save the city $50 million a year. Requiring city employees to work a 40 hour week (not just 35 hours) could eliminate 8,500 jobs and save $500 million a year . . ." The writers point out that despite all of these opportunities, "Mr. Bloomberg has taken no significant structural steps to eliminate the deficit."

An independent Rockaway City would, of course, have had to "stand on its own two feet" and so, to do that, the Secession Exploratory Committee headed by John Baxter was looking into all these options (and more) to find a more efficient way to operate. The committee was initiating a study that would have determined the value of the current Rockaway real estate tax base, as well as other revenue sources for a free-standing municipality out here, in order to compare these with the actual costs New York City incurs annually to operate and maintain services in our community. The plan was to identify what the city currently expends for us (including all direct manpower and assets in Rockaway as well as the costs for indirect services and administration) and then to determine if we couldn't just do it more cheaply by private contracting and/or maintaining a radically leaner administrative structure.

Despite the common idea that you get economies of scale by centralizing, there is very good prima facie evidence that the opposite may occur. A study by a Rockaway group in 1914 found that Rockaway got back only 75 cents for every dollar in taxes it paid to New York City and that a comparable upstate municipality (approximately the same size as Rockaway in land area and population) actually obtained significantly more for every dollar it spent than New York City obtained for Rockaway. Combined with a recent study reported in The New York Sun showing how New York State, itself, currently gives back less to New York City overall than it takes away in state taxes, one has to conclude that there is a definite cost to centralizing in some cases, a cost arising from top heavy administration and waste (due to the reduced accountability that comes along with such heavy centralization).

The Secession Feasibility Study that John Baxter's group was pursuing would have gotten directly at this by determining what exactly New York City really pays to "keep" us, what it should reasonably cost (without all the waste and excess built into the current bureaucracy) and whether we could actually do better as a stand-alone concern. Even if such a study did not finally lead to secession, it surely would have demonstrated that we are being taxed at an excessive and wasteful level relative to what is actually needed to run our community.

Seeing this in black and white would have been good for all of New York City's communities, not just Rockaway, because it would have served as a wake-up call to our putative leaders, showing them a better path and putting them on notice that they must either find ways to run government more economically and within taxpayers' means . . . or make way for new political realities. After all, who says that just because New York City has existed as a huge municipal white elephant since 1898, it must continue to do so? Who says there's no better way to hold officials accountable for how they spend our money than via a huge, insulated and centralized city administration? Or that there aren't plenty of perfectly rational alternatives for voters facing ever-increasing government inefficiencies, exploding taxes and another downward economic spiral in the city they call home?

SCENIC ROCKAWAY

(July 4, 2003)

Some years back my wife insisted we take a vacation, something I was averse to doing, being too tied up, then, in the responsibilities of my job. Where did she want to go I asked her? Cape Cod, as it turned out. My objections were numerous. I said why should we go to a beach community when we already live in one? But that didn't cut any ice with her and off we went. Afterwards, I had to admit she'd had a point. The general Cape Cod area, and each of the beach communities within it, was beautiful. It was all so clean, quaint, well kept up, etc. Scenic too. You had to love those beautiful vistas of seemingly endless, untouched coastal wilderness . . . along with all the yachts and sailing vessels plying the local waters, the lovely shoppes, the restaurants, etc. The traffic was a bit congested, true, but on balance she'd made her point.

After that, we went back a number of times, visiting Martha's Vineyard, Nantucket, and Block Island, as well as sojourning in Montauk and the Hamptons on Long Island's east end in other years. All beach communities, of course . . . the kind that were fun to visit.

Why do I bring this up now? A week ago I got a call from a reporter at Newsday doing a story on the new ferry service which will be transporting beachgoers from Manhattan to our shores this summer. The reporter wanted to know what there was to see out here? She noted that the Park Service planned to provide a free shuttle bus to ferry-users (it should be free since the ferry's charging $26 per adult, round trip!), to take them on a tour of the "sights". What did we have that was worth seeing, the reporter asked?

Well, I told her about Ft. Tilden with its abandoned gun batteries, now made available to visitors as observation posts (you get a nice view on a clear day from them, too). And I mentioned the nascent art gallery installed on the old fort grounds. And the wildlife Preserve which is really the old fort's "target and maneuvers" area which has been encouraged to go back to its wild state. There you can find a number of nature trails to share with the local flora and fauna, including opossums, raccoons and rabbits. (Not to mention ticks and mosquitoes . . . we city folk just have to learn to live with wildlife all over again . . . just last fall, in fact, a stray raccoon wandered into our backyard while we were having a cool evening meal; our cat, being less tolerant than we, chased it off.)

And then there's the beautiful view of New York Harbor one can get from Breezy Point . . . though tourists are not encouraged to go touring there! Of course, there's also our own answer to Jones' Beach: Jacob Riis Park where sweaty and overheated city-dwellers can find a broad public beachfront with a boardwalk, ball fields, and large picnic grounds as well as showers and changing facilities.

I told the reporter all about these and, while doing so, I found myself thinking again of other beachfront communities up and down the coast. In fact, I couldn't help wondering what made them so different from our town and why I preferred to go off to any of these with my wife, despite having a nice little beach only blocks away from my home. Of course, the answer is precisely what the Newsday reporter was asking me about. What did we have here?

I had to admit that, aside from the rather mundane amenities of Riis Park and the overgrown scrub lands of the old fort, we don't have a lot to offer. Besides a few prosperous pocket communities, a drive down the length of our peninsula only offers the visitor vista upon vista of vacant and weedy lots, a crumbling elevated train trestle, deteriorating houses . . . and not a great deal more. Why is this beachfront community different from others? The answer's not hard to discern when you think about it. No one seems to be looking after this area with any kind of proprietary interest. Our roads are broken up and shabby-looking, for the most part, while in Cape Cod or Montauk you'd never see anything like that. In those places the local governments take a special pride in the appearance of their towns. And it shows.

So who is taking pride in Rockaway? City Hall is a long way off and seems to have very little interest in us except insofar as we have some empty land that can be rolled into new housing. But what we really need out here is an economic revival. How do you get that? Well, you have to take advantage of what you have . . . like beaches! But are beaches enough? We've had beaches for years and where has that gotten us since 1898, when Rockaway lost its independence in order to be rolled up, along with other outlying communities, into so-called Greater New York. As a result of that event, we find ourselves, today, an outlying province of a distant government whose interests seem to lie elsewhere. Who's looking out for us today? Who's trying to develop this area and ensure that it's restored to the scenic peninsula it once was? Should we really be depending on a group of politicians in faraway Manhattan who haven't exactly distinguished themselves in this regard over the course of the last century? In fact, isn't it New York City's various governments, over the years, that have let this area go to seed? So I keep coming back to that reporter's question: "What do you have out there and why would people want to pay $26 to take a ferry ride to Rockaway?" What can they see? Well, I told her all about the raccoons and the opossums and the old gunnery batteries and, of course, our public beaches. And then I got my wife on the phone and asked where she wanted to go this year for our summer vacation.

ODD AND ENDS

IT'S THE STATS, STUPID

(July 26th, 1994)

Statistics are a wonderful way to make a point. They lend credibility and a measure of authority to any argument and enhance the prestige of the arguer, making the person presenting them seem marvelously erudite. Unfortunately they can also be misleading . . . or downright wrong.

Two cases come to mind from the recent July 15th issue of this newspaper. In one, a fellow columnist here led off her piece on the O.J. Simpson murder trial by asserting that: "One out of every four women in a relationship is a battered woman." That's 25%, a startlingly high figure, but, our columnist tells us, it's a "fact."

Where did this "fact" come from? Well, she doesn't tell us that. But she goes on to use this, and a couple of other "facts" to launch into a fanciful scenario on what Nicole Simpson's life with O.J. must have been like, culminating with a brief, apocryphal tale about how the male police officers, responding to Mrs. Simpson's calls for help on previous occasions no doubt identified with her "sports hero" husband and may even have been involved in a little spousal abuse of their own and so chose to look the other way. All speculation, of course, but a 25% abuse rate certainly implies that some police officers, perhaps quite a number of them, must be doing it too.

The only problem with this is who says the 25% rate is true? My colleague doesn't cite any sources for this figure, she just seems to take it for granted. I consulted with my own life-partner (who, to my knowledge, has never alleged or contemplated alleging, or even considered herself to be a victim of, spousal abuse), and she tells me she's seen this statistic elsewhere, too. So if it's out there and people are quoting it, it must be true, right?

Wrong. Even if some study was done somewhere and numbers were generated purporting to show this 25% rate, we still have to examine it logically. If one of every four women in a relationship is, indeed, the victim of battering from abusive partners, it suggests that most of us should know some women who have experienced this. Yet, my wife and I both considered all the married women we knew, and those with boyfriends, and had to admit we couldn't think of any who fit this category. We do know some women who have had some pretty aggressive fights with their mates (generally giving as good as they got), but we could not think of any who had been beaten, knocked around, bruised, cowed into submission, etc. Well, maybe it's how you define abuse? If the wife shouts and raises her hand in anger, that's just vigorous advocacy . . . she's only a woman, after all. But if the husband does this . . . it's abuse? On such a view, a vigorous battle between mates might count as spousal abuse of the female, even if she gets the better of the encounter.

But my colleague in this newspaper implies another answer to this conundrum. In her article she says that Nicole Simpson must have been a victim of far more extensive abuse than she actually reported, giving us a speculative picture of a life lived in terror of her celebrity husband from the earliest days of their marriage. Although we cannot really know what went on in those days, my colleague assures us that Nicole, like many women, was probably just "afraid to tell." Perhaps, of course, this is true, though we have no way of knowing at this time whether the abuse that resulted in Mrs. Simpson's death was truly part of a lifelong pattern characterizing her marriage to O.J. Simpson or if it was simply a sudden eruption of rage that may have occurred at one specific moment in time and ended her life.

But perhaps, if my colleague's supposition is correct, the 25% abuse rate she cites is believable and the friends and acquaintances my wife and I have in common just aren't telling us? Possible, but highly unlikely, since we could not recall seeing any evidence of abuse: no bruises, no broken bones, no haunted glances, no cryptic allusions even to the possibility that this sort of thing might be happening to the women we know. Besides, the supposition that many women just aren't telling has to make you wonder how, in this case, the statistics gatherers could have found out about it in order to include it in their results?

A final possibility: my wife and I may be in a sub-group of people where spousal abuse is far less frequent. But then, to get your overall 25% rate, abuse must be far more common in other groups, maybe up to 50% and higher in some. While not denying this possibility, I would suggest that it's highly unlikely real abuse (beatings with bruises, bloody noses, broken bones, etc.) is *that* common. Just look at your own experience as my wife and I looked at ours.

Now none of this is to suggest that abuse of this sort does not exist at all or that it's not more common than it should be. But we have to hold the hysteria in check. It's very alarming to cite a statistic that says one out of every four women in a relationship in this country is the victim of abuse by a partner. Without anything solid to back it up, you have to wonder if making a claim like this is any less problematic than crying fire in a crowded theater when there isn't anything ablaze.

And what was the other example of spurious statistics I had in mind? In the same issue of this paper, another individual wrote in about the evils of bringing casino gambling to the Rockaways. He attacked the "real estate shysters," "the mob," and "our elected officials" who, he says, "have sat on their fat prats (sic) while Rockaway goes to pot." He did not argue his case so much as hurl assertions, laced with invectives. At one point, in support of his angry claims, he says "about 50% of (Rockaway's) people" are "in need of some kind of assistance," and that "25% . . . (are) on fixed incomes" and "only 25% . . . (are) economically viable." In this way he seemingly accounts for 100% of Rockaway residents.

Now it's not my intention to address the value (or lack of it) of the proposal this gentleman so clearly derides, the idea of bringing casino gambling to Rockaway. Or even to discuss his allegations against the types of people he mentions. However, I do want to ask where he gets his stats from and on what basis we are to believe they accurately depict circumstances in Rockaway? Of course, putting aside the question of source, you have to ask yourself if these numbers accord with our real life experience. Just because they are numbers on the printed page doesn't mean they are reliable. More, they don't even make a lot of sense when looked at closely.

If our correspondent is talking about heads of households rather than all individuals living on the peninsula, this claim of only 25% "economically viable" looks particularly suspect since dependents who do not earn their own incomes may be perfectly viable, economically, as part of a family where the head of the household and other members do.

And what does "economically viable" mean as used here? Are retired people who aren't on any form of assistance and who get by on savings, social security, pensions, etc., not economically viable because of that? And are some of the "25% . . . on fixed incomes" (presumably retirees) also included among those receiving some kind of assistance? In that case you couldn't simply conclude that, after subtracting the 25% and the 50% you are left with only 25% who are economically viable.

The point is that talk is cheap and so are statistics. Like any other weapon, this sort of intellectual artillery may be put to better or worse use. But what you shouldn't do is go around shooting off this particular quantitative scatter gun without also exercising a little judgment when you do it.

BEING FAIR

(December 21, 2002)

So there I was sitting in the jury box, trying to figure out if I wanted out or not. The notice I'd gotten had said "must serve" and, though I could have figured out a way to get another postponement, it didn't seem to make sense since they'd probably just catch up with me eventually anyway. Of course, I hadn't counted on the fact that the week they called me was also the week I'd be putting together a big event for the Commissioner of my agency, complete with a re-hanging of two long lost World War I and World War II memorial plaques, a Color Guard from Ft. Hamilton, and VIPs from three city agencies in the audience. Sure didn't want to miss that one, especially since I was the one who'd pushed so hard for it. But I figured if I didn't answer the summons and serve this time, who knew how inconvenient it might be the next time they called. And then, since it would be a third postponement, getting out of it would be much, much tougher, wouldn't it?

So that's how I ended up sitting there in front of a judge, two young attorneys and a miserable and very guilty looking defendant who sat hunched over, most of the time, with his head down, lifting it only occasionally to glower at us or glance around the courtroom in apparent disbelief that he was even there. A drug charge, they said, but we weren't to think him guilty unless proved, never mind how sneaky the guy looked. You had to be fair said the judge. Can you be fair? That was the question the judge kept asking us. Can you be fair to this defendant and withhold judgment until the matter was proved or not? And can you give the witnesses the benefit of the doubt, even if some are policemen? Undercover cops to boot?

Do you believe a cop can go undercover to get his suspect, asked the judge? Or do you think that's just trickery?

And always the judge came back to the same refrain: Can you be fair?

The judge, himself, was a lean, impeccably dressed African-American man; the attorneys were both white. The assistant DA was nattily dressed and a smooth talker, an "up and comer," I thought, who'd be running for something some day. The defendant's lawyer was less sharp looking, more of a working man's type. Both were young, but the assistant DA was lean and gentlemanly while the other guy was definitely "St. John's Law School."

The defendant's attorney wore a sport jacket that was poorly fitted to his torso; his face and physique were burly and blue collarish.

But it was the judge who dominated the courtroom.

He began by reading to us, in an almost bored voice, a lengthy list of what serving on a jury was all about. His tone said he'd done this a hundred times before. He was pedantic and seemed to be talking down to us, laying everything out in terms that would suit the lowest common denominator among us. And then he started to go through his questions.

Anyone here a police officer or related to one, he asked? Anyone an attorney or related to one? Anyone ever been the victim of a crime?

Lots of affirmatives, to this last question. Me too, in fact. Interestingly, when we all went through our litanies, almost all of us had experiences that harked back to the eighties and early nineties. And all the reported violent crimes were from that period, too. You'd have thought crime had died out in the last decade, except for the round-faced black guy sitting forlornly before us, nervously scanning our faces.

In answer to the judge's queries, one guy piped up and said he had been a narcotics officer, himself, and that he figured he would automatically believe anything a narcotics officer said because of that.

"So" asked the judge, "does that mean you think narcotics officers can't lie?"

"Not exactly," answered the ex-narc, "but I would tend to believe them. Because I used to be one."

"But is that fair?" asked the judge.

The former narc just shrugged.

A dark-haired lady spoke up, when it was her turn, and said she was related to a police officer and would automatically believe anything a police officer said, too, just like the former narc.

"So in your opinion a policeman can't lie?" asked the judge.

"Sure they can lie," said the lady, "but I would generally believe whatever they said."

"If you just want to be excused from serving, why don't you say so?" asked the judge in obvious frustration. "But don't sit there and tell me that you don't believe the police are human just like the rest of us and could never be mistaken in something they offered as testimony. Or misstate a fact."

Still the lady would not budge and at last the judge, exhausted and obviously frustrated, excused her.

Then a young guy said he had once been rousted by the police and so he "could never believe anything they'd say." The judge asked this fellow if he thought all police were like the ones who had apparently mistaken him for a criminal. He shook his head but added that he just didn't trust cops anymore and so could never, ever believe any of them.

Another young lady, blonde and sleek looking, said that her brother was an assistant DA out in Oregon.

"So can you be fair?" asked the judge in what seemed, by now, to be an almost exhausted refrain.

"I guess so," said the lady at last, having given it a little thought. "But I'm pregnant," she added somewhat tentatively. "Can I go to the bathroom when I have to . . . if I get selected?"

"Of course," said the judge, a relieved grin on his face. "All you have to do is tell me or the officer here and we'll excuse you for that."

She seemed okay with his answer though she added she was also a diabetic and so had to be extra careful. The judge nodded reassuringly.

Another fellow announced that he was a "distinguished professor" at Brooklyn College (I guess that's some sort of title, as opposed to an undistinguished professor?) and that a close member of his family had previously been addicted to drugs. As a result, he said, he could not fairly react when confronted with an accused drug dealer such as the defendant.

Though obviously in his fifties this Brooklyn College type was dressed in jeans, his long gray hair tied back, a canvas backpack slung over his shoulder whenever he walked, with the rest of us, to and from the courtroom.

"Does this mean you can't be fair?" the judge asked the prof, beginning to betray some real exasperation.

The professor said he could not, "distinguished" though he might be.

One after another they raised their hands around me and told the judge why, for this or that reason, they could not be expected to sit on his jury. One after another, the judge let them go, shaking his head, wondering aloud about fairness and how these folks could claim they weren't, or couldn't be, and declare their prejudices so openly, either against the police or against the alleged perpetrator. The judge was annoyed, but his demeanor and tired tone said he'd seen it all before.

One after another he dismissed those who demanded it because of their self-proclaimed inability to be fair. But he did not let them off lightly, telling them they were to go back to the pool and sit there, awaiting another call-up.

He knew what they were doing, he told them darkly, as did all the rest of us there.

We broke for lunch then and the judge gave us two hours of respite. After calling my office and straightening a few things out, I took a long walk in nearby Forest Park, a place I'd known when I was growing up, before moving to the Rockaways. I'd always loved that old growth forest with its canopy of towering oaks, the darkened forest floor, the heavy undergrowth and the hills and little rift valleys which cut the undisturbed landscape here and there.

I wandered into the woods and found the old LIRR tracks and crossed them, just as I had as a boy, keeping alert not only for trains on the trestle but for lurking muggers and robbers as I'd learned to do back in the eighties. I wandered about, lost in my own world, admiring the rippling forest floor and the great trees that rose up all around me, darkening the sky and creating a sense of otherworldliness, as though I were somewhere far off and not in New York City at all.

Of course, I lost track of the time as I pressed more and more deeply into the park and when I glanced at my watch I was astonished at how late it was and at how far I had wandered into the depths of the old forest. Remembering the judge's charge to us, that we had to be back on time so as not to impede his proceedings, I turned about and reluctantly left the forest. Soon it became clear enough that I was too far away, that I might not make it back to the courthouse within the allotted time. I began to race through the woods, cutting across dirt paths, hopping barriers, running down rock strewn hillsides and through dense tree stands. The judge had been very specific about our obligation not to hold him up.

As I ran through the woods and at last reached the streets, I finally saw what I had to do. I was racing back to be part of the process, I was racing back because I knew that I, at least, could be fair and that I could accept a seat on this judge's jury if I had to . . . even if it would cause me to miss that ceremony I'd worked so hard on for five months, to bring it to fruition. I knew that, like so many of the others, I, too, could tell this judge stories, tales of being mugged and of how cops and DAs had mishandled things afterwards. In my case I was convinced that the cops and DAs had been bumblers at best, ill-intentioned at worst (since the police, in my case, had seemingly guided me to make an uncertain identification based on a few photographs, while the DA had waited almost a year before seeking an actual in-person identification by me of the suspect charged with the crime).

I could have it either way if I wanted to get off this jury, I knew. But I also knew that in the end I could and would be fair.

All this rolled about in my mind as I raced desperately back through Forest Park and finally gained the streets. Then I had to half-run all the way across Park Lane, down to Queens Boulevard and finally back to the courthouse itself.

There I was stopped at the gates as long lines formed and filed up to the array of metal detectors. I'd forgotten how much metal I was toting around on my person!

Off came the cell phone that had been attached to my belt, and the pager and the watch. Then from my pockets came wallet and keys. The EZ pass next (would that trigger an alarm?). The badge I carried, too. Still didn't get through though, and they made me spread my arms while they traced the outline of my body with an electronic wand. Sweating and panting from all the exertion, I finally made it up to the courtroom . . . just in time, too.

They were showing us in as I got there, still sweating from my ordeal and breathing heavily. I quickly fell in at the back of the group and struggled to calm my racing pulse.

I could be fair, I was thinking, when I was finally inside again, the crisp, clear voice of the judge still ringing in my ears with his trademark question from the morning. Forget all the business about whether I liked cops or not, or whether I thought that fellow with the guilty demeanor at the defendant's table really looked guilty or reminded me of any of the guys who'd ever accosted me in my life. Or the ones who once held me up at gunpoint and tried to blow me away after shooting my two dogs one dark winter's night in a schoolyard. I knew, at last, as I sat there under the judge's keen scrutiny again that I could, as he had so cogently put it, be fair. And that I wanted to be.

By that time I was back in my seat and the judge was finally turning to me and asking his questions. I said, in what I'd intended to be a strong voice, but really came out as a kind of nervous croak, that yes, I could certainly be fair. Nothing would prejudice me I wanted to tell him, you can count on me, judge!

But there was only that nervous, gulping, "yes" that escaped my lips and hung there in the air between us.

I was not like those others, those hypocrites, I was thinking to myself, even as I answered the perfunctory questions the judge fired at me after my barely enunciated affirmative response.

Hadn't I run all the way back over what must have been a good three miles to make sure I would not be the cause of a breakdown in the system, I was thinking? If not me, who here could be fair?

Then it was the lawyers' turn. The up-and-coming DA's assistant and the young, burly Perry Mason-for-the-defense.

The judge cut them off here and there, impatiently, and urged them to stop their dithering, equally curt with both, betraying his impatience. Maybe a shade too arrogant, I thought, an old lawyer measuring those coming up. But they swallowed their words and bit back their pride and did as he told them, questioning those of us who seemed to interest them.

One of our number, a professed newspaper reporter, interested them more than the rest. They came back to him again and again. He could be fair, he said. He was a reporter, albeit for a union newspaper, accustomed to looking for the truth in things. He knew that people didn't always tell the truth and that this applied to law enforcement officials as much as to civilians, he said.

I sat straighter in my seat, waiting for the lawyers to come to me. I knew about fairness, too, I would tell them.

But they never asked me a thing, though the DA looked my way once or twice throughout the proceedings.

Then the judge said we were to go outside and up we got and walked around the lower partition between the jury box and the rest of the courtroom, up and filing out in orderly procession, down the incline, which equalized access for the fit and the disabled, and out into the sleek modern hallway with tall glass windows facing the busy streets and the highway beyond. We stood about or sat on the window ledge. A few folks struck up conversations with one another. Muted talk throughout. I made another phone call to the office. We had a bill that needed collecting and I was concerned as the budget year was winding down.

Abruptly, the bailiff appeared again and called us all back. Once more, obediently, we filed in uneasy silence back to our seats. We each took the seat that had been assigned to us because that's how they know you in the courtroom: juror number 1, juror number 2, and so on. I was juror number 11 and I dutifully found the properly numbered seat and sat down.

Then the judge told us that everyone whose name was called was to remain in place. All the rest of us, if we didn't hear our names called, were to get up and leave the courtroom, he said, and go back to the jury pool.

I sat there, ears cocked, as they started reading the names, three I think, in all.

And then they stopped.

The judge said thanks again and something like "those who have not been chosen will be getting their tickets punched when they get back to the pool" and I was up again, with the others, and filing past the jury box and out into the corridor.

The only one they kept who stuck in my mind was that reporter fellow. Two others and the reporter and the rest of us were shown the door. Some were relieved I think and glad to be out of there. But I had wrestled mightily with myself, wrestled and won, for I had no tales to tell or excuses to give or blame to lay on anyone, cop or defendant. I was ready to be fair. I wanted to be. I had even found in myself a sense of pity for the poor befuddled, and sometimes resentful-looking, defendant who sat in the middle of the jury room, under the searching and imperious eyes of the judge and his bailiff.

Yep, I could have been fair. But they promised us no more jury duty for four years thereafter, and that seemed like a respectable enough reward for our having given up a couple of days to sit through the judge's harangues and the lawyers' sporadic questions . . . though even the hypocrites got the same promise I did. Fair or not, we all got off with a promised four-year hiatus in jury duty to boot. And I even got to attend that plaque re-hanging in my agency at the end of the week that I'd been so worried about. But I left the courthouse with a profound sense of having missed something real, something important, something I'd worked hard to steel myself for, although to no avail. What kind of jury was I leaving behind in that courtroom? Who would ultimately be chosen to sit in judgment on that befuddled and angry-looking guy hunched over at the defendant's table . . . and would they, as I knew I would have been, be fair?

THOUGHTS ON THE ISRAELI DAY PARADE

(June 11, 2004)

My wife teaches at a yeshiva high school for girls and her contract calls for her to attend the annual Israeli Day Parade along Fifth Avenue with her school each year. My contract with my wife calls for me to attend whatever she wants me to, so I generally go along for the ride. This year, as in past years, we were there. We drove into Manhattan early, found street parking, had a nice leisurely breakfast (at about twice what we normally pay for a better one in Cedarhurst) and then we ambled on up to the staging area.

This year, as in past years, the weather was miserably hot and my wife's school contingent typically disorganized. But we primed ourselves with some overpriced bottled water and iced tea, and set off uptown, roughly on schedule, along the parade route. There were the usual ragged lines and singing students . . . just what you find in parades of this sort. And, as we came to the southeast corner of Central Park, there was the usual group of protesters as well, a disparate group of grim, angry people . . . some demanding Israeli withdrawal from the occupied territories and some demanding Israel's demise altogether. Among these were a group of renegade Hasidim, a sect of orthodox Jews who do not believe that Jews as a people have a right to a state of Israel until the messiah finally arrives to establish it.

At one time, in the formative days of Zionism (the movement that called on Jews to take matters into their own hands and return to Zion to escape European anti-Semitism), the idea that one should not act until the messiah had come was prevalent among

many of the Hasidic sects. But, after Hitler, and with the successful
birth of a Jewish state in the ancient homeland, most Hasidim
moderated their views. But one small group never did. So there
they were, in long black coats and hats, with curls hanging down
their faces in the 90+ degree heat, praying intensely and, in some
cases, shouting angrily as the paraders passed by. A motley group
of anti-war activists and Palestinian nationalists stood just behind
them, glowering in their own righteous anger. One sign said "Zionist
Hoodlums Get Out of Gaza". Other signs said things that were far
worse. Harsh glances and some angry words were exchanged
between the marchers and the protestors. The police separating
the two groups uneasily hurried us along, plainly concerned about
the risks of an unpleasant clash ballooning into something beyond
a mere exchange of radically divergent viewpoints.

In the hot sun, as we moved toward the shade of the trees
overhanging the edges of Central Park, I felt a terrible sadness.
Neither side seemed able to hear or see the other's viewpoint.
Though I'm a lifelong supporter of the State of Israel, I couldn't
help thinking of the opportunity we had lost over the years, an
opportunity to change the dynamic of this conflict. After the Six-
Day War in 1967, when the Arab population on the West Bank
and Gaza suddenly found itself under Israeli rule, there was only
shock and passivity on their part. That was the time, I thought, to
have reached out to these people and changed the perceptions on
the ground. Instead, by the late seventies, the Likud party had
come to power in Israel and was actively pushing a policy of creeping
annexation of the conquered territories at the expense of the native
Arab population.

It's easy to see why Israeli voters were eager for this. The West
Bank is, in fact, the ancient Jewish homeland, not the marginal
coastal areas and desert that make up much of the modern Israeli
state. More, the pre-1967 borders were barely defensible and the
land these borders contained was so limited (about the size of the
state of New Jersey) it was barely sufficient for a growing
population. So, instead of reaching out to work with, and reassure,
the Arab population they had just annexed, by the late seventies

Israelis began planting settlements in earnest on undeveloped land in the Arab territories. The message this sent to the local Arabs was that they were destined to lose more and more of their territory to encroaching foreigners, the longer the Israelis remained in charge.

Now many people say these Arabs always hated the Jews anyway, from the time the first Zionists began trickling into the old Turkish province of Palestine, and that the local Arab population was always unwilling to share the land with the newcomers. In fact I think this is probably true. Nor was it guaranteed that a pre-emptive Israeli effort to share and reach out to the local populace after 1967 could have changed this fundamental dynamic. But surely an active settlement policy, such as the one begun in the seventies under Likud's Menachem Begin, foreclosed even the chance of that.

I supported the Oslo Accords in 1993 which brought the Palestinian leader Yasser Arafat to the West Bank and made him a "partner for peace." And I supported former Israeli Prime Minister Ehud Barak's efforts to reach a final accommodation with Arafat in the last year of the Clinton administration, even when Barak offered roughly 97% of the occupied territories plus shared sovereignty of Jerusalem (something no Israeli leader had been willing to do before him) along with dismantlement of the majority of Israeli settlements in the territories in order to provide the basis for a new Palestinian state. I supported every chance for peace. And I was as shocked as anyone when Arafat walked away from the deal Barak put on the table and initiated the intifida that has led to the present bloody impasse.

I'd always suspected the Palestinian leadership wasn't seriously interested in a two state solution, that their unspoken aim, from the beginning, had been the complete eradication of Israel (just as they teach and preach in their native Arabic). I'd hoped otherwise, of course, but suspected the worst. And Arafat's actions confirmed the worst. But walking along the Fifth Avenue parade route on that burning hot Sunday afternoon, seeing the awful tension and anger on both sides, I couldn't help thinking that a wonderful opportunity had been missed, years ago, when Israelis gave in to their worst impulses and initiated a policy of settlement and expansion. What could be worse than human beings so divided like this over a little piece of real estate too small to accommodate these two peoples? Do not the Palestinians have their pain, just as Jews do? And while I happen to think their pain is mostly self-inflicted, since, unlike the Israelis, they have never once been willing to compromise, yet self-inflicted pain is real pain, too.

The current trouble in the world today is clearly about a clash of cultures since there are strong elements within Islam that retain a somewhat medieval mindset. Indeed Islam's very emergence occurred in the context of the conquest and defeat of non-believers. Christianity and Judaism once shared this "crusading" viewpoint but both grew out of it centuries ago. Yet a substantial part of today's Islamic world has not. The very existence of the State of Israel remains an irritant to a vast number of Muslims today who see it as an affront to their beliefs and rights as followers of the "true faith." Our present struggle with the Islamo-fascism of Osama bin Laden et al is certainly not only about Israel. But Israel is a red flag for them in this conflict.

What a chance was lost back in the seventies, to change the rules of the game and defuse the nascent Palestinian jihadism that was then being born. As many tell me today, there's no way to know if an Israel less eager for its historical homeland in the hills of Judea and Samaria after 1967 would have made any real difference in the continued development of today's barbaric Middle Eastern sensibilities. And I can't disagree. But looking at the glowering faces as we walked by, on parade, and contrasting these with the indifferent jubilance of my fellow paraders, inured to real Palestinian anguish, I couldn't help thinking we could have been so much better off today if we had been able, back then, to think for a few moments about what the other fellow's needs and hopes were and given up one small part of the Zionist dream, waiting more patiently, perhaps, for the intervention of that higher power.

WHAT AM I MISSING?

(June 6, 2004)[25]

The June 6th Sunday edition of the New York Times ran a lead article in its Metro section concerning one Ansar Mahmoud, a green card-holder from Pakistan who fell afoul of authorities in the weeks following 9/11. According to the reporter, Lisa Fodero, Mr. Mahmoud, a pizza delivery man, stopped one day on a delivery run to photograph the scenic Hudson River Valley so he could send pictures back to his relatives in Pakistan. Alas, the site Mr. Mahmoud chose to photograph from was next to a New York City water treatment plant and authorities scooped him up when they learned of his actions. Ms. Fodero says "the nation was panicked" after 9/11 and feared "poisoned drinking water."

Well, Mr. Mahmoud, Ms. Fodero tells us, was soon cleared of any taint of terrorism but it turned out he had been helping Pakistani friends whose visas had expired, "an offense that led to his detention and pending deportation."

Ms. Fodero goes on to note that "with his arrest, Mr. Mahmoud became part of the wave of Arab and Muslim aliens and citizens who were detained for questioning in the two months after Sept. 11th." Estimated at about 1200 people by the U.S. Justice Department, "advocates for the detainees," says Fodero, "say the number is much higher."

A local community of "peace activists" soon became aware of Mr. Mahmoud's plight, according to Ms. Fodero, and stepped in to aid him, winning "letters of support from seven United States Senators including Hillary Rodham Clinton." Calling the authorities' actions in arresting Mr. Mahmoud "racial profiling" one local activist is reported to have said that Mr. Mahmoud is "very spiritual and loves beauty and that's why he took the picture that got him into trouble in the first place."

Though cleared of suspicions of terrorism, evidence surfaced that Mr. Mahmoud had assisted other immigrants from Pakistan, who were here illegally, to remain. Mr. Mahmoud, on the advice of his attorney, pled guilty when this became known, and was sentenced to five years probation along with time served. But, by pleading guilty, he automatically became subject to deportation and detention. Mr. Mahmoud is now contesting this, represented by a new attorney, according to Fodero, and awaiting the decision of the Homeland Security Department.

"They can't afford to deport him, not in the face of Abu Ghraib and seven senators," one of his supporters told Ms. Fodero. "Indeed," Fodero adds, the group's "latest coup was a May 21 letter of support from five Democratic senators addressed to the homeland security secretary, Tom Ridge. The letter—signed by Edward M. Kennedy of Massachusetts, Richard J. Durbin of Illinois, Jon S. Corzine of New Jersey, Russell D. Feingold of Wisconsin and Patrick Leahy of Vermont—cited a report last year from the Justice Department's own Inspector General that criticized the round-up and detention of hundreds of Muslim and Arab immigrants after Sept. 11th."

According to Fodero, the letter noted that the report said "it is unlikely that most if not all of the individuals arrested would have been pursued by law enforcement" except, she notes, "for the Sept. 11th investigation."

There are, of course, some dissenters in the upstate town where Mr. Mahmoud's activist supporters reside. Ms. Fodero notes that one, "a 32-year-old construction worker" says of Mr. Mahmoud that "he got caught trespassing and that led to this other thing he got in trouble for. If you break the law, you should be punished."

Still the tone of Ms. Fodero's article is best summed up by her final quote from a Mahmoud-supporter: "There have been thousands of deportations since 9/11 for very bureaucratic reasons and glitches. But he is someone taken from our midst. He was taken 20 minutes from where I live and that's not okay."

Of course, we can all sympathize with this individual's sense of concern and with Mr. Mahmoud's plight. Obviously there are quite a few highly placed politicians who also sympathize. In fact, if Mr. Mahmoud's actions with regard to the immigration law violations are shown to be merely minor and/or inadvertent (as he claims) and if he has demonstrated good intentions while in this country on his green card otherwise, I would not have a problem with the Department of Homeland Security ruling in his favor.

But my concern here is for something else: when you break the law, shouldn't you have to pay the price? There may be all sorts of extenuating circumstances and our system of justice enables these to be considered through the sort of process Mr. Mahmoud is now pursuing. But the bottom line is *he pled guilty to a criminal act* that placed his green card status in jeopardy. What kind of an argument is it that, since his lawbreaking wouldn't have become known if he hadn't been picked up because of his suspicious behavior after 9/11, he should not, therefore, be held to account for breaking other laws? In fact, people stopped by the police for all sorts of reasons always run the risk of arrest if they have outstanding warrants against them or are legally discovered, in the course of the arrest, to have broken other laws.

And then there's this business about "racial profiling" which seems to be taking some of us off the deep-end. The people who gave us 9/11 happen to fall into a particular, and very recognizable, category . . . as do the people who persistently promise us more of the same. They all hail from a certain part of the world, espouse certain views, belong to certain ethnic backgrounds, etc. This is just a matter of fact. Certainly neither Mr. Mahmoud, nor anyone else, should be considered guilty of a crime just because of their ethnicity or what they happen to look like. But it's not wrong to be on the alert if people fitting certain descriptions are seen to be performing certain suspicious and potentially threatening actions.

Mr. Mahmoud was rightly picked up in the aftermath of 9/11 for doing something that could have signaled great danger to this country. In the light of what we now know, it's not paranoid or irrational to fear the poisoning of our drinking water by some individuals who come from the Middle East or related areas of the world. And Mr. Mahmoud, innocent or guilty of charges of terrorism, apparently did break other laws . . . which has, and should have, consequences.

You don't have to be an American citizen to be expected to abide by American laws when you are a guest in this country. Nor is a green card a get-out-of-jail-free card.

LAST THOUGHT, BEST THOUGHT

My wife is a poet, among other things, and, while still in college, she studied with the famous beat poet and godfather of the hippie movement, Allen Ginsburg. She used to bring back many of his little aphorisms, along with tales of some of his less edifying idiosyncrasies. One of the things he would often say to them, she told me, was this little writer's rule of thumb:

"First thought, best thought."

Basically he was telling them to stop second guessing themselves and go with the first idea they had when crafting a bit of poetry. As a writer myself, though without the name and notoriety of an Allen Ginsburg, I've often seen the value of this approach. However much we may agonize and revise, there is something to be said for those first words as they come pouring out of the depths of our unconscious. There's something pure about them, something unmarred by artifice and the analyzing mind. But compiling this present collection has prompted me to reconsider Ginsburg's adage.

The first piece I used here, "Ushering in an Era," was not the first Rockaway Irregular article ever written. But it was one of the earliest ones. In it, I recall my reactions to Rudolph Giuliani's first mayoral inauguration; and to the reception he got at the fringes of the crowd that had turned out to hear him that day from a motley assortment of demonstrators representing the protest culture of New York's political left.

So much seemed possible then as Giuliani began the process that was to return New York City to governability after decades of sliding ever more deeply into chaos. And yet, I was appalled at the remarkable inability of the demonstrators who had arrayed themselves at the outer edge of the crowd to see any of the good Giuliani's election seemed to promise . . . . and none of the hope in the faces of the larger mass of people who had come to hear, and cheer, the new mayor on. The protesters were focused on one thing only, denying the mayor his "win" through their antics, if they could, and promising to work against him as he moved resolutely into governing mode. But it didn't seem to faze him, then or after, despite the rearguard battles that were to be fought by these people against him in the subsequent years of his administration.

It was still a time of shock for those on the left, though. They seemed unable to conceive of granting a "win" to a Republican in New York City, not even to one who actually shared at least some of their views (which Giuliani, as a social liberal, most assuredly did). The Soviet Union had only recently imploded, in response to Ronald Reagan's prodding, and the prior incumbent, Democratic Mayor David Dinkins, had just gone down to a narrow defeat in the face of Giuliani's second challenge to him for the top city job. It looked like the world was turning inside out for the folks on the left, that they were becoming progressively more irrelevant . . . and that, perhaps, they even knew it. They knew, too, that they were mounting an ineffective protest against the new mayor and yet they pressed on, determined to make a statement in a raucous display of picketing, shouting and boisterous street theater.

Over the years Giuliani actually did much of what he had promised on that first morning and was elected resoundingly to a second term. But in looking at all the stuff that's passed under the bridge since that time, I can't help comparing the promise offered in that early article about the first Giuliani inauguration with the results of his two terms as mayor reflected in some of the later pieces.

As I argue later on, in "Who 'Lost' the City?" (May 9, 2003), Giuliani only partially succeeded in what he set out to do. In his first term, faced with difficult fiscal hurdles and recalcitrant political resistance on the part of the advocacy community and the political left, he made great strides in pushing city agencies to be more effective with leaner resources. He also reformed the city's dinosaur-like welfare system while rolling back a crime-ridden street culture that had for years infected and sullied our neighborhoods. But Giuliani was only human and he loosened his hold on the reins, once he'd won his second term. Re-reading the later article I am struck by how much the man left undone when he turned City Hall over to his successor.

The city inherited by Michael Bloomberg was rife with fiscal problems that seemed to dwarf what Giuliani had initially faced. Of course the terrible attacks of 9/11 were a huge part of the problem. They helped tip the nation into economic recession (by slowing down business activity, as fear and previously undreamed of security costs kicked in), while sucking up city resources for the massive response city agencies were forced to mount. Giuliani, in his last years, had left us unprepared for such an eventuality because he had become focused on pleasing us more than doing his job. He wanted to move on to higher office, since term limits prevented him from succeeding himself, and to do that he needed voters' approval. But even when securing a new political perch no longer seemed feasible for him, at least in the immediate future, he didn't cease wanting to be loved or, at the least, no longer despised by those who had so vehemently opposed him in his early years in office. He had a rough, somewhat abrasive manner but underneath he was like most of the rest of us . . . just a guy who wanted to be appreciated.

It's probably inevitable that many of the things we set ourselves to do are often left undone, or only partly done, when we move on. Sometimes, if we're not particularly lucky, they are even systematically dismantled. I had that experience myself when I left a post I'd held in the city's Human Resources Administration in 1990 as a new crew under a new mayor took over that agency and began to undo a facilities project tracking system I had previously worked untold hours to build. It meant nothing to those who came after me. They hadn't known about the problems it was intended to fix and couldn't see its relevance to their own concerns and so they simply discarded it. A friend of mine, a Deputy Commissioner in another city agency, saw the same thing happen to his work after he left his agency, too.

On the other hand, sometimes what we leave behind does have an impact, even if it isn't always credited to us. I think some of my own contributions, in some of the agencies I've served in, still survive and continue to do the job I set them to do, though others certainly "own" them now. City government is just not the kind of place where you can leave much of yourself behind. Things move on and new people bring their own ideas and priorities in with them and don't much care what their predecessors thought was important or needed doing. Sooner, rather than later, your presence there just gets erased.

Still, no one can argue that Giuliani didn't leave a substantial imprint behind him when he left City Hall. But it's the nature of government, not unlike most things we're engaged in, to spawn new problems even as old ones evade our grasp. It's probably unrealistic to think that anyone who manages to win a bit of power or influence can permanently and irrevocably change things. There's always more to do.

But that's no reason to give up. Our lives are about striving and straining, which is one of the reasons socialism, a wonderful system in theory, just doesn't cut it in the larger world. Socialism wants to make us all equal and take the struggle out of our lives. Would that we could do that! But the truth is we're born to struggle and it's in the struggling itself that we find what we need. Politics, in this sense, is only a reflection of that. We set ourselves a task, here and there, and go about getting it done. And when we have, we find a new task to do. Or if we can't finish it as we'd like, we just move on. There's no standing pat.

Looking over these articles now, I'm struck by their somewhat limited range as well as by the sometimes simplistic mindset that had me in its grip when I wrote some of them. But writing is like everything else. It comes from the soul. You just have to keep at it, doing it over and over again and then, no matter how good the first thought was, the last is likely to be better. The only thing is that there never really is a "last," not while we're alive and still working, anyway.

And when we're not?

Then there are others doing much the same as we have done, pushing ahead and doing this or that, trying their best to make an impact and get something worthwhile done. I'm not sorry for the years I spent as a bureaucrat. They always seemed worthwhile to me, even when I was frustrated and had to stand by and see my work spilled off like so much old foam. Perhaps Ginsburg did have it right, that the first thought is our best. But if things never really end for us, if we just keep going until we can't any longer, then maybe there is no real "first thought" to speak of. The first one really is no different from the last.

ENDNOTES

1. The date shown is roughly when this piece was written as it had not run in the Irregular at the time this book went to press.
2. From an interview in the New York Observer.
3. Erica Walter in an American Enterprise Institute magazine article.
4. President George H. W. Bush, of course, is meant.
5. I'd guess Clinton's I.Q. is probably higher.
6. Most Americans had come to believe, and probably rightly, that these crises now posed grave problems for our continued economic well-being.
7. The first President Bush again, of course, since this was written during Bill Clinton's presidency.
8. The name of the letter writer has been changed since the exchange referenced here took place roughly ten years ago and I am now unable to find the original letter writer to request permission to use her actual name. Still, her letter was published in a local newspaper and subsequently referenced by me in the original article so a pseudonym here should serve the present purpose.
9. Clinton's statist instincts were actually curbed early on by a Republican Congress which resulted in legislative gridlock. This helped foster an economic boom in the nineties which Clinton partisans subsequently ascribed to his stewardship and which Republicans claim as their legacy. The truth probably lies somewhere between. Clinton was not as left-leaning as his Democratic base and he did put in place Bush's previously negotiated NAFTA agreement, while pushing through Welfare reform, against the left's wishes, even as the Republicans in Congress were keeping the lid on his broader, statist ambitions. These factors combined with the "peace dividend" following the end of the Cold War and skillful Fed management of the money supply to drive an unprecedented U.S. economic boom in the nineties. The long pent-up economic forces released by the Reagan-Bush tax and regulation-reduction policies of the preceding decade

further fueled this economic juggernaut which only peaked, with the dot.com bubble in the last year of Clinton's term. George W. Bush, who succeeded Clinton, inherited the subsequent declining economic situation which was then exacerbated by the infamous terrorist attacks of September 11th, 2001.

[10]   Of course the presidency of the second George Bush is meant.

[11]   Note that in the run-up to the election in 2004, the knock on Bush switched again to his alleged incompetence and lack of intellectual heft, after his critics briefly played around with the notion that Bush was some sort of a Hitler incarnate. This last charge even struck many in the opposition as over the top so the best thing seemed to be to switch back to the old claim that the president was just too much of a simpleton to be trusted to deal with America's enemies . . . or its friends.

[12]   Of course, history has shown that, to a large extent, Ms. Razuki called it right as many Iraqis turned away from their initial joy at the removal of Saddam Hussein, in the face of ongoing resistance by elements in Iraq devoted to the elimination of the American presence. But at this writing, the full story is not yet in. We can only hope we got this right!

[13]   This did seem to me to be true at the time but it didn't stay true. The subsequent presidential campaign and the failure to find the anticipated weapons of mass destruction, compounded by continuing unrest in post-Saddam Iraq, revived all the old arguments and brought the question of whether we should have, or shouldn't have, removed Saddam to the fore again. At this writing this issue still seems to be monopolizing much of the debate.

[14]   The recent reports of the U.S. Senate, of the Butler Commission in Britain and of the 9/11 Commission all bear out the supposition that Saddam had had longstanding contacts with al Qaeda, among his other terrorist relationships, and that the evidence available to the Bush administration, pre-war, supported a good faith belief that Saddam possessed and was concealing wmd killing technologies and materiel. None of this has done anything, however, to still the continued claims that Bush and his administration lied about these two matters rather than, as in the case of the wmd, apparently getting the facts wrong because of faulty intelligence. The fact that a record of ongoing apparent contacts between Saddam's regime and al Qaeda does not reveal the content of those contacts (whether

there was actual operational collaboration or not) continues to leave this issue unresolved in the minds of those who opposed the president's policies in this matter.

15   Although the text taken from the letters-to-the-editor cited in this article is accurately reported, I decided to re-write the article itself to exclude the names of the two correspondents writing the letters since I have had no subsequent contact with them and, therefore, no opportunity to obtain permission to use their names.

16   February 15, 2004

17   Deconstructing Kerry (April 2, 2004)

18   That's the term used for this sort of contract in New York City municipal agencies, though I believe the feds have a different name for the same kind of contract.

19   Although written on this date, this piece had not actually run in the Irregular at the time this book went to press and so it's presented out of sequence here.

20   Poor quality cleaning supplies, for instance, one very simple example, actually result in the need for more frequent cleanings and the use of overtime to fund these, more than offsetting any gains realized by paying less for product.

21   Although the enlarged, over-funded and dismally inefficient pest control program ended up being base-lined into the Department's budget and became a permanent institutional fixture in this new politically-driven, over-inflated form.

22   In the summer of 2004, I again drove down to Dubos to check on the status of the magnets. The areas in which the equipment was housed had become overgrown with weeds, making it difficult to get close without exposing oneself to a mosquito attack. However as I slowly drove along the street, it appeared that a number of the units were in a state of disrepair though some did seem to be operating. The cages themselves were somewhat banged up and a number of them were empty. As I drove by, with my window open, I was suddenly attacked by a swarm of mosquitoes and had to skedaddle. If the units were operating optimally, it was plain they weren't doing much good. What I was able to observe, however, suggested that the Health Department wasn't doing any better job in setting up and maintaining this equipment in 2004 than it had done in prior years.

23   Although written on this date, this piece had not actually run at the time this book went to press.

24   Scholars suggest that an Algonquin tribe in this region, with the name "Reckouwacky," was the source of the current "Rockaway." This tribal group is thought to have been an offshoot of the Canarsies. However the etymology remains speculative, at best.

25   Although written on this date, this piece had not actually run at the time this book went to press.